SCOTT AND SOCIETY

SCOTT AND SOCIETY

Graham McMaster

CAMBRIDGE UNIVERSITY PRESS

CAMBRIDGE

LONDON NEW YORK NEW ROCHELLE

MELBOURNE SYDNEY

Published by the Press Syndicate of the University of Cambridge
The Pitt Building, Trumpington Street, Cambridge CB2 1RP
32 East 57th Street, New York, NY 10022, USA
296 Beaconsfield Parade, Middle Park, Melbourne 3206, Australia

First published 1981

Printed in Great Britain by
Western Printing Services Ltd, Bristol

British Library cataloguing in publication data

McMaster, Graham
Scott and society.
I. Title
823'.7'09   PR5341   80–42074
ISBN 0 521 23769 6

CONTENTS

Contents

INTRODUCTION

One or two of the propositions advanced in this book about Scott's novels may seem to some readers to be unnecessarily exaggerated and blamefully dismissive of other people's work, indeed, of the common experience of readers. As in the accommodating tradition of literary scholarship disparate and even opposing views of a single topic can be asserted simultaneously, the resulting paradoxes being nothing more than evidence of a plenitude of life that refuses to be so easily docketed, I would like my arguments to be understood as a complement to, rather than a contradiction of, scholarship on Scott of the last few decades.

One major critical problem, or more accurately a problem for critics, still exists. How can the distance between Scott's enormous historical reputation, his current general neglect and a minority contemporary opinion that he is a writer of the first order be contracted? In the beginning of the modernist period Scott's novels, for obvious reasons, had come to seem little more than trivial, nostalgic boy's adventure stories, origins of a tradition that descended to the underground of the popular press. The first task of criticism in the academic period was the restoration to the novels of a sense of seriousness and importance. Two short accounts have been overwhelmingly influential: David Daiches' *Scott's Achievement as a Novelist*, and a chapter by Lukacs in *The Historical Novel*.

In Professor Daiches' view, Scott is above all important as a man who stands astride a division between two epochs, epochs that have their own actual importance and also importance as types of change. Seeing, accepting and regretting an irreversible change from one type of society to another, Scott turned to narrative to record the passage, to give the likeness of both the old and the new, and as far as possible to mediate between them, to find, for example, some sort of relevance for glamorous heroism in the 'dull but necessary' world of modern commerce. How can honour become honesty, martial courage civil courage? The answers have overtones of tragedy: many of the virtues of the old society cannot be made available to the new – they are simply lost, and their protagonists defeated. The Waverley novels, at least the 'nine plus one' series, are the only synthesis. Professor Daiches' arguments have been of enormous value because they brought Scott into the realms of serious literary discussion, opening up a way for his novels to be seen as something worthy of adult attention.

If Daiches' account perhaps unnecessarily favoured the 'nine plus one' series, Lukacs redressed the balance. From his point of view, novels such as *Durward* and *Kenilworth* are far from inferior to *The Antiquary*. In Lukacs' view, Scott was great exactly as a historical novelist, a man who embodied the truth of history – more poignantly and memorably than academic historians, but also more deeply honestly – in fiction. He excelled in fairness, objectivity, in the ability to find just the right embodiment for a given class, age or group. It must be admitted that Lukacs' arguments have lost something in credibility from his own mistakes with periods and dates. Lukacs also invented, or re-invented, what is frequently called 'Scott's dualism'. Though a bigoted Tory in private life, Scott overcame his prejudices in the act of composition to arrive at a more radical view of history than was achieved by almost any of his nineteenth-century successors. The first enunciation of this idea that I know came from W. Howitt in 1834, an article published in *Tait's Edinburgh Magazine* called 'Great Poets, Great Reformers'.

It has been said that rank, knighthood, feudalism – all that pertained to the past rather than to the present, all that sanctioned caste and the subjection of the interest of the multitude to the interests of the few – were his favourite topics and breathed through all he wrote . . . Decided Radical as I esteem myself . . . I must confess I never felt it in him ... Genius, when it retires from the consideration of everyday subjects, from the party topic and feelings of the common moment, into its closet and gives itself up to its own glorious visions and emotions, is too noble to see anything but the broad light of everlasting truth, to feel anything but the majestic presence of nature, and the quickest sympathies with struggling humanity.

Lukacs' argument, allowing for a certain variation of vocabulary, does not seem very different: 'Scott ranks among those great writers whose depth is mainly manifest in their work, a depth which they often do not understand themselves, because it has sprung from a truly realistic mastery of their material in conflict with their personal views and prejudices.' There is to me something very ungenerous in ascribing all decent feelings to members, even non-paid-up members, of one's own party. But the theory of 'Scott's dualism' seems very unconvincing also in the sort of model of humanity it proposes. Large parts of creative writing may spring from 'the unconscious', but they must surely be assisted by – or not hindered by, at least – the conscious, organising mind; there must be a free flow of information between the active, social individual and the creative artist. A condition of such aggravated schizophrenia as would be implied by the division of the artist into Radical Wully and Tory Sir Walter might perhaps produce some sort of literary expression but could hardly be expected to result in such a high-level, sustained and organised type of intellectual activity as the creation of major novels.

If the dualism theory is unconvincing, the description of Scott as a cool, mature, social-realist historicist, however respectable, has in fact failed to find Scott many new admirers. Principally, I think, it has concentrated too heavily on interpretation, and neglected discussion of Scott's literary art. Attempting to persuade us of the seriousness of his work, it has failed to account for, or even to acknowledge, Scott's vein of grotesque or farcical humour, his interest in fantasy and in states of anxiety, the patterning, poetry and symbolism of the novels. And yet some very interesting work on Scott's oeuvre as a chain of obsessional images has been done by

Alexander Welsh. I find Welsh's Scott unattractive because the critic makes the novels too English and too Burkean. Welsh has attributed a particular type of conservatism to Scott too easily, without venturing outside the novels to see what the novelist's real-life politics really were.

One of the principal aims of this book is to show that the novels are in fact dominated not by figures and situations that are rationally calculated to make certain historical (to Scott) trends palpable, but by patterns, metaphors and symbols, and by a very restricted range of them. Can the interest, however, proper to a *historical* novel, as we usually understand the term, drive an artist, as I believe Scott is driven, to the creation of myths, to the forcing of his material into a series of repeated patterns? Surely the impulse to mythologise comes from an imperfectly or unwillingly grasped vision of the present – whether it is the political and social, or religious, sexual, familial or metaphysical present – and its impingement upon the author's sense of security and his perceptions of his own relation to the whole. According to his vision, either fully or tentatively registered, he will feel a need to give or to deny life to particular shapes. The presence of particular shapes, vigorous and quasi-independent life forms, in novel after novel, quite independent of the overt historical backgrounds, is the best clue there is to Scott's purpose.

It would be possible to argue that the many images I shall discuss below are essentially private, and neurotically in-spired. Scott's life provides ample opportunities for speculation about unsatisfactory filial, marital and paternal roles, about a longing for success and a terror of disgrace. Yet the images are embedded in contexts that are overwhelmingly public, asking to be read in some way that makes sense in the political, social world – how different to the much more private worlds of novels like *Adam Blair* and *The Confessions of a Justified Sinner*. If a personal neurosis did lend its impetus, there is no sign that one is being cherished to distort the passionate, dangerous and tendentious portions of the novels. A comparison of scenes of violence in the Porteous riots in *The Heart of*

Midlothian with similar scenes in *Barnaby Rudge*, which they partially influenced, shows very well the absence in Scott of any sort of personal violence and a very impressive and objective sense of the reality of others' grievances and of the corruption of authority – in sharp contrast to Dickens. And since in *Midlothian* the seemingly private heroism of Jeannie is a parallel to the public defiance of an unjust authority, the work as a whole, with its own curious unity, is pulled into the public sphere.

In the public world of the Waverley novels, the world of social and political action, a sequence can be observed. Partly, one novel builds upon its predecessor, though not necessarily its immediate predecessor. Yet the sequence is not smooth; the generation of new events and images is obviously affected by terms outside the system of novel-writing. Mood, tone and imagery undergo profound modification and changes of emphasis at certain points in ways that can most probably be best explained by reference to events in the real world. The two systems need to be held together – the development of a personal fictional language with the changing perception of, and response to, a world that was itself being subjected to violent and far-reaching changes.

Thus we need to know the origins of Scott's attitudes, and his political prejudices and assumptions, before we can possibly know how they were affected by events in the outer world and in the inner world of novel-writing. And before we can permit ourselves to draw conclusions from our knowledge of Scott's political opinions, we should be sure that we really know what these were. We should be sure too that the political and social world we know about is the one that Scott inhabited.

Scott's intellectual debt to the Scottish Enlightenment is well known. The account given here, in chapter 2, is a little more detailed than, I believe, any that has appeared in print before. However, in the area of the relevant social background, some misconceptions need to be corrected. Most writers unjustly assimilate Scott to English social history, while writers with a knowledge of Scottish social history, for obvious reasons usually themselves Scots, are frequently either so consciously democratic or so nationalist that they are seldom able to do justice to Scott's position. With regard to Scott's politics, a great deal of misinformation is still being distributed. My conviction is that as a politician Scott was far from being the figure of fun that his own enemies, or Carlyle, or Lockhart – Oedipus Lockhart – would like to foist upon us. My middle chapters will show what Scott did with his intellectual and social inheritances in the vital years after Waterloo, describe the quality of his attention and response, and define the nature of his reaction to, and partial despair over, a society whose problems seemed to be becoming more and more intractable and less explicable in terms of the Enlightenment philosophy that had seemed to provide a clue to all processes in the first decade of the century. The final chapters will show how the novels assimilated his uneasy apprehensions, embodying in fiction criticisms of society similar to those that he was to make in more public and acknowledged contexts, but earlier and more logically.

Logically, these conclusions entail dissent from many currently accepted ideas about Scott's novels. Novels that express a view progressively more critical of the capitalist transformation of traditional society can hardly advocate wise acceptance of the new, can hardly indeed be expected to stand back from events at all. Stories and persons that repeat a small number of seemingly obsessional experiences and situations cannot at the same time embody the objective truth about the history of a wide variety of British and European settings from the Middle Ages onwards. Yet, obviously, Scott's novels may be imperfectly integrated and subordinated to a single theme. Contradictory impulses may in fact exist. However much I am convinced that Scott wrote from a need to keep the social relationships of his own day under his imaginative control, there is also no doubt that one major creative impulse was the desire to fix and record styles of life that were passing out of currency. With a writer like Scott, particularly at the present time, it is important not to try to force his writings into any one narrow mould but to demonstrate the largeness and complexity of his work, while insisting at the same time on the fundamental unity of his life and his art.

NOTE: Quotations from the Waverley Novels are taken from the Oxford University Press edition of 1912

PART I

1. 'WAVERLEY' AND 'REDGAUNTLET': DEFINITION OF A CRITICAL PROBLEM

'By the author of *Waverley*': and so a whole shelf-full of books have come to be known as The Waverley Novels. It is very reasonable, and yet, how odd it would be if there were a similar shelf-full called The Pickwick Novels. In many respects, *Waverley* is very different from the novels it was reputed to have sired, so different that a number of critical propositions founded upon a supposed continuity of subject and technique have proved highly dubious. The nature of this difference will be demonstrated here through a comparison with *Redgauntlet*, a novel that is superficially very similar to *Waverley*. Both novels involve young men with Jacobite plots. Yet *Waverley* is obviously much concerned with a judging and balancing of the old and the new, all the changes conveniently symbolised by Stuart and Hanover. It is a highly ordered work, thoroughly known and coolly deliberate. *Redgauntlet* is another type of novel, murkily symbolic, romantic rather than rationalist, and relatively unconcerned with the weighing of social pros and cons that forms the stuff of the early novel, although material covered in *Waverley* still forms part of its background.

One account of *Waverley* sees it as fundamentally a *bildungsroman*: point and shape is given to the story by ironic confrontations between 'reality', known to the mature author, and the undisciplined fancy of the hero, a fancy that results from an inadequate and sentimental education. The key in such an account is Waverley's reflection by the side of Windermere that the romance of his life has ended and the reality begun. His spirit has been 'tamed by adversity', and he has learned to live with the real world and turn his back on romance. Such a view, which centres on Waverley's realisation of his

9

own 'indolence and vanity', is representatively voiced by S. S. Gordon's important essay.[1] But Gordon, in rightly drawing our attention to the fact that something important as a novel is happening in *Waverley*, and that a novel is not the same thing as social and political history, tends to withdraw altogether from the facts of society and politics. A tale that is only a dramatisation of the hero's 'sound' and 'unsound' judgements would not need a historical, political, social novel at all; the novel of manners would be an adequate medium. But Scott draws the reader's attention to the fact that the internal drama of the protagonist is something that cannot be divorced from the substantial and important happenings of the outside world. Human nature is the same through a thousand editions, but 'Some favourable opportunities of contrast have been afforded me, by the state of society in the northern part of the island at the period of my history, and may serve at once to vary and to illustrate the moral lessons, which I would willingly consider as the most important part of my plan' (chapter 1). We might treat this claim with some scepticism since it was written long before the bulk of the novel. In my view, however, the moral intention can be strongly felt throughout the novel.

At about the time he wrote the first seven chapters, Scott was very critical of some things in Scottish society. Money was at the root of it: 'in general the vulgar saying of no longer pipe no longer dance applies to landlord and tenant and clan superior and vassal and in short to all the relations of mankind'.[2] Scott had been talking about the coming of the sheep; nostalgia for the older and 'kindlier' society was balanced by the knowledge that social relations were bound to follow economic changes. The greatest hope Scott had at this time was that things would work themselves out, that things that looked bad would produce their own cure. He reported, for example, that it had been found impossible to stock a farm to its full capacity with sheep in summer unless they are fed in the winter, which requires turnips, which in turn require a greater number of hands:

the farmers who do not lie near a town or village are as anxious to have cottagers upon their estates as they formerly were of banishing them – and this the more as they find that they are more regular sober and manageable than hired servants or labourers. In this way we may hope that our vallies will gradually be repeopled with a hardy and virtuous peasantry.[3]

A similar sense that basic economic laws had been and would be obeyed is very strongly felt in *Waverley*, in both the Highland and the Lowland scenes. In the scenes at Glennaquoich, Scott's aim is to portray, realistically, pre-1748 clan society. The authorial comments are throughout in the same key as the many accounts of the Highlands in Scott's letters and prose works. When we read of Fergus MacIvor that

his own patriarchal power, he strengthened at every expense which his fortune would permit, and indeed stretched his means to the uttermost to maintain the rude and plentiful hospitality which was the most valued attribute of a chieftain. For the same reason he crowded his estate with a tenantry, hardy indeed, and fit for the purposes of war, but greatly outnumbering what the soil was calculated to maintain (chapter 19).

we know that sixty years later this had all disappeared; the place of the clansmen had been taken by sheep. We know that Fergus' character is seen in a critical light, although his care for his clansman is noted, for its basis is a sort of egotism, the desire for the furtherance of his own power and prestige. When the clansmen no longer served this purpose, as after 1748, the Ferguses would look around for some other means of personal aggrandisement, based usually on conspicuous consumption and requiring the economic exploitation of their old tenants. Not that Scott is against economic exploitation in this passage: the economic unreality of the old system is hinted at in the reference to the productivity of the soil. The agriculture was primitive: 'a scanty crop of barley, liable to constant depredations from herds of wild ponies'. And of Tully Veolan, the first view we have is its material poverty, backwardness and squalor:

The whole scene was depressing; for it argued, at the first glance, at least a stagnation of industry, and perhaps of intellect ... poverty,

11

and indolence . . . were combining to depress the natural genius and acquired information of a hardy, intelligent and reflecting peasantry . . . the common field, where the joint labour of the villagers cultivated alternate ridges and patches of rye, oats, barley, and peas, each of such minute extent that at a little distance the unprofitable variety of the surface resembled a tailor's book of patterns (chapter 8).

This is improver's talk; the whole chapter is a description of the tenures, land-usage and unimproved agriculture of pre-'Scottish economic miracle' society. The frequent relish with which Bradwardine outlines the extent of his feudal powers – '*cum fossa et furca*' – is more than a grotesque humour. It is seriously related to the 'habits of solitary and secluded authority' exercised over the 'half cultivated estate'. The Baron's pride in his feudal tenure is, for all of Scott's readers, although the connection is not made explicit, the origin of the material poverty of the village.

Scott's purpose in *Waverley*, however, is not to praise the new while castigating the old. The background of economic rationalism is part of his rhetorical strategy. It helps to convince us that this novel is the work of a clear-sighted, objective and knowledgeable informant. Scott knew that his contemporaries, Scots of education, would immediately recognise the 'old', 'runrig' field-system in the 'tailor's book of patterns' and would unhesitatingly agree with him in condemning it. Scott was perhaps more knowledgeable about Highland customs than many of his contemporaries, though by no means all of them. His comments are certainly not remarkable or unusual; great numbers of his fellow-countrymen had been saying the same things since about 1785. The reader knows that Scott is fully informed about the economy that supported the old Highland manners and is the more disposed to accept Scott's word when he nevertheless finds something of counterbalancing value in this world, and that in a completely original and novelistic way. Most writers, not novelists, but parsons, squires and farmers, could only contrast 'lazy' and 'unproductive' with 'sturdy' and 'good soldiers'. Subtler evaluations slipped through their fingers. Scott uses a series of dramatic confrontations – the 'contrasts' and 'moral lessons' – to place the 'Highland question' in a wholly new light. It is the same technique he was to use later in *The Pirate*: the hero is exposed to a communal way of life that he, as bourgeois individualist, is incapable of participating in or even fully comprehending, which neverthe-less makes a deep impression on him and, more importantly, prompts the unembarrassed, uninvolved reader to develop new insights of his own.

There is one important difference between *Waverley* and *The Pirate*, and indeed other later novels. In *Waverley* Scott's moral lessons are not entirely beyond the capabilities of discursive prose. Later, there will be doubt about the very idea of giving 'moral lessons' at all, in a situation that is so intractable as to be approachable only obliquely, through drama, myth, symbol, metaphor. In *Waverley*, the intention of the novel comes out quite openly in two or three strongly marked scenes in which the reader is clearly asked to make moral judgements. These scenes are close to the novel's centre, and they deal with class-relationships.

The first of these scenes is Waverley's discovery of his wounded sergeant, Houghton, dying in a hut. In the first part of the scene, before we know all the details, we are prepared to admire Waverley, to recognise in him the epitome of Christian charity, the Good Samaritan:

'For the love of God,' said the wounded man . . . 'give me a single drop of water!'
'You shall have it,' answered Waverley, at the same time raising him in his arms' (chapter 45).

The dignified, near-Scriptural language, invites the reader to applaud Waverley's action. Although the deed is in itself a worthy one, we are made to feel in an instant that Waverley himself is not worthy of the action, that he is reprehensible and contemptible. '"I should know that voice," said the man; but looking on Waverley's dress with a bewildered look – "no, this is not the young squire!"' The implications of this, in their dramatic way, are obvious; it is the person of the young squire, but he is not playing his part as he should. He has, as both squire and captain, shamefully betrayed his charges to 'that fiend of the pit, Ruffin'. His self-justification sounds pathetically weak: 'I assure you, Houghton, you have been vilely imposed upon.' It is contrasted strongly with the sergeant's rejoinder, with its uncomprehending, matter-of-fact despair: 'I often thought so . . . though they showed us your very seal; and so Timms was shot, and I was reduced to the ranks.' Waverley's failure to look after his men makes doubly ironical the opinion of the Clan MacIvor that 'Waverley's conduct was that of a kind and considerate chieftain who merited the attachment of his people.'

It is important at this stage to draw attention to one of Scott's fundamental techniques. Depth of character creation is attained through manipulation of the reader's attitude, externally to the character. Scott seldom gives us introspection, and when he does it is frequently false or banal. Nor will he reflect at length on the niceties of conduct. He relies on a change of feeling about the character by the reader to substitute for authorial commentary.

Another moment of recognition is Evan's speech at the trial of Fergus MacIvor. We have found Evan's speech comical for its verbal oddity and we have been invited to laugh with the fictional audience. Evan rebukes the audience for their scorn:

'If they laugh because they think I would not keep my word, and come back to redeem him, I can tell them they ken neither the heart of a Hielandman, nor the honour of a gentleman.'

There was no further inclination to laugh among the audience, and a dead silence ensued (chapter 68).

This notion of 'gentlemanly honour', with its absolute and unswerving claims, is contrasted with the more flexible 'Waverley honour'.

A third moment, which is less clearly a pointer, in being unmarked rhetorically, is Bradwardine's restoration to his estate in chapter 71. On being shown the restored avenue to the house, the felled trees removed, the stone bears replaced, and on Edward's asking him if he would like to visit the gentleman who had 'purchased [his] ancient patrimonial property', the Baron replies that he will be 'happy to see the new master of [his] old tenants'. With all his antiquarian pedantry, he still puts the social relationship first, as Waverley is unable to do.

The Baron's deficiencies in political economy have been made very obvious. But he grows in moral stature towards the end of the book, as Waverley falls, in spite of all his absurdities, through his kindness and delicacy in his dealings with his dependents and through their reciprocal affection for him. His inability to make agriculture work is implicitly related to his refusal to assign human beings a market value. He supports and countenances economically useless and derelict, outcast people – old Janet and her pair of sons, the poor scholar and the idiot. It was a gentle, patriarchal and Wordsworthian society. It might even have existed: James Russell celebrated this kind of community in his nostalgic portrait of the Selkirkshire of the turn of the century.[4] At a very short interval after the writing of this scene, Scott was to comment on something similar in the Orkneys. What to do with the useless indigenous population, if you are an Orcadian lord: 'it is the hardest chapter in Economicks'; Scott claimed that he would be tempted, against his better judgement, 'to shuffle on with the useless old creatures'.[5] In *Waverley* Scott does not make explicit the connection between economic and political backwardness and social kindliness; but there is meaning in the mere juxtaposition. Scott nowhere gives a utopian or sentimental account of old or Highland manners. Compared with similar scenes in *The Pirate*, the Highland feasting and hospitality episodes are seen crisply and from the outside, full of hints of material brutality and of the strictly necessitarian ordering of manners and customs: 'Everyone present understood that his taste was to be formed according to the rank which he held at table, and, consequently, the tacksmen and their dependants always professed the wine was too cold for their stomachs, and called, apparently out of choice, for the

15

liquor which was assigned to them from economy' (chapter 20). Dramatic confrontation between two ways of life is curiously avoided since the moral of the story never enters the consciousness of the hero. Waverley is quite unaware of his own failures as a leader of men. He sees his own 'education' as a progress from an undisciplined romanticism to a chastened realism. It is perhaps part of the novel's conception that he cannot see what we do. After Fergus' death, Waverley becomes the munificent friend of the sons of Ivor. He cannot take the chief's place; his sentiments are based on friendship and general philanthropy, not on ties of family and place.

Waverley comes from a divided family; his father is traitor to his hereditary cause. He himself lays claim to Sir Everard's coach because of his proprietorial instincts with regard to its coat of arms; but he has no sense of the traditional code of conduct associated with a coat of arms. Having got his troop of horse and his uniform, he is content to leave his post and continue his tour of Scotland, during which he observes the strange society around him. We are content to follow this, but as the plot is unfolded, the reader's sense of his folly is sharpened.

Waverley 'represents' English or modern society. The only way he can fulfil his role is to adopt a certain style – of dress, aesthetic taste, attitude. His faults, compared with those of later young aristocrats of the series, are quite venial, but they are still those of vanity and egotism. I shall show below in accounts of the poor-laws and income tax how Scott saw these at work in Britain during this period, attacking the bases of society and alienating class from class. The moral surprises and rebuffs that Waverley experiences during his adventures help to point up the contrast between a feudal and a modern society. Nostalgia is at a minimum; the respective vices and virtues of the two societies are allowed to stand. We note that Jacobite Scotland was violent, economically irrational but homogeneous and loving; and that Hanoverian Scotland was more rational, cooler, less closely knit. We understand that there are losses and gains, and seem to look forward, from a secure, confident base, to a future that will achieve a credible synthesis.

This discussion of *Waverley* has been brief, not because I think it is of little interest, but because I am in principle in agreement with the direct and implicit judgements made by the consensus of modern critical opinion on the novel. Largely, it is a novel that dramatises a contrast of cultures; it is true that there is a sharper side to it, which is related to the busy social questions that were soon to engross Scott completely. However, *Waverley* is an academic novel, literally, in that it discusses questions that were then current in the Scottish schools, and it generates an interest and an emotion not more than is appropriate to an academic novel. The contrast of life-styles is something that we can approach easily, with relish but no pain. *Redgauntlet*, by contrast, is a difficult and obscure novel, and one that has been ill served by being forced into the mould of *Waverley*, with which it has only very accidental connections.

A composite modern reading of *Redgauntlet* would say that it stresses the inevitability of the fall of Jacobitism and shows its irrelevance to the modern world. There is Darsie Latimer, understood to be a standard Scott youth poised between two worlds, whose final choice will express a judgement endorsed by the author. The representatives of the two worlds are Herries and Geddes, one of whom Latimer must choose as a surrogate father. In choosing Geddes, Darsie commits himself, and us, to the modern world. And yet, how odd: did anyone in the 1820s feel anything for Jacobitism, and if not, how could it be important? Of course, we can say that 'Jacobitism' means something else. D. D. Devlin has this explanation:

Redgauntlet and *Waverley* are Scott's most successful attempts to define his feelings towards the old Scotland and the new . . . [His] dramatic aim may, very briefly, be described as the attempt to answer the question: 'What qualities of mind and character are necessary to reconcile a deep love of the past with successful living in the present?' It is a great historical novel because Scott tackles with art and energy this urgent question which lies at the heart of all the Waverley novels, and because this urgency is concerned not only with the rapid social and economic changes of post-Culloden Scotland (Scott writes historical, not social, novels), but with the central and perennial question of man's relationship with the past and the present, and the need and cost of movement, change and survival.

Scott . . . sees Jacobitism not as a political faith, but as an older way of life, a different culture; and he recognises that it is partly 'the gradual influx of wealth and the extension of commerce' that have killed it . . . Scott's attitude to this past and to the less glamourous present is what gives pressure to all his finest Scottish novels.[6]

Other readers will have their own opinion, yet I must voice mine that the 'question' that Devlin isolates – living in the present yet retaining a deep interest in the past – does not seem either very real or very interesting, and certainly not absorbing enough to write even ten novels about. It is true that such topics are raised and discussed in traditional societies that are undergoing modernisation – and sociologists write papers, and urban personnel take their relaxation in styles derived aesthetically from tradition. But this 'question' does not arouse passion, and if it ever seems to, then it is usually a cover for something else: who is to wield the power, where are resources to be allocated, what are the limits of American influence, how is wealth to be shared out?

However, if we accept Devlin's definition of the theme, we might be inclined to attempt a sketch of the novel that runs like this: in the midst of a general prosperity and stability, a few malcontents who have nothing to lose attempt to stir up rebellion among those whose economic interests are entirely opposed to change. Within this political drama is the personal story of a young man who must choose between past and present . . . Yet this is not the novel we read in *Redgauntlet*. There is no circumstantial account of peace and plenty. Edinburgh and county society are both described with great selectivity. There is no bustle of commerce, no mention of the agricultural improvements that were in reality stirring at this time, no university, no bleachfields, antimony mines, cotton-mills and the rest. There is Saunders Fairford, and there is Joshua Geddes – but they have very different parts to play in the novel. Nor is Herries cast in any appropriate mould. We do not see his plots. The last quarter of the novel, the part that deals with the Jacobite rebellion in some detail, is by far the weakest section. The inferiority is in a decline of local richness: Scott's 'invention', his capacity to engage with life at its most physical level and to endow it with rich suggestiveness, was in abeyance in this section. Nor, in the earlier portion, is Herries' position as reactionary or as distressed gentleman presented with any clarity. When we do see him, it is through the eyes of Darsie and Alan, and his meaning is his meaning for them. The legend that the House of Redgauntlet is on the losing side saves Scott from having to be more circumstantial. And, in fact, neither Alan nor Darsie really does make a choice. We might feel that they would opt for Hanover, but the moment of decision does not form part of the novel.

So much attention has been paid to what the novel is not to illustrate the dangers of deciding what it is about from a bare description of the plot. The action does have its own significance, but so do other structural elements, notably the various narrative devices and the technique of doubling or repetition. Close analysis will reveal both a kind of realism, or 'psychological truth to life' and 'the creation of a palpable fictional world', and poetry, the employment of images that have universal reverberations or make sense within the literary tradition or serve to link the novel into one whole. Current critical enthusiasm for Scott the realist should not drive out our memory that he was also a romantic poet.

This novel begins with 'character'. The opening interchange of letters between Alan and Darsie is designed to reveal individual lineaments within the generic figure of 'young hero' and to place them within an economic and social context, although the context is hardly designed to evoke 'Scotland, 176–', not in the same way that *Waverley* located its economic setting very precisely, just before 1745. The fact of *a* social background is important, but not the particular time. To begin with, the novel is more interested in the relations between Alan and Darsie, in the dynamics of their exchanges, their likenesses, dissimilarities, their respective positions in society, their friendship.

Darsie to begin with adopts a rather haughty attitude to Alan: he comments on Alan's 'miserable hack' and his 'law drudgery'. But his own aristocratic pretensions rest on a financial easiness of dubious origins; he is a mere rentier. There is the early half-suggestion that he is the bastard son of an English merchant. Darsie has no *connections*. Alan's father reckons him a 'lone thing', while Darsie denigrates what he does not have by saying that he can 'take no interest in the common herd'. He feels his isolation severely in Scotland 'where all the world have a circle of consanguinity extending to sixth cousins at least'. Here is a cultural contrast: but it is related to living social concerns, not to academic and aesthetic sociology. The tenacity of the Scots in preserving their family ties to the most obscure reaches of relationship was, as we shall see below, what distinguished post-Waterloo Scotland from England, and was manifested in the operation of the Scottish poor-laws, which seemed to the Scots to stand for much more. Yet Darsie intends to conform to the English model he believes his own: the novel shows how far such an ambition will take him. Darsie is not connected even economically to society: not being 'condemned to labour for [his] bread' he does not feel even 'that necessary communication of master and servant [which] would be at least a tie which would attach [him] to the rest of [his] kind'. His economic independence aggravates his isolation: he characterises his own relationship with society in a telling image that makes physical the meaning of the phrase 'cash-nexus': 'I am in the world as a stranger in the crowded coffee-house, where he enters, calls for what refreshment he wants, pays his bill, and is forgotten as soon as the waiter's mouth has pronounced his "thank ye, sir"' (chapter 1). Unable to make his way in the law, he is determined to be Alan's first client and to give him his first fee.

This portrait is darkened by critical attitudes that are taken up with regard to Darsie. At times, he seems to be sliding into what is called an 'unmanly' self-pity; by his own account, he was an over-indulged child. Old Fairford sneers at the implications of the hamlet called 'Noble House', while Alan convicts Darsie of want of ambition and of hoping to secure wealth and position without 'any exertion of [his] own'. This hints at weaknesses of character to be further explained. Yet the novel does not develop this strand realistically. The source of future development is located elsewhere: the prohibition upon Darsie's going to England. In terms of plot, Darsie can only come legally under his uncle's rule in England, where he possesses property. There is probably a clear moral lesson in chapter 19 when Darsie reflects that it was those 'possessions which had occasioned [his] loss of freedom'. To say that Darsie would have remained free had he not got into the ambiguous position he was in by the side of the Solway is beside the point since Scott shows how inevitably he is drawn there.

Alan Fairford is a character of equal importance. Like Darsie, he is extremely self-conscious. Their letters are artificial, narcissistic, anxious. They brood over their own characters and observe each other ironically, trying to prepare for the parting they see ahead, subtly running down each other. Neither Darsie's 'Quixotry' nor Alan's dour pedantry are facts in the novel since each is reported by the other. Alan's life is as circumscribed as Darsie's is apparently free. It is directed by his father; his motions are ordered and restrained. He regrets that his father 'does not allow him a little more exercise of [his] own free will' but keeps him 'caged up like a cobbler's linnet'. But Alan, if not free, is not alone. He is part of a family and a community – that of the law: 'The law is my vocation – in an especial, and I may say, in an hereditary way, my vocation.' There is something paradoxical about a hereditary vocation, but Alan accepts it, as he does the necessity of making his way up the ladder of legal promotion. Alan concurs in his not-free situation by giving himself over to study and ambition. The law sustains him. When Darsie writes that he will 'go on doubting with Dirleton, resolving these doubts with Stewart' it is as if the dry authorities of the law were intimate daily acquaintances. Alan and his father carry the flavour of shop into their breakfast and supper, their conversation is replete with precedents and decrees. The law is not merely Alan's occupation and hope of advancement, it is an integral part of his character.

Freedom and restraint, money and the law, isolation and community: these are the important concepts outlined in the opening pair of letters. Much of the rest of the novel is a development of them. There is no suggestion of any contrast between the old and the new.

Darsie is an isolated figure without a community. But there are some things he believes in: his freedom, his wealth, his superior, enlightened 'Englishness'. All these beliefs prove to be illusions. Darsie is hypnotised by England. (I suspect, yet cannot prove, wider symbolism; Darsie is the whole of Scotland about to cast away its cultural heritage and social traditions in favour of a disastrously inappropriate southern model.) He is led towards the Solway in spite of himself. 'The anxious thoughts which haunt me began to muster in my bosom, and my feet slowly and insensibly approached the river which divided me from the forbidden precincts, though without any formed intention' (Letter IV). There is irony, in view of later developments, in Darsie's apostrophisation of England as 'the land of the brave and the wise and the free' (Letter III).

Darsie images his freedom as freedom from control, but it becomes freedom to lose himself. This is the point of the first Solway episode. Darsie, wandering among the pools and quicksands of the Solway, with a storm coming up and the tide racing in, is the first urgent image of deracination in the novel. It is a version of an image used again and again by Scott: that of the maze or labyrinth. Very often it is associated with a complementary or opposite image: that of the pilot, the man who can find his way. In *Redgauntlet*, the pilot is Herries: he can negotiate his way to dry land, from one pool to another. Another important image for him is the rider, the skilled horseman. As is traditional in literature, horsemanship represents control, discipline and authority. Control may be political or personal; the horseman is either a ruler or a man in control of his own passions. Interestingly enough the image of horse is twice applied to Darsie (though not to Alan). In not being allowed to go to England, Darsie thinks he is like a 'tethered horse'. Darsie's 'cock-a-hoop' courage is like a 'hot mettled horse', which will carry its owner into 'some scrape', says Alan. When Herries appears as a man who has iron control of his horse, it is accompanied by the exercise of another sort of authority: 'He was a tall man, well mounted on a strong black horse, which he caused to turn and wind like a bird in the air . . . He seemed to hold some sort of authority among [the fishermen] and occasionally directed their motions both by voice and hand' (Letter IV). He places Darsie behind him and then shows his authority: 'The horse was soon compelled to submit to the discipline of the spur and bridle.' And so, shortly, will Darsie. The symbolism is not immediately obvious, although it becomes clear later when the relations between uncle and nephew are developed. At the moment though, Darsie is frightened and hurt at being beholden to one he considers his inferior. He makes what is to be a typical gesture with him – he reaches for his purse. Herries snubs him: 'Your presence will no doubt give me trouble, sir, but it is of a kind which your purse cannot compensate; in a word, although I am content to receive you as a guest, I am no publican to call a reckoning.' Darsie remains in debt, with the uncomfortable feeling that he has behaved churlishly. The power of his purse and the extent of his liberty have already been called in question; the direction of the novel is towards his complete helplessness and dependence.

The steps by which this is reached will be outlined below, but this first picture is instructive for its demonstration of the variety of techniques at Scott's disposal. The figure of the Laird is rendered in prose that uses Gothic sensationalism to convey his impressiveness. It will also render the physicality of the action, and the awkward, half-aware-of-itself egotism of the narrator. It is also highly suggestive: the figure of the narrator/helpless passenger, the flood tide of the Solway, its labyrinthine bed, and the tall, capable horseman: all these are physically real and vibrant with symbolic life.

To describe part of the prose as Gothic sensationalism is not to pass an adverse judgement. Almost always in Scott, as well as the physical-realistic, the psychological-realistic and the poetic or symbolic, there is an extra or literary dimension. The writing reaches out to enfold by pastiche or quotation another epoch, author or dramatic moment. The Gothic novel is one quarry; Shakespeare is more important; there is Restoration and eighteenth-century drama, Milton, Dryden, balladry, the Renaissance epic. In this novel Darsie writes like an eighteenth-century novel, now Johnsonian and now Gulliverian: 'I never saw finer animals, or which seemed to be more influenced by a sense of decorum, excepting that they slobbered a little as the rich scent from the chimney was wafted past their noses' (Letter IV). Secure young men of the eighteenth century, on the Grand Tour say, might well adopt such a magisterial attitude to what they see and report upon. The irony about Darsie is that he is reporting upon something he imagines to be foreign and outside himself while it is in fact a part of his past and his make-up. Such literary references are far from mere decorativeness, they involve large areas of the cultural inheritance and allow it to participate in the novel.

The novel moves towards Darsie's imprisonment and the establishment of his identity. But before this occurs there are some episodes that should be considered: Darsie's stay at the Laird's and at Geddes', his trip to the dance with Willie, and Alan's encounter with the Laird in Edinburgh. A comparison is established between Herries and Geddes and it would be useful to inquire into the real nature and purpose of this juxtaposition. For it is a very deliberate pairing. Both Geddes and Herries are met in the wilderness on horseback; both guide Darsie to their houses; both houses are isolated areas of life in the wilderness; both are surrounded by woods and bordered by a stream. These repetitions emphasise their moral unlikeness; as Darsie writes: 'they might have formed no bad emblem of

Peace and War' (Letter VI). Geddes' plainness is a matter of principle, while Herries' expresses contempt for his company. The houses are not similar in the comfort they offer; Darsie dines better at Mt Sharon and is more kindly treated. These are details of action and description. They create a physical contrast that implies to the reader that a further, more abstract, one is intended. But what is its real significance? As outlined above, some critics would have it that the two represent a landed/feudal society and an urban/commercial one, the past and the future of Scotland.

There is a grain of truth in it. At one point the Laird and the Quaker do seem to assume representative economic roles. The Laird is fisherman, hunter, while Geddes is a couple of stages on in the 'progress of society'. The Laird appeals to tradition: 'we . . . fish fairly, and like men, as our fathers did'. He accuses the stake-net company in these terms: 'You will destroy the salmon which makes the livelihood of fifty poor families and then wipe your mouth, and go to make a speech at meeting.' The phraseology reminds us of the way in which the big sheep farms were criticised in the early nineteenth century: one man and a dog would occupy the ground that previously supported twenty (or thirty or fifty) poor families. Joshua's reply, confident that his fishing system better serves the ends of Providence (it makes use of the ebb and flow of the tides) reminds us of those who argued that God seemed to have destined the Highlands to oviculture. The Laird makes a gesture towards linking Joshua's Protestantism with his capitalism: 'this pious pattern of primitive simplicity will teach thee the right way to the Shepherd's Bush – aye, and will himself shear thee like a sheep, if you come to buying and selling with him'.

Nevertheless, this sort of opposition cannot remain convincing. It is, first, quite wrong to suggest that the past of Scotland belonged to the aristocratic and landed interest and the future to the urban, commercial middle classes. At least as Scott wrote, the hereditary gentry and aristocracy was far more powerful in Scotland than any men of commerce (see

25

below, chapter 4). Perhaps, though, Herries might represent the old-fashioned, unimproved, retrogressive gentry? In that case he is not presented as one would expect. He would care for his tail or retinue, like Fergus MacIvor, to maintain his influence. But his fields would remain uncultivated and squalid. He would be surrounded by a mixture of ostentation and squalor. Then again, something of the social virtues of past times might be shown, hospitality, care for tenants and so on. But the Laird hardly exists at this level of interest. His fomenting of the fishermen's riot was aimed at securing Darsie's person and had nothing economic in it. His house exhibits neither waste nor squalor but an almost Puritan frugality and cleanliness. There are no old-world social values of openness and hospitality. It is not in any very easily recognisable way that Herries represents the economic and social past.

Does Geddes represent the drab but necessary future? What about his commercial activities, his thriving country house? Joshua is a rentier. As his sister explains to Darsie, the family fortune was made by his fathers, while he himself has chosen withdrawal: 'my brother Joshua withdrew from an active share in the commercial concerns of my father, being satisfied with the portion of worldly substance which he already possessed' (Letter VII). This is no Jarvie. Joshua's sole reason for taking part in the stake-net enterprise is that 'his withdrawing might have been prejudicial to friends, or because he wished to retain some mode of occupying his time'. R. J. Gordon calls Joshua's house, Mt Sharon, 'an earthly paradise'.[7] But is it really so ideal, and what is its meaning? Is there an implication that Joshua was one of the first agricultural improvers, who were at this very minute beginning their work? There is certainly something; as Darsie comes close to the house

conducted by the meanders of the brook, we left the common behind us, and entered a more cultivated and enclosed country, where arable and pasture ground was agreeably variegated with groves and hedges . . .

If there was a little vanity in the complacent smile with which Joshua Geddes saw me gaze with delight on a scene so different

26

from the naked waste we had that day traversed in company, it might surely be permitted to one who cultivating and improving the beauties of nature . . .

Here is fertility, enclosure of commons, afforestation, the harmonious regulation of nature and the works of man: Scott's own practice, and what he recommended to all his friends. We would not expect physical details of the agriculturist's art. This sort of observation may be understood to be subsumed into implicit generalisations, where practicality and the picturesque are carefully united: 'A rivulet which spread into a pond for the convenience of the aquatic birds, trickled over gravel as it passed through the yards dedicated to the land poultry, which were thus amply supplied with the means they use for digestion.' And yet, it is still impossible to see Geddes as improver, man of the future. Improvement was never something perfected: it was an ongoing activity. The imaginations of commentators were fired by the bustle of labour, the way one achievement would be the start of another activity, 'new wants' be uncovered, the 'bonds of community' be strengthened. Geddes' house is truly in a wilderness; although labour must have been required to complete it, there is no suggestion that at present it is the centre of any economic activity – it is very different from Scott's own attempts with Abbotsford and Abbotstown. Labourers, cottagers, a village – all are strikingly absent. Joshua's existence is more similar to the Laird's than he would want to admit. Darsie does refer to the house as a 'little Eden'; but he is to report on it more truly than he realises.

The first clue that something is not quite right with the house is given in the account of the gardens:

The space contained close alleys and open walks; a very pretty artificial water fall; a fountain also, consisting of a considerable jet d'eau . . . There was a cabinet of verdure as the French call it . . .

I know that you, Alan, will condemn all this as bad and antiquated; for, ever since Dodsley has described the Leasowes, and talked of Brown's imitation of nature . . . you are all for simple nature (Letter VII).

In real life, a man can admire a French formal garden without prejudice to his character, but in this context, it would seem that at the very least the owner of this property is not fashionably progressive and that he attempts to mould nature to the ways of man, to impose geometrical designs upon her. By itself this would be inconclusive, but it is followed by a long passage that deserves quoting at length:

At any rate, Alan, had you condemned as artificial the rest of Friend Geddes's grounds, there is a willow walk by the very verge of the stream, so sad, so solemn, and so silent, that it must have commanded your admiration. The brook, restrained at the ultimate boundary of the grounds by a natural dam-dike or ledge of rocks, seemed, even in its present swollen state scarcely to glide along; and the pale willow trees, dropping their long branches into the stream, gathered around them little coronals of the foam that floated down from the more rapid stream above. The high rock, which formed the opposite bank of the brook, was seen dimly through the branches, and its pale and splintered front, garlanded with long streamers of briers and other creeping plants, seemed a barrier between the quiet path which we trod, and the toiling and bustling world beyond. The path itself, following the sweep of the stream, made a very gentle curve; enough, however, served by its inflection completely to hide the end of the walk until you arrived at it. A deep and sullen sound, which increased as you proceeded, prepared you for this termination, which was indeed only a plain root-seat, from which you looked on a fall of about six or seven feet, where the brook flung itself over the ledge of natural rock I have already mentioned, which there crossed its course.

The quiet and twilight seclusion of this walk rendered it a fit scene for confidential communing; and having nothing more interesting to say to my fair Quaker, I took the liberty of questioning her about the laird (Letter VII).

While the stream outside Joshua's house and outside the Laird's is swollen and roaring, it is here so dammed up that it scarcely seems to move. The brook is emblematic of life in the garden, with its studied, peaceful beauty, and a barrier against the outside world. 'River' in the novel represents process, life, and time; the slowing down of the river would then suggest that life and time are halted, dammed up, inside the garden. When the pent-up water is thrown down with a sullen sound, the conversation turns naturally to Herries. A few pages later, Darsie and Rachel are still walking down this willow walk. Rachel is describing her brother's difficulties, explaining that he will neither retreat nor compromise in the salmon war:

'but what can I say? Even in the best-trained temper there may remain some leaven of the old Adam . . . [he] will not resist force by force, neither will he yield up his right' . . . This observation convinced me that the spirit of the old sharers of the spoil was not utterly departed even from the bosom of the peaceful Quaker . . .

As we approached the further end of the willow walk, the sullen and continuous sound of the dashing waters became still more and more audible . . . we obtained a view of the cascade, where the swollen brook flung itself in foam and tumult over the natural barrier of rock, which seemed in vain to attempt to bar its course.

Surely this counterpointing of character and scenery cannot be accidental. The river is stilled in the garden, but time and passion will intrude here, hints of them occurring when the water bursts over the dam. Joshua cannot really shut out the world, any more than he can restrain himself. It reminds us of those moments in the novel when Joshua's habitual restraint fails him, and he utters hasty words, grips his cudgel tighter and defies his enemies. Darsie feels obliged to leave the Quaker's domain. In Letter x he explains why: 'there was, in the whole routine, a uniformity, a want of interest, a helpless and hopeless languor, which rendered life insipid . . . on the whole, time glided softly and imperceptibly on with them, though to me, who long for stream and cataract, it seemed absolutely to stand still'. How similar this account of time is to the description of the river: compare 'time glided softly and impercep- tibly' with 'The brook . . . seemed . . . scarcely to glide along.' Mt Sharon then would appear to have its meaning in a set of moral/symbolic terms. And if it is an island of would-be still- ness, attempting rather selfishly and inadequately to oppose, the world of process, then it cannot be, in another, metonymic, realistic world, representative of an ethos that accelerates social and economic change.

There are two similar passages in *Waverley*, which nicely

illustrate the differences between the two novels. In chapter 22, Waverley chooses to follow the course of a stream that is 'rapid and furious' rather than one that is 'placid and sullen'. This ironically illustrates the hero's narcissistic romanticism, but it is not linked in any precise way with the plotting. The garden at Tully Veolan is very like that of Mt Sharon:

[it] seemed to be kept with great accuracy, abounded in fruit trees, and exhibited a profusion of flowers and evergreens, cut into grotesque forms. It was laid out in terraces, which descended rank by rank from the western wall to a large brook, which had a tranquil and smooth appearance, where it served as a boundary to the garden; but, near the extremity, leapt in tumult over a strong dam, or weir-head . . . After this feat, the brook, assuming its natural rapid and fierce character, escaped from the eye . . . (chapter 9).

One would assume that Scott derived both streams from the same original, yet his use of it varies strikingly in the two novels. The *Waverley* passages may, perhaps, hint at violence and turbulence beyond the bounds of cultivated life. But it seems much more to represent simply its own existence, or the fact that this garden might be like this. It does not enter Waverley's consciousness, its meaning can only be ironically perceived by the reader. There is certainly none of the precise linking of image with narrative and character so strikingly exhibited in *Redgauntlet*.

Why did Scott choose to bring in a Quaker? It may be true that he was reworking early biographical material: but why here, in his eighteenth novel? If he wanted an opposite to reactionary Catholicism why did he not choose to include the Presbyterianism he knew so well? A mere fear of staleness? The vital point about the Quaker, in the novel, is that he does not participate in ordinary society. He cannot swear, and so will not be able to be protected by, or to serve, the law. In Scott's terms, he is neither a full citizen nor a free man. When Darsie bursts out of the garden he is in fact making a correct choice. He rejects the Quaker, if not for quite the right reasons. Geddes is like the Laird in another way: if the Laird is an outlaw, Geddes is outside the law. Old Fairford links the two quite straightforwardly. Only the determination of modern criticism to see Herries and Geddes as the two terms of a polarity has prevented this connection from being generally recognised. Fairford remarks: 'ye are to judge for yourself whether ye can safely to your soul's weal remain longer among these Papists and Quakers'. Quakers are 'a people who own neither priest nor king, nor civil magistrate, nor the fabric of our law and will not depone either *in civilibus* or *criminalibus* be the loss to the lieges what it may' (Letter IX). This inevitably involves the Quaker in some paradoxes, unkindly but understandably labelled by the multitude as hypocrisy. Geddes, to defend his property, is bound to resort to the law that he cannot support and to invoke the aid of force that in principle he rejects:

'John Davies,' he said, 'will, I trust, soon be at Dumfries –'

'To fetch down redcoats and dragoons against us, you canting old villain!' (chapter 4).

Scott makes a likeable figure of the old man, but the anomalies of his position are underlined at every turn. He was not interested in, and clearly did not even consider, a figure who would embody extreme Christian virtues of self-abnegation. This Quaker is a man who would be benevolent and prosperous and quietist; Scott wants to tell us that it is impossible.

The party at Brokenburn shows Darsie in a new light; here he has to try to relate himself to a more general and unfamiliar sort of society. The reader's attitude to Darsie changes. Our reaction has been one of sympathetic indulgence; he has been a friendless wanderer and our representative against both Papist and Quaker. Now we see him in a less sympathetic light. He offers Willie money to take him with him. '"Damn your crowns!" said the disinterested man of music.' Darsie is made to prove his worth as a musician in a revealing little section. He puts all his technical skill into a performance 'as [he] thought must have turned Crowdero into a pillar of stone with envy and wonder'. Willie parodies his efforts, angering and embarrassing him. Darsie will 'play very well wi' a little practice and some gude teaching. But ye maun learn to put the heart into it, man – to put the heart into it.' At the dance itself he is amused, condescending, insufferable. By the end of the party he has to escape to mutterings of dislike: 'flory conceited chap', 'haflins gentle'. He has been conceited, refused to dance with the principal lady, Dame Martin. He offers to dance a minuet with Lilias: 'She thanked me, and told me haughtily enough, "She was here to encourage the harmless pleasures of these good folks, but was not disposed to make an exhibition of her own indifferent dancing for their amusement" ' (Letter XII). This is a matter of character: egotism, inability to discriminate. It also exhibits at the level of character what the symbolic–metaphorical side of the novel is busily establishing: Darsie's social isolation.

Here the presentation of Darsie takes on an ethical dimension. Lilias rebukes him for mingling in society unfitting to his station. Darsie replies that he does not know his station or birth. This reminds us that he is in disguise, that he has paid Willie money for 'naething, but saying ae man's name instead of anither'. The ambiguity over names is an important recurring theme in the novel. It links Darsie with Herries, who has no name and many names. Lilias says she sees Darsie running into danger and would wish to help him as she would 'a blind man whom [she] might observe approaching the verge of a precipice'. Darsie has entrusted himself to a blind man as to 'an experienced pilot'. If he is being led by a blind man, we can expect that he is approaching a precipice. Another important concept that is raised in this exchange is that of manhood. Lilias asks if it is manly to wait for good furtune when with his own hands or mind he could make his own way: 'Reason, common sense, manhood . . . give the same counsel.' Her advice is like the Fairfords'. But it is irrelevant to his real position. Darsie's reply, that manhood calls him to face danger, also begs the question. But the dialogue formulates a very important question that has underpinned the novel: what is manhood, manliness, courage, what does being a man entail? Darsie does not play a very manly role in the novel, yet before examining the second part, where he is a prisoner and a woman, I should like to explore the contrast that is implied between him and Alan.

For all the similarity of their epistolary styles. Alan is in a different position in life. He and Darsie play at considering which is the more enviable mode of life, but Scott shows that neither has any choice. For all his penetration of his father's egotism, and his regret that his life is so circumscribed by study and ambition, Alan has no real wish to turn his back on Edinburgh law society. He is smugly proud of his middle-class 'free-born Scotsman's' status. He upbraids what he regards as his father's slavish awe of the great and is incensed by Herries' treatment of them:

What was it to him if we chose to imitate some of the conveniences or luxuries of an English dwelling-house, instead of living piled up above each other in flats? Have his patrician birth and aristocratic fortunes given him any right to censure those who dispose of the fruits of their own industry, according to their own pleasures? (Letter IV).

Alan is whole-heartedly in favour of this much-commented-on middle-class revolution. In fact, the difference between Alan and Darsie is early summed up as being one of security and self-confidence. While Alan is on home ground, in Edinburgh, he is strong. He chides Darsie for making histories out of nothing, being a Quixote, looking through a Claude Lorraine glass. Yet we know this is unjust; against all odds, Darsie's fears are justified. In Edinburgh, Alan can see Herries only as a rather antiquated outlaw, who has no power to disturb the young advocate. Yet Alan, confident as he is, is also unfree. The prose brings in constantly, almost gratuitously, images of restraint in the Fairford passages:

. . . my father having contrived to clog my heels with fetters of a professional nature . . . (Letter XIII).

Would to Heaven he was yoked to some tight piece of business . . . Some job that would hamshackle him.

A philosopher would have given way to this tide of feeling . . . but Mr Fairford only saw the more direct mode of continued restraint (chapter 1).

This restraint is thoroughly internalised. There is an amusing scene in which Alan shows for us how strongly his spontaneous life is checked, although he himself does not perhaps realise it. He plans to receive Lilias: 'I disarranged books to give them the appearance of a graceful confusion . . . I endeavoured to dispose my dress so as to resemble an elegant morning dishabille.' The persona Alan would like to assume is the one he is least fitted for: nothing could be stranger in his father's house than graceful confusion. When Lilias withdraws, Alan stands some time dumbfounded:

Then it darted on my mind that I might dog her . . . Off I set – ran down the close . . . demanded of one of the dyer's lads whether he had seen a lady go down the close . . . 'A leddy!' . . . 'Mr Alan, what takes you out, rinning like daft without your hat?'

'The devil take my hat!' answered I, running back, however, in quest of it . . . I saw my friend, the journeyman dyer, in close confabulation with a pea-green personage of his own profession, and was conscious, like Scrub, that they talked of me, because they laughed consumedly . . . and so slunk back within my own hole again (Letter VIII).

The presence of Lilias, the laughter of the commons, link this episode with Darsie's experience at the Brokenburn Foot dance. Alan is allowed one conspicuous success to complement Darsie's obvious exercise of his freedom. The primary function of Peter Peebles is that his law case provides a context to show Alan's competence as a lawyer. Peter Peebles' function as anti-masque to Stuart legitimacy is not to be denied but I believe it to be an afterthought. It is only apparent at scattered points and does not really touch the basis of Peebles' case. Scott could not resist making use of a ready symbol, but the greater part of the creation has little to do with Herries or Jacobitism. Satire on the law is not in question either: comparison with the Man from Shropshire serves to show how different Scott's purposes are from Dickens'. The Man from Shropshire is part of a fabric of legal injustice, while Peebles is part of the personal drama of Alan Fairford. Scott does not show us the mechanical details of the lawsuit – which he would have been undoubtedly

capable of doing. The complications of the case and its injustices are presented emblematically in the broken-down figure
of Peter and his pokes of documents, in the endless terminology
and legal jokes he is surrounded by. When Alan pleads his case,
all his gaucherie fades away, replaced by the commanding
presence of the advocate. It is not exciting, but it is economically done, and we are asked to enjoy and identify with this
triumph, especially when Fairford shows his emotion: 'Aye,
aye, I kend Alan was the lad to make a spoon or spoil a horn.'
Alan's success is related to his 'long and sedulous training', to
his 'father's experience and knowledge of business'. Tradition
and hereditary experience have been vindicated and Alan is
thoroughly a man on this, his own 'his native land'.

And yet this chapter (1) ends in confusion and disorder, the
confident and steady rhetoric dissolves as Alan reads the
letter from Mr Crosbie: 'He stopped short in his harangue –
gazed on the paper with a look of surprise and horror – uttered
an exclamation, and flinging down the brief which he had in
his hand, hurried out of the court.' This is similar to the
moment when Darsie flings out of the Quaker's garden. Law
and garden represent a sort of peacefulness, order and propriety. As the Quaker's hypocrisy is criticised, Fairford's mean-
ness and deceitfulness are exposed. Alan breaks through all his
father's bonds to 'obey the calls of friendship and humanity'.

Alan puts his trust in his status, his years, and his legal
training: 'I shall know, I trust, how to conduct myself with due
caution in any emergence which may occur, otherwise my legal
studies for so many years have been to little purpose (chapter
2). Just as Alan establishes his freedom, Darsie's is curtailed.
The turning-point of the action in the Darsie plot is where
Darsie stands helpless beside Joshua, is stunned and overpowered. Everything in this narrative now establishes his
helplessness and vulnerability.

Physical and mental weakness are stressed in this new part
of the novel. Darsie is unheroic; he and Geddes 'stood perfectly
passive' and Darsie is unconscious within half a dozen lines;
then he wonders if he has dreamed the tumult, then he is

bound and in bed. 'Aware of my utterly captive condition, I groaned betwixt bodily pain and mental distress' (chapter 4). Later, he seems to enter infancy again, while drugged and in pain:

the appearance of things around me became indistinct; the woman's form seemed to multiply itself, and to flit in various figures around me . . . the discordant noises and cries of those without the cottage seemed to die away in a hum like that with which a nurse hushes her babe. At length I fell into a deep sound sleep, or rather, a state of absolute insensibility (chapter 4).

Then Darsie is aware of himself prostrate and bound in a cart crossing the Solway. He relates his fears of being abandoned helpless:

I soon not only heard the roar of this dreadful torrent, but saw, by the fitful moonlight, the foaming crests of the devouring waves as they advanced with the speed and fury of a pack of hungry wolves.
    The consciousness that the slightest ray of hope, or power of struggling, was not left me, quite overcame the constancy which I had hitherto maintained. My eyes began to swim – my head grew giddy and mad with fear – I chattered and howled to the howling and roaring sea (chapter 4).

In this condition Darsie is seized by Herries in a scene that reinforces the echoes we have already had of the first Solway scene: 'he seized me as if I had been a child of six months old, threw me across the horse . . . supporting with one hand while he directed the animal with the other'. Darsie has been overpowered, drugged, concussed, bound. Naturally he is helpless and weak: but why has Scott engineered the scene, and why are there echoes of an action that occurred when Darsie was officially free? Scott wills us to have this image of Darsie's helplessness. There is an inevitable feeling of impatience, which the reader – with certain literary expectations – will feel at Darsie's 'lack of spirit'. Darsie relates the causes of our dissatisfaction himself, but is unable to change things:

In the meantime, there has stolen on me insensibly an indifference to my freedom – a carelessness about my situation, for which I am unable to account . . . I have said to myself that no one who is possessed of a fragment of freestone, or a rusty nail . . . need continue the inhabitant of a prison. Here, however, I sit, day after day without a single effort to effect my liberation (chapter 5).

He humiliates himself by the letter he sends to Herries:

Perhaps this letter was expressed in a tone too humble for the situation of an injured man, and I am inclined to think so when I recapitulate its tenor. But what could I do?

Darsie is made the subject of a number of humiliating comparisons: child, baby, madman. Darsie's early ideas about freedom and manhood have gone. This is accompanied by the discovery that some of the external resources he relied on have disappeared. He attempts to bribe the old woman but cannot reach his wallet. And when he would bribe Nixon:

'I will give you earnest directly, and that in banknotes,' said I; but thrusting my hand into my side pocket, I found my pocket book was gone . . . Cristal Nixon . . . no longer suppressed his laughter.

'Oh ho, my young master,' he said; 'we have taken good care you have not kept the means of bribing poor folk's fidelity' (chapter 4).

Darsie's trust in the law, in his rights as a freeborn Englishman, appears equally illusory in his interview with Justice Foxley, a scene of obvious satirical humour. The idea that justice is liable to upset is reinforced by the entry of Peter Peebles, himself ruined by the law, anxious to buy a 'fugie warrant' so that Alan can be caught in the mesh of the law's injustices. Darsie's particular weakness appears to be his lack of name and family. Illogical though it is, we feel that his helplessness is to do with his namelessness. He has to face his fate with his solitary 'I', with no help from family, friends, tradition: and he is inadequate. A conversation with Mr Nixon reinforces this point:

I asked him whether his name was not Cristal Nixon.

'What is other folk's names to you,' he replied gruffly, 'who cannot tell your own father and mother?'

. . . 'Tell me the cause of my misfortunes, or rather help me to my liberty, and I will reward you richly.'

'Ay aye,' replied my keeper; 'but what use to give you liberty, who know nothing how to use it like a gentleman but spend your time with Quakers and fiddlers, and such like raff?'

Somewhere in the tension between the scorn expressed for Darsie, his lack of propriety, his namelessness and our sense that after all he is not really responsible for the actions of his ancestors, the stirrings of some problems of moral and social existence are felt. What is manhood? What role does society play in its formation and self-experience? The past/present dichotomy is subsumed within these problems, as are many of the themes that have been discussed. 'Who are you?' is bound up with 'What is your name?' The dilemma of Geddes' existence is mirrored in the associations of his name: Ged is pike – a taker of fish – a border bandit; his house, Mt Sharon, was previously Sharing Knowe. There is a division between his 'profession' and his heredity, as between his utopian isolationism and his forced acknowledgement of the old Adam within him. Redgauntlet is known by a multiplicity of names. His safety demands that his real name should not be acknowledged, while his power is shown by his assuming a number of names at will; his lack of 'a certain name' points to his own real weakness as an outlaw. When Peter Peebles addresses him as Mr Herries in the presence of Justice Foxley, he is disconcerted:

standing like one petrified by the assurance of this speech.

Darsie observed:

It was evident that our friend, Peter Peebles, had unwarily let out something which altered the sentiments of Justice Foxley and his clerk towards Mr Herries, with whom, until he was known and acknowledged under that name, they had appeared to be so intimate . . . Herries made a different and far more interesting figure. However little Peter Peebles might resemble the angel Ithuriel, the appearance of Herries, his high and scornful demeanour, vexed at what seemed detection, yet fearless of the consequences and regarding the whispering magistrate and his clerk with looks in which contempt predominated over anger or anxiety, bore, in my opinion, no slight resemblance to

> The regal port
> And faded splendour wan

with which the poet has invested the detected King of the powers of the air.

Redgauntlet undergoes one of those moments of dreamlike

impotence that are common in the Waverley novels, and are by no means restricted to juvenile leads. The reference to Milton reinforces the notion of identity and disguise, and draws our attention back to Wandering Willie's Tale. The various literary traditions meet: ballad, Milton, Gothicism, all of which openly or covertly refer to the devil.

There seems to be a very wide range of critical opinions about the meaning of the Tale, although most critics are anxious to see the work as an integral part of the novel. Is it an account of the workings of folk memory[8] or of feudal master-and-tenant relations?[9] Both of these accounts seem to touch the tale only adventitiously. If we were reading the tale by itself, as an independent work, we would have much less doubt about its meaning. The true significance of it must lie in its legendary heart: the man riding through the forest, the stranger, the quest and the trial in the castle. Out of this, a few sentences seem to glow with an intensity of meaning that distinguishes them from everything else. There is the devil's speech after taming Steenie's horse with a touch of his wand: 'But his spunk's soon out of him, I think . . . and that is like many a man's courage, that thinks he wad do great things till he come to the proof' and 'So he spoke up like a man and said he came neither to eat or drink or make minstrelsy; but simply for his ain.' These little passages are distinguished by their simple language and by the transparency – in their ballad manner – of their moral purpose. They fix our attention because they are moments of quiet and seriousness within the baroque welter of detail of the story.

The first passage, of the devil on horseback, touches the novel proper at a number of points. There are echoes of Darsie's being accosted by Herries, of Herries' almost superhuman control of his horse and of his sardonic attitude. The 'man's courage, that thinks he wad do great things' is an ironic echo of Darsie's reflections on his inability to escape from prison (chapter 5).

Before I consider the meaning of the second passage, I would like to look at Alan's adventure, which has been strangely neglected by critical accounts of the novel, as if it were largely irrelevant, as indeed it would be if the novel's centre were Jacobitism or 'the two cultures'. In keeping with the main structural device of the novel, Alan's adventure repeats Darsie's.

On arrival in Dumfries, Alan seeks an interview with the Provost on the subject of Darsie's disappearance. At once, his certainties – his confidence in his birth-right, his law, his hard work – begin to fade. The Provost is very uncertainly a man of the law – he would prefer Alan to consult the sheriff rather than himself. He is uncertain whether he really is a JP or not: 'I cannot remember that I have ever qualified' (chapter 10). The riot is difficult to investigate: 'the Quaker would not swear', and the men are ambiguous: 'a kind of amphibious deevils, neither land nor water beasts – neither English nor Scots – neither county nor stewartry, as we say – they are dispersed like so much quicksilver'. The law itself is in dispute. Darsie has disappeared in a quarrel over the stake nets, and there is no certainty that the rioters were not in the right:

[The stake nets] are not over and above lawful, and the town clerk thinks that they may be lawfully removed *via facti* – but that is by the way (chapter 10).

the scoundrels had so much pluck left as to right themselves against a fashion which would make the upper heritors a sort of clocking-hens to hatch the fish the folk below them were to catch and eat (chapter 11).

As Scott wrote *Redgauntlet*, the legal status of the stake nets was a topical affair. In 1824 the first Blue Book on Salmon Fishing appeared and was followed by a number of others. Most of the arguments used by witnesses called by the committee appear in the novel, especially that of the injustice to the 'upper heritors'. However, the Solway was *singled out* as having been fished by stake nets for at least half a century. And in 1824 they still used 'the stake net, the pock net, the halve net and the hang net; and there is a mode of fishing by spears practised'.[10] Cockburn expected that there would be 'formidable opposition' to the legalisation of stake nets.[11] Spear-fishing was not then such an anachronism, since it was still practised; stake nets were not so very new, nor so very respectable. The parliamentary report does not come down in favour of any one method; nor does the novel. There is certainly no suggestion that we should automatically favour Geddes against Herries for his fishing methods. This point is laboured because it is crucial, because it shows that Scott is not contrasting a picturesque past with a dull but efficient present. What can clearly be understood is that there was in the mid-1820s a hopeless confusion in the laws respecting salmon-fishing in Scotland. It was this that appealed to Scott. Alan left the legal centre of Edinburgh, went to an area that was anyway lawless and involved himself in a cause where the judges were uncertain of what the law said.

Alan's strength is undermined at the level of dialogue and character, and very vividly and economically, in the interview he has with Crosbie and in the dinner party at the latter's house. At the beginning of the interview, Alan is on top, his language is full and stately, with finely balanced clauses on the character of Redgauntlet the traitor: 'has not only ventured to take up his abode in this realm . . . but is suspected of having proceeded, by open force and violence, against the person of one of the lieges, a young man who is neither without friends or property to secure his being righted' (chapter 10). Alan directs the conversation and lays down his conditions. Yet by the end of it the Provost has made his escape and left Alan 'at a loss how to proceed'. He has introduced human complexities Alan has never dreamed of, has hinted at obstinacy, corruption, family loyalty, self-interest – all things that are impervious to Alan's rhetoric. Alan is convinced that the law in this society is fairly helpless, for the old county families would be unwilling to prosecute Redgauntlet. He resolves 'not to have recourse to the higher authorities' but to 'collect all the information within his power' – a course that would be 'attended with much danger to his own person'. The impotence of the law is comically restated in the episode in which Crosbie must reinstate a Jacobite bell-ringer in order to have his dinners on time.

Throughout the dinner party, Maxwell snipes at lawyers and the injustices committed at Carlisle. Alan's own pride is rebuffed by Maxwell:

'. . . it is sometimes our duty to ask questions, Mr Maxwell.'

'Ay, sir, when you have your bag-wig and your gown on, we must allow you the usual privilege of both gown and petticoat, to ask what questions you please. But when you are out of your canonicals, the case is altered.'

Alan's trip to Dumfries is an uncomfortable episode for him. He has learned that the law may be unjust, that it will not always work as it should in theory, and that there are times when he will have to confront society as a man, not as a lawyer. This is put in so many words at the end of the chapter:

[Alan] saw plainly, that were he to take the course most safe for himself, and call in the assistance of the law, it was clear he would either be deprived of the intelligence necessary to guide him or that Redgauntlet would be apprised of his danger, and might probably leave the country, carrying his captive along with him. He therefore repeated, 'I put myself on your honour, Mr Maxwell; and I will go alone to visit your friend.'

What has already been established at the level of dialogue, character and image now seems to be an inevitable part of the plot as well. The situation here approaches the mythic: the hero has to face his ordeal alone and unassisted. Also mythical are the temptations he must face on his way: at Tom Trumbull's he is clumsy with the password and refuses to accept any name but his own. We are reminded of Steenie Steenson at Redgauntlet's castle. Gradually, however, we come to see that these adventures are taking a toll on Alan's nerves. He is confused by Trumbull's hypocrisy – the obscenities within the book of devotions. He is disoriented by being led through the maze of smuggler's cellars: 'Fairford followed his gruff guide among a labyrinth of barrels . . . Fairford . . . was involved in another tortuous and dark passage, which involuntarily re-minded him of Peter Peebles' law suit. At the end of this labyrinth, when he had little guess where he had been conducted, and was . . . totally *désorienté*, Job suddenly set down the lantern.' What of the reference to Peter Peebles? Within that labyrinth, Alan was perfectly at home, he himself was guide; but in this, deprived of the fabric of the law, he is lost. At this stage Alan's adventures begin to resemble Darsie's more precisely. He becomes lost and takes on a guide or pilot – Nanty Ewart is his Wandering Willie; as Willie is blind, he is drunk and yet appears to be equally confident: 'the very touch of the helm seemed to dispel the remaining influence of the liquor which he had drunk, since, through a troublesome and intricate channel, he was able to direct the course of his little vessel with the most perfect accuracy and safety' (chapter 14). At another moment Ewart doubles for the Laird; there is a memory of Darsie's fears when Alan 'could not withstand the passing impulse of terror which crossed him, when thus reminded that he was so absolutely in the power of a man who . . . had been a pirate, and who was at present . . . an outlaw as well as a contraband trader' (chapter 14). Both Alan and Darsie are taken over the Solway in a more or less passive condition, in a half-conscious state, prostrate. Alan's is a physical weakness, illness and fever; Darsie's state is the result of physical violence. Probably such a physical condition is the only way Scott has of making obvious their sense of strain and desertion. The parallel becomes unmistakeable when Alan reaches England:

Perfectly passive . . . his own bodily distress was now so great and engrossing, that to think of his situation was impossible . . . Their course was inland; but in what direction Alan had no means of ascertaining . . . very small fields or closes, by high banks overgrown with underwood and surmounted by hedgerow trees, amongst which winded a number of impracticable and complicated lanes . . . But through this labyrinth the experience of the guides conducted them without a blunder (chapter 15).

This was Darsie's account:

still numbed and torpid in all my limbs, [I] permitted myself without reluctance to be placed on a horse brought for the purpose

. . . we travelled forward at a considerable rate and by bye-roads, with which my attendant seemed as familiar as with the perilous passages of the Solway . . . At length, after stumbling through a labyrinth of dark and deep lanes, and crossing more than one rough and barren heath . . . (chapter 4).

At the end of their journeys, both boys reach lonely houses where they are locked in rooms and kept alone. The houses are physically similar:

When [Alan] dragged himself to the window . . . behold it was closely grated and commanded no view except of a little paved court.

. . . the windows of my chamber had lately been secured with iron stanchions . . . the window, two stories high, looked into a back yard or court . . . the servants who brought me victuals . . . always locked the door when they returned (chapter 5).

This was Darsie. Alan is also locked in each time:

Fairford observed that whoever entered or left the room always locked the door with great care and circumspection (chapter 16).

So much repetition can hardly be accidental; nor is it likely to be mere laziness. We understand that Darsie and Alan have undergone journeys or experiences that are psychologically similar. Differences indicate that they started off from their own individual positions and also show a realistic novelist's desire to remain faithful to probability. The climax of the comparison comes when Alan Fairford has his interview with Charles Edward. This is a repetition of Darsie's interviews with Redgauntlet and Foxley. Both interviews should be compared with Steenie Steenson's interview in hell with old Redgauntlet. Steenie's heroism, his straightforward manliness, his refusal to compromise, his determination to get 'his ain', represent a standard by which to measure their behaviour.

Darsie, as his position deteriorates, finds himself more and more under the influence of Redgauntlet. The beginning of chapter 6 has a scene in which Herries enters Darsie's room unexpectedly: 'The figure of this man is peculiarly noble and stately, and his voice has that deep fulness of accent which implies unresisted authority. I had risen involuntarily as he entered.' Alan too rises as Buonaventura enters his room. However, the real point of comparison occurs when the Father tells him to take a seat: 'Fairford, somewhat surprised to find himself overawed by the airs of superiority . . . sat down at his bidding, as if moved by springs, and was at a loss how to assert the footing of equality on which he felt they ought to stand' (chapter 16). Darsie, too, is told to sit by Foxley, and 'used the permission given, for [he] had been more reduced by his illness than he was aware of'. Alan is convinced by the 'Father' that he should remain silent about what he has seen. It is a problem of conscience, a repetition of the one he has considered before in Dumfries: 'you will bring ruin on these hospitable ladies, to whom, in all human probability, you owe your life. You cannot obtain a warrant for your purpose, without giving a clear detail of all the late scenes through which you have passed.' Alan has to quibble with himself, however much he suspects treason: 'On the other hand, whatever he might think or suspect, he could not take upon himself to say that the man was a priest, whom he had never seen in the dress of his order . . . he felt himself at liberty to doubt of that respecting which he possessed no legal proof.' We are reminded, particularly by the rhythm and syntax, of those sections in which Darsie justifies his remaining in custody.

There is then in *Redgauntlet* an interest in symbol and patterning that is missing in *Waverley*. At the same time, there is no longer any great interest in time and history as expressed in sets of contrasts between epochs and life-styles. Indeed, we are made aware that there are fundamental similarities between persons and milieux that at first glance seem strikingly different. Yet *Redgauntlet* is still a novel about society, one in my opinion more original and profound than *Waverley*, and full of psychological subtlety for which Scott has received little credit.

Scott's portrayal of society in *Redgauntlet* has much in it that is realistic. Fear, interest and inertia are shown to account for much of social behaviour. Society may be unkind, irrational and oppressive. Yet, he urges, at one with the 'Scottish school' of Smith and Ferguson, without his society a man is neither free, safe nor himself. Not only do particular characters reflect in their language and behaviour the institutions of their societies (Scott's particular contribution to the history of the realist novel) but some of them take part in myths that represent the struggle that the individual has to define himself in relation to his community. Darsie Latimer is seemingly at first without a community. He is offered various false alternatives to communal living. We see his failure to adapt at the dance. He is confident in his rank, his purse, his abstract rights as a 'freeborn Englishman'. Later, he is degraded from the rank of manhood, a child, a woman. All this takes place when he has been deprived of his social rights: his individual liberty is possible only within a social situation. Qualities that are seemingly personal and inherent – courage, confidence, perseverance – are closely related to social background. According to the Scottish philosophers, liberty was a social invention: it meant protection of rights of property and person. As if to prove that Darsie's experiences are not merely the result of individual weakness of character, they are repeated by Alan. We see his ambiguous relationship with his own particular community, how he is irked and oppressed by it, and how it is an essential condition for his being. We see his gradual removal from this community and his arrival at a state of impotence similar to Darsie's. Both heroes go through a series of episodes that might be called temptations. The temptations put in the way of Steenie to eat, drink and pipe are similar to those put to Alan and Darsie by the strangers they meet on the wayside. His resolute sticking-out 'for his ain' is a touchstone by which to judge the integrity of their actions. The novel has, however, put them in situations that make such simple courage desperately far off.

Colin Campbell comes like a wish. Civil, dignified, but backed by overwhelming forces, he resolves all problems, frees and restores the innocent, pardons the nearly guilty and drives no one to desperation. If only governments were always like this! Scott needed to allow himself this hope. But the major part of the novel has been devoted to showing the consequences to individuals when just such an instrument of central sanity is lacking or when its functions are usurped.

Formally, *Waverley* is in a recognisable eighteenth-century tradition. Its fundamental shape is that of the journey that takes the reader into socially and geographically novel areas and the hero into unrecognised regions of his own character. The drama of social and class conflict that coexists with this inherited form should dispel any notion however that *Waverley* is really an eighteenth-century novel. It is a transitional novel, and the drama of social conflict is the growth point. How rapidly Scott's imagination developed, in tune with his analysis of society, is shown by *Redgauntlet*, a novel that obviously comes from a totally different age and reminds me of no novel so strongly as *Great Expectations*, thematically and technically. There are analogues of character. Darsie, principally, and Alan, play the part of Pip. They have to recognise their own relationship to an unfree and oppressive society, a dual relationship in which they are simultaneously victims and oppressors. Darsie imagines, like Pip, that his money comes from a clean source; he has to recognise that it is derived from a world in which the reality is of power struggles, exploitation and oppression. Darsie has to recognise the Redgauntlet in himself when he sees the horseshoe mark on his brow, the ancestral mark of guilt. Geddes shows us a variation on the theme that money and wealth are not clean and cannot except in fantasy isolate their possessor from the world: he is remarkably like Wemmick. Cristal Nixon's sardonic role is that of Orlick, while Lilias has an affinity with Estella. The role of the convict is not clearly echoed, but as I shall show below. the victim or scapegoat is such an important figure in the middle novels of the series that we can see Magwitch's role being split up among various characters: Peter Peebles, Redgauntlet, Nanty Ewart. Both novels contain betrayals and ordeals, and involve the heroes in dreamlike situations of loss, ridicule and guilt. Both novels feature flat, waste landscapes, tides, ships, exile, illness, friendship. I do not think that Dickens borrowed from *Red-*

47

gauntlet, even unconsciously. I have adduced what I hope is an authentic comparison to show how far *Redgauntlet* is from both traditional accounts of it and *Waverley*. How Scott made the journey from *Waverley* to *Redgauntlet* is the subject of the remainder of this book.

PART II

2. SCOTT AND THE ENLIGHTENMENT

Waverley, then, bids a regretful farewell to the past and looks forwards with a jaunty optimism to the future. There are no constraints upon the hero's power to act for good other than his own failures in sympathy and understanding. *Redgauntlet* imagines a world in which the past is even more unavailable, but the future questionable. However, in the later novel, the past/present confrontation is really not very important. Instead, Scott's subject is one that has a far greater relevance to us: the societal basis of personal identity, and the limits imposed by society upon autonomous action and feeling.

Later novels, even those with medieval or Reformation settings, do not, with the possible exception of group IV (according to my division in chapter 6), offer worlds with fewer constraints or simpler choices. As far back as Scott goes in time, the world is a dauntingly complicated and arbitrary place. Only in ballads or poems, or in tales like Wandering Willie's, are men able to stretch out their hands courageously for 'their ain'; 'modern' characters like Darsie Latimer do not know what their ain is.

This is not the place for a detailed consideration of Scott's shift from verse to prose, from narrative poetry to novels. To my mind, the suggestion that it was hurried about by Byron's superior competitiveness in the field seems unsatisfying. Certainly, Scott needed the greater scope for complex social analysis that was given him by prose fiction. But, above all, the poems, and *Waverley* (1814), were products of the war years. This does not only mean that the martial virtues were celebrated – military skill, strength, courage, patriotism – though they were. The world they were written in and for was a simplified and, paradoxically, an easier and more comfortable one. Divisions between classes were suppressed in the face of the external enemy; and, more importantly, not only did the wartime economy not exacerbate class divisions, it actually went some way towards narrowing them, on the surface. For the war was a period of prosperity in which all classes shared: landlord, farmer, labourer, merchant, manufacturer and artisan. Nowhere was this prosperity more pronounced than in Scotland, or the post-war contrast more alarming. Future literary historians will doubtless note a marked contrast between the novels of the 1950s and 1960s and those of the 1970s and 1980s, especially in the United States. Novels that, reflecting the confidence and self-satisfaction of academic liberals (with professorships), are bouncily satirical, must differ markedly in content and tone from those written by graduates in the liberal arts and social sciences for whom there is no room in the employment market, who will have a much less confident relationship with the world around them and be more given to uneasy contemplation of failures that they both will and will not accept responsibility for. And the future literary historians will not be doing their jobs properly if they do not at least partially explain this literary phenomenon by reference to the collapse of expansionist economic policies caused or accelerated by the petroleum crisis.

The economic problems of post-war Scottish society will be dealt with in chapter 4, but one small example will be adduced here as an introduction to the economic background of the history of ideas, for Western prosperity of the sixties fuelled by cheap petroleum has its tiny analogue in the prosperity of the Western Highlands and Islands during the Napoleonic wars. With the Orders in Council and the Continental System, the kelp that could be gathered on the Atlantic beaches was of considerable importance as a fertiliser, for neither foreign substitutes, nor indeed foreign agricultural products to depress local demand for fertiliser, could be imported. The little prosperity that was built up in the war years seems pathetically brief in retrospect, but ten or fifteen years are quite long enough to accustom a man to a rising standard of living, and to bring large families into the world. With 1815, cheap Spanish *barilla* entered the United Kingdom freely, completely destroying the market for kelp. In today's Britain, looking back over the mingled emotions of despair, bewilderment and resignation that have attended the destruction of so many of our national industries, can we wonder that Scott should have written novels that image man's inability to shape his own future? We should rather wonder if the opposite were true.

One other result of the end of the war and the economic collapse is that Scott at least, and in this he is perhaps not typical, began to develop and question ideas, or perhaps it is better to call them assumptions, that had swayed him for the better part of a quarter of a century. Scott was in his mid-forties when he began his career as a novelist, and he began it with intellectual equipment he had acquired in his early twenties. Scott never rejected rationalist doctrines *in toto*. Indeed, a sense of the inextricability of the categories of economic activity, manners, laws and morality, in approximately that order of primacy, was fundamental to his perception of the social world. And this sense, which he bequeathed to the nineteenth-century novel, was, in turn, an inheritance from the Enlightenment. What he came more and more to doubt was the Enlightenment belief in progress, progress in the sense that life is constantly improving in terms of individual satisfaction, not merely changing. However, even in this he was to a certain extent developing ideas that had been latent in the Enlightenment itself.

THE EVIDENCE FOR SCOTT'S ACCEPTANCE OF ENLIGHTENMENT IDEAS

Critical opinion today largely accepts the proposition that Scott's political and social views make most sense when seen against the background of eighteenth-century rationalism, especially the brand developed in the universities of Glasgow and Edinburgh.[1] However, although well known in principle, Scott's debt to Smith, Hume and Millar, has not been thoroughly elucidated. This must be very largely owing to there being no one convenient locus for a demonstration of an influence that can frequently be sensed, but seldom traced for any number of consecutive pages. Scott was neither teacher nor philosopher, and too original a mind to be a mere plagiariser. He drew upon the findings and constatations of the Scottish school when and as he needed them, largely for rhetorical and persuasive purposes. His utterances are those of a man who accepts a particular philosophy, politics, view of history as 'correct'; he does not subject it to extended discussion because it is not controversial for him. Only twice is there anything approaching an extended theoretical treatment (in *The Visionary* and in *Tales of a Grandfather II*) and even to say this is to water down the notion of what theory amounts to, for in the one Scott was composing an extremely partial exposé of democracy and in the other giving a popularised, children's account of the growth of social organisations: in other words, in contexts in which great simplification is appropriate and expected, in which what he would normally regard as truisms might be repeated with justification.

Scott has disappointingly little to say about Smith, Hume, Millar and the other elders of the Scottish school.[2] However, he is quite open about his debt to John Bruce, Dugald Stewart and Baron David Hume:

I made some progress in Ethics under Professor John Bruce and was selected as one of his students of whose progress he approved to read an essay before Principal Robertson. I was further instructed in Moral Philosophy at the class of Mr Dugald Stewart whose striking and impressive eloquence riveted the attention of even the most volatile student.[3]

Such an architect has Mr Hume been to the law of Scotland, neither wandering into fanciful and abstruse disquisitions, which are the more proper subject of the antiquary, nor satisfied with a dry and undigested detail of the laws in their present state, but combining the past state of our legal enactments with the present and tracing clearly and judiciously the changes which took place and the causes which led to them.[4]

John Bruce, who approved of Scott's progress (and we can assume that, as a teacher, he would have expected at least a modicum of repetition of his own ideas) was the author of a book called *Elements of the Science of Ethics on the Principles of Natural Philosophy*, which had had, according to its preface, the approval of 'the late Dr Smith'. In substance the book is the same as Bruce's course of lectures delivered to Edinburgh students during 1786–7; Scott must have been familiar with its contents.

Ethics, says Bruce, have been practised as an art and consequently have produced only elegant speculations. His will be the task to raise it to the level of the sciences of Galileo and Newton: 'The proper subject of all philosophy is Nature; and the simple means of obtaining a knowledge of its laws are observation and experiment.'[5] A reiteration of the necessity of employing the experimental method in moral as in natural science was commonplace in the Scottish eighteenth-century philosophers. Yet 'experimental', with its modern connotations, is perhaps misleading: in the moral sciences, the key word is 'experience'. Introduced by Hutcheson, the word has an impressive structural function first in Hume: his *Treatise* is professedly an attempt to introduce the 'experimental' method of reasoning into moral subjects. Hume uses the word 'experimental', but it is to experience that he refers over and over. There is a vast body of completed experiments for us to draw upon – the entire history of the race – why should we require more? History 'expands our experience to all past ages and to the most distant nations; making them contribute as much to our improvement in wisdom as if they had actually lain under our observation'.[5] Reference to actual experience is a constant in their method. This is how Smith bridges the gap between *is* and *ought*:

It is thus that the general rules of morality are formed. They are ultimately founded upon experience of what in particular instances our moral faculties, our natural sense of merit and propriety, approve or disapprove .... The general rule . . . is formed by finding from experience that all actions of a certain kind . . . are approved or disapproved of.[6]

Scott's subscription to this doctrine was visible to Bagehot, who said that his mind had a 'Baconian tendency to work upon stuff'.[7] Yet only at one point, as far as I know, does Scott's allegiance to the Scottish school's 'inductive method' surface in an acknowledgement. In the *Life of Dryden* he writes:

[Dryden] was the first to hail the dawn of experimental physics, to gratulate his country on possessing Bacon, Harvey and Boyle, and to exult over the downfall of the Aristotelian tyranny. Had he lived to see a similar revolution in ethics commenced, there can be little doubt that he would have welcomed it with the same delight.[8]

Obviously, Scott considered himself to be living in a time when the revolution had already been completed.

Baron David Hume was one of the most distinguished of John Millar's pupils. Interestingly, Scott's account, quoted above, of Hume's claim to be considered a philosopher of the law and no mere jurist (a claim not borne out by Hume's surviving Lectures[9]) is strikingly similar to W. C. Lehman's account of Millar himself: 'Millar treated law not as a set of lifeless rules, merely prescriptive in character, enforceable by the instrument of the state but otherwise having little to do with the daily vital concerns of life ...'[10] Scott's legal education led back through Hume to Millar, and beyond, to Montesquieu, to inquiries that attempted to combine law and sociology and to relate alterations and change in common law and statute to growth in manners and the economy. However banally obvious such truths may seem today, for Scott they were not so; they were established, but they enabled him to make original and satisfying correlations. Consider this passage from the introduction to the *Minstrelsy*, in which he describes the power of the border chiefs:

By the same statutes, the chieftains and landlords presiding over Border clans were obliged to find caution, to grant hostages, that

they would submit themselves to the due course of the law . . .
From these enactments the power of the Border chieftains may be
conceived; for it had been hard and useless to have punished them
for the trespasses of their tribes, unless they possessed over them
unlimited authority.[11]

Bruce's *Elements*, a highly derivative book, which draws on
most of the original thinkers of the Scottish school, is a useful
guide to the items that Scott must have learned as part of the
new orthodoxy. Bruce's plan was to 'give such a history to
moral phenomena, as may directly lead to the law of this
part of nature'.[12] Bruce's argument is that ethical rules are
an expression of a particular society, or, better, a particular
type of society, and can be understood only with reference
to it. The 'history' that follows is an account of the way in
which 'rights' and 'obligations' come to be claimed and admitted
in the various stages of society – hunting, pastoral, agricultural
and commercial, according to Smith's classification.

Although behaviour patterns vary in different ages and
nations, they do so in a way that can be seen, retrospectively,
to be compelled by the interaction of certain basic conditions
of human existence, which are unchanging. One of the favourite phrases of the Scottish school is: 'common to all nations
at such a stage in the progress of society'. Of course, such a
doctrine was not promulgated without political intentions. It
proved a useful weapon to use against the natural-rights school,
for if a given social rule could be shown to have existed in all
similar societies then there is a good chance that it answers
to certain needs in the human make-up: in other words (for
example), in an agricultural community in which the maintenance of the fertility of the land from generation to generation
is very important, and, consequently, so is the interest of a
man in his children's and grandchildren's future, the rule that
women should be chaste is a correct rule.

All this is behind the celebrated passage in *Waverley*, chapter
1, which refers to 'those passions common to men in all stages
of society and which have alike agitated the human heart,
whether it throbbed under the steel corselet of the fifteenth

century, the brocaded coat of the eighteenth or the blue frock and white dimity waistcoat of the present day.' This statement has puzzled critics who recognise a neo-classic principle but know that Scott wrote no *Rasselas*. However, the explanation is very simple: Scott is saying that man is always moved by the same springs, that he is always, for example, acquisitive and philoprogenitive, but in societies that differ economically, the sorts of behaviour that express these drives will not be the same. The conflict D. D. Devlin has discovered between 'Enlightenment' and 'historicism' is, I believe, an unnecessary complication of a simple and consistent, if not unassailable, principle.[13]

If there is a core of human nature that can only be channelled and directed by social conditions and not fundamentally altered (there is a deep fund of conservatism in the ideology of the Enlightenment philosophers) then it is logical to expect all societies to change and develop in the same way. Robertson expresses this with particular clarity:

the characters of nations depend on the state of society in which they live and on the political institutions established among them; and . . . the human mind whenever it is placed in the same situation will in all ages the most distant and in countries the most remote assume the same form and be distinguished by the same manners.
If we suppose two tribes, though placed in the most remote regions of the globe to live in a climate of the same temperature, to be in the same state of society and to resemble each other in the degrees of their improvement, they must feel the same wants and exert the same endeavours to supply them . . . the disposition and manners of men are formed by their situation and arise from the state of society in which they live.[14]

The uniformitarianism here proposed is understood to apply over the whole spectrum of human activities and relations: laws, ranks, property institutions, marriage, the arts and sciences. Scott's adherence to this doctrine in part accounts for his lack of hesitation about describing societies in his novels that he had no personal or first-hand knowledge of. In *Anne of Geierstein*, for example, pastoral, mountain Switzerland would greatly resemble parts of Scotland, the troubled Rhineland, in which no king's authority ran, the Borders between England and Scotland.

This whole area of sociological concern brought Scott to his most original contribution to literary criticism when, in the editions of Swift and Dryden, he always attempted to place poets and works against their economic and political backgrounds. He was fully aware of how radical a departure this was from neo-classic practice. Discussing the canons of literary taste, he says that there are rules, but they must be

drawn not from the mechanical jargon of French criticism but from accurate consideration of the springs and movements of the human heart. These doubtless are changed and modified in different stages of society as the outward figure is disguised or altered by the progressive changes of dress. But the nature of the human mind in the one case as the conformation of the limbs in the other remain unaltered.[15]

In the essay on Romance, Scott claims that tales of chivalry, 'modified according to the manners and the state of society, must necessarily be invented in every part of the world'.[16] To understand romance, the economic activities of the whole society and the particular occupations and pleasures of the consumers of literature must be taken into account. He criticises Ellis and Ritson for failing to cast ' a philosophic glance on the necessary conditions of [the romance writers] . . . who were by profession the instruments of the pleasure of others during such a period of society as was presented in the middle ages'.[17] Scott describes a fall in the status of poets from the relatively exalted and independent position they held in the non-hierarchical Dark Ages to thier dependence on the wealthy in the Middle Ages. However weakly his account is documented, it shows a sociological depth to his criticism that was deeply at variance with neo-classic practice.

Closely related to the Scottish school's perception of a basic human nature under different institutional guises are their essays in comparative sociology. They use accounts of existing societies at varying stages of development, whether examined *in vivo* or in the *vitro* of classical, biblical or travel literature, to fill out their sketch of the growth of society from its most primitive origins to its modern culmination. In all societies, a steady and essentially similar progress from identical beginnings is assumed. Synchronic differences existing between societies are indices of their respective speeds towards the common, if unrecognised, goal.

Comparative sociology provokes reflection too. Societies are compared for the satisfactions they offer. Usually, except in Monboddo's works, the 'advanced' or commercial stage of society is preferred. But in contrast with other eighteenth-century writers on the primitivism-v-progress debate[18] (no less universal than our ecological debate) the Scots neither pitied the savage for his deprivations nor envied him his freedom and 'magnanimity'. Such qualities are data, related to particular stages of society, and ought not to be the object of either regret or self-congratulation. It is true that there is the hypothesis that all men are driven by restless ambition to improve their material conditions – this is necessary to account for material progress and technological change. Except for their different degrees of success in attaining more and better possessions, all societies are really equal inasmuch as they all equally satisfy the present needs of their members:

Nature with the most benificent intention conciliates and forms the mind to its condition; the ideas and wishes of man extend not beyond that state of society to which he is habituated. What it presents as objects of contemplation or enjoyment fills and satisfies his mind and he can hardly conceive of any other mode of life to be pleasant or tolerable . . . the rude Americans, fond of their own pursuits and satisfied with their own lot, are equally unable to comprehend the intention or utility of the various accommodations which in more polished societies are deemed essential to the comfort of life . . . Unaccustomed to any restraint upon their will or their actions they behold with amazement the inequality of rank and subordination which takes place in civilized life and consider the voluntary sub-mission of one man to another as a renunciation, no less base than unaccountable, of the first distinction of humanity.[19]

Imagining a barbarian and his reactions to modern society, Scott asks:

Will the simple and unsophisticated being, we ask ourselves, be more inclined to reverence us who direct the thunder and lightning by our command of electricity – control the winds by our steam engines . . . or take us as individuals and despise the effeminate child of social policy whom the community have deprived of half his rights – who dares not avenge a blow without having recourse to the constable – who like a pampered jade cannot go thirty miles a day without a halt.[20]

Of all the novels, it is *Waverley* that springs to mind here, for it deals at length with such contrasts. Edward ignominiously fails to challenge Balmawhapple when he has been insulted by him, and is weakly short-winded when required to run by the side of the Highland gillies.[21] Once again, *Waverley* exemplifies text-book doctrine.

ENLIGHTENMENT IDEAS AT WORK IN SCOTT'S HANDLING OF PROGRESS AND FEUDALISM

The Scottish writers, as we have seen, discounted the idea that the sum of happiness was much greater in one age or society than another, unless a particular society (pre-revolutionary France, for example) were severely distorted. But they did affirm the idea of progress, although a progress of a very particular nature.

There was obviously the progress represented by technical innovation and the superior satisfaction of consumer desires. Dugald Stewart expresses it this way: 'It seems to be the intention of Providence that as soon as one class of our wants is supplied, another, whether real or imaginary, makes its appearance.' Repetitions by Scott of this sort of language confirm how much he took for granted this sort of analysis. Discussing post-war inflation in Edinburgh, he talks of 'the high price of necessaries – both real and rendered such by custom'.

Progress in Millar's account is strictly linked to material causes but Scott does stress the progress that is willed and results from education and the 'diffusion of knowledge' consequent upon the invention of moveable type. Not only, he states, does an individual progress in wisdom and skill as he matures, but 'tribes and nations of men assembled together for mutual protection and defence have the same power of alteration and improvement and may if circumstances are favourable go on by gradual steps from being a wild horde of naked barbarians till they become a powerful and civilised people'.[22] Once again, a comparison can be made with the Scottish school. Ferguson wrote: 'Not only the individual advances from infancy to manhood but the species itself from rudeness to civilisation.'[23]

Scott's account of *the progress of society* follows the standard hypothetical model of the Scottish school. Primitive society is a family unit, founded on 'affection between the sexes' and the love and affection of parents for children who must, by contrast with the animals, be nourished and reared for an extraordinary long period before they reach independence.[24] The family unit is maintained after this period is past out of the child's habitual respect for patriarchal authority. Such family units will combine, and a leader be chosen as arbiter or general. This is the origin of monarchical government, though several writers, Scott included, found it no more than a useful fiction rather than a literal history dangerous for its legitimisation of tyrannies. Primitive tendencies towards republics were halted by material progress. Scott, in common with most of these writers, imagined a republic as a society where both property and power were shared equally. In the hunting economy, this might be the case, but as society moved into the pastoral and even more into the agricultural stage, the rights of individuals to property had to be recognised, otherwise there would have been no guarantee of adequate productiveness. According to Kames 'a lasting division of the land among the members of the state, securing to each man the product of his own skill and labour, was a great spur to industry and multiplied goods exceedingly'.[25] The establishment of property is followed by the division of labour, Scott's account of which is inspired by the first three chapters of *The Wealth of Nations*. Then society is stratified into ranks according to wealth 'According to the accidental difference of wealth possessed by individuals a subordination of ranks is gradually introduced and different degrees of power and authority are assumed without opposition by particular persons.'[26] This is John Millar; Scott's view of the process by which technical changes and economic specialisations lead to a hierarchical society is very comparable. He affirms what he sees as the necessity – if the goals of material improvement are to be maintained and extended – of passing from simple, egalitarian societies to 'artificial', highly organised inegalitarian ones:

the whole order of society is changed and instead of presenting the uniform appearance of one large family, each member of which has nearly the same rights, it seems a confederacy or association of different ranks, classes and conditions of men, each rank filling up a certain department in society and discharging a class of duties totally distinct from those of the others. The steps by which a nation advances from the natural or simple state which we have just described into the more complicated system in which ranks are distinguished from each other are called the progress of society or civilisation. This is attended like all things human with much of evil as well as of good; but it seems to be a law of our moral nature that faster or slower, such alterations must take place in consequence of the inventions and improvements of succeeding generations of mankind.[27]

Whenever Scott is asked to formulate his assumptions about society, history and politics, he returns to the lessons he learned as a student. *Tales of a Grandfather II* is a late work (1828) and a continuity of allusion and reference to the Scottish school can be traced up to it through *The Visionary* and the historical registers for 1814 and 1815[28] right from the life of Dryden (published 1808). More and more, however, in his private writings such as journals and letters, and, as I shall suggest later, in the novels, progress, particularly technological (the steam engine) seems a decidedly ambiguous gift.

Tales of a Grandfather II was reviewed by the *Westminster* in 1829.[29] The reviewer compares Scott to Hume 'whose history the author may be presumed to have had frequently in his hands of late'. The account of the 'progress of society' that I have sketched above he declares 'an intelligible account of a difficult subject'. Yet, however much the rationalist inheritance crossed party lines, those lines did still exist, and the *Westminster* was right, in its own terms, to take exception to Scott's handling of the constitutional and political controversy, which was never far out of sight in all the writings of the Scottish Enlightenment. The reviewer objected strongly to Scott's claims that 'the spirit of the constitution possessed all the freedom which was inherent in the ancient feudal institutions'. Frequently stated (by Scott and others) but seldom explained, this seeming paradox is fully intelligible in the Scottish school's own terms. Two points are crucial: the definition of liberty, and the acceptance of the sketch of northern European history since the fall of Rome. According to one's point of view, their arguments are either a crude apology for the Hanoverian establishment and *laissez-faire* capitalism, or the first attempt to base political argument on something more solid than wilful assertions of principle.

But they did seem to have cogent reasons for accepting the model, reasons that will be discussed later (pp. 74–5) in this chapter (Mackintosh). And then, they admitted quite freely that there was a propaganda element in their history, although they did not put it quite as crudely as that. Dugald Stewart, in his introduction to Robertson's *Works* (1822) is particularly instructive. He boasts (knowing he is boasting) of the progress that has been made in Scotland during the last fifty years in tracing the 'origin and progress of the present establishments in Europe' and goes on:

in the whole history of human affairs no spectacle occurs so wonderful in itself or so momentous in its effects as the growth of that system which took its rise from the conquests of the Barbarians. This event . . . laid the foundation of a state of society far more favourable to the general and permanent happiness of the human race than any which the world had hitherto seen – a state of society which required many ages to bring it to that condition which it has now attained.[30]

Scott's claim that feudal society was 'free' reads oddly until we realise how closely defined freedom is, and understand that

Scott, in common with other Enlightenment writers, knew full well that his descriptions of feudal and Gothic constitutions were models and not literal descriptions.

Freedom had a particular set of meanings for the Scottish school. It was not a natural right that every man, today, was born with, but something achieved for its own utilitarian aims by society itself. This philosophy, which may be traced ultimately to Hobbes, is conveniently stated by Millar:

When the citizen is supposed to have rights of property and of station and is protected in the exercise of them, he is said to be free; and the very restraints by which he is hindered from the commission of crimes are a part of his liberty. No person is free where any person is suffered to do wrong with impunity. Even the despotic prince on his throne is not an exception to this general rule.[31]

Utilitarian, for, without this freedom, the progress of society will not be accomplished: who will labour to increase his stock if he is not free to enjoy his life and property? The feudal system was understood to guarantee, in its ideal form, just these freedoms. Scott wrote:

The feudal system of France like that of the rest of Europe had in its original composition all the germs of national freedom. The great peers in whose hands the common defence was reposed acknowledged the king's power as suzerain . . but recognised no despotic authority in the crown and were prompt to defend the slightest encroachment upon their rights . . . The tendency and spirit of these singular institutions were to preserve to each individual his just and natural rights.[32]

If these comments seem romantic, we should remember that they were by no means exclusive to Scott but were common to a number of men who are today called rationalists.

Ivanhoe has come to seem the archetypal romantic historical novel of the type ridiculed by Twain. A recent critic, however, has found 'anti-romantic' elements in the novel – satire on savagery and warfare.[33] Yet the truth is that those elements that have come to seem most romantic are those most closely associated with rationalism. *Ivanhoe* is, like other group IV novels, very much an academic work. One version of the novel treats it as a way of seeing how the tragic defeat of Saxon by Norman was made good. To my mind, however, it was much more to Scott's purpose to show how an allodial proprietor (Cedric) finally enters the feudal system because it is his only protection against lawlessness. Isaac of York shows the response of merchants, especially Jews, to the same lawlessness: they invented bills of exchange.[34] But the eponymous chivalric hero himself is the most closely related of all the characters to rationalism. Millar, Robertson, Stuart (G.) all dwell on the chivalric hero's Gothic ancestry and his function as a lonely well-spring of justice and probity in a barbarous age. Most of them repeat a particular story about the Black Prince. Millar, after his retelling of it, goes on: 'we are led . . . to conceive an exalted idea of the institutions and manners of chivalry which in so rude a state of society were capable among people of the better sort of promoting so much delicacy of sentiment, and of encouraging any individual to form such a perfect model of propriety and refinement'.[35] Gilbert Stuart's account of 'feudal freedom' has a close affinity to Scott's: 'Of this system, the intention and the spirit were national defence and domestic independence. While it called out the inhabitant and the citizen to defend his property and secure his tranquillity, it opposed barriers to despotism. Growing out of liberty, it was to promote the freedom of the subject.'[36] We should recall that there had been an enormous expansion of knowledge about other societies and political systems during the eighteenth century. History and travel-writing had shown the Enlightenment that their political institutions were both unique and precious. Far removed from the spirit of Augustanism, their most frequent comment about Rome was that it had been a 'gloomy despotism'. Although we call these writers rationalists, not all of their arguments were very cool and scientific. They did not hold themselves aloof from the fashion for 'northern' wildness, poetry, barbarism and independence that took England by storm in the late eighteenth century, of which Mallet and Ossian are notable symptoms, as indeed are the Waverley novels. Only Robertson was able to preserve a degree of scepticism about the 'Germans' of Tacitus. Millar and Stuart, for example, were completely spellbound by them. Millar adduced a great variety of reasons for 'a set of customs and institutions of which we have no example in any other age or country'.[37] Altogether, these things 'gave rise to' a wonderful sense of personal honour and independence, a martial spirit and a high degree of delicacy and restraint in the 'commerce between the sexes'. Scott swallowed Tacitus whole.[38] We shall see below how Scott resurrected these Enlightenment savages in *Count Robert of Paris*. As a Scotch lawyer he felt entitled to pronounce: 'The Scottish judicial system contained, like the criminal procedure of all nations derived from the noble Gothic stem, the principles of freedom, the darling attributes of those gallant tribes.'[39] But once again it should be stressed that Scott's reaction was not eccentric. Gilbert Stuart was one of many who had exactly the same thing to say about the Goths: 'the spirit of liberty and independence which animated their actions was to produce that limited and legal administration which still gives distinction and dignity to the Kingdoms of Europe'.[40] Of course, these noble Germans did not live in the feudal system: their landholding system was allodial, not feudal (a trace of this term is preserved in the 'Udaller' of *The Pirate*). The Scottish writers tried to account for the growth of the feudal system upon a base of already-existing institutions that still preserved their nurture of liberty in a more disciplined and hierarchical organisation. Scott was one of many to see a link between the English Parliament and the councils of the Free Franks, with the Wittanegemot as intermediary. Also, if the Frankish society was so ideal, the origin of the feudal system had to be explained. There is a particular strain of English radical-conservatism that says it was imposed by conquest, and calls it the Norman Yoke.[41] But this had for Scott too little inevitability in it. A mere military imposition of a system does not have in it the satisfying sense of a system working itself out according to its own logic.

According to a letter written to an uncle in 1789, Scott had presented a paper at the Edinburgh Literary Society called 'The origin of the feudal system'. Scott says that he has attempted to deny two commonly held propositions: that it was invented by the Lombards and that it depended on the vassals' acknowledgement of the king as sole lord of all the land in the country. 'I have endeavoured to assign it to a more general origin and to prove it proceeds upon principles common to all nations when placed in a certain situation.'[42] How familiar such an account sounds. Since the paper has not survived, and since Scott nowhere reworks that particular body of material, it is fortunate that we are able to reconstruct it with the help of Col J. Tod's *Annals of Rajasthan*, which Scott, in later life, found to be a striking confirmation of his views of the origin of the feudal system. Tod himself is a disciple of the rationalist historians, and admits that he has been guided in his researches by Hume, Montesquieu and Millar.[43] Tod was struck by the organisation of the Rajput states which was 'so analogous to the ancient feudal system of Europe that I have not hesitated to hazard a comparison'. Tod repeats the uniformitarianism of the Scottish school: 'In the same stage of society, the wants of men must everywhere be similar and will produce analogies which are observed to regulate the Tartar hordes or German tribes, Caledonian clans and Rajput tribes.'[44] Scott made the same point about the Highlanders and the Afghans, Robertson about the Mexicans.[45] Tod found that allodial had been *voluntarily* converted into feudal tenures in the Rajput states. In a state that was now settled and no longer engaged in external belligerence, the existence of 'fiefs' was highly disruptive, with the king and the great proprietors fighting each other. The feudal system, in which lands were nominally exchanged in return for fidelity and military service, arose to cope with this violence. Millar's account of the origins of feudalism was just this: we may assume that Scott's was too.

Nevertheless, the disadvantages of the feudal system were not invisible to our historians. They were quick to agree that it soon hardened into a mere form, with the unity of the state disappearing and the independence of the barons becoming an instrument of oppression for their vassals. Although the barons and king were supposed to check each other's power, in practice the pendulum would swing to extremes of either anarchy or despotism. Scott, like Robertson, thought that the autonomy of the barons 'formed but a feeble system of government and gave an insecurity to the ties which bound together the national compact'.[46] To most writers the period of Louis XI was a particularly interesting one for the insight it gave into the struggles between king and nobility. And it was this period that Scott chose for his one novelistic essay at French history – *Quentin Durward*. But it was Scott's most original contribution to extend their work into the one area they never paid any attention to: the Scottish eighteenth century. Their silence about matters taking place on their own doorstep offers scope for malicious speculation; it can be safely assumed however that their accounts of the breakdown of feudal society must have been inspired at least in part by the course taken by Scotland during their own lives.

In the decline of feudalism in general, Robertson and Millar both regarded the abolition of baronial courts as one of the most decisive causes – or symptoms – of the decline of the aristocracy. When a baron had been both plaintiff and judge, it could not have been expected that justice would result.[47] Scott applied this to Scottish society:

The ancient laws which vested the administration of justice in the aristocracy continued to be a cause of poverty amongst the tenantry of the country. Every gentleman of considerable estate possessed the power of a baron or lord of regality, and by means of a deputy who was usually his factor or land steward exercised the power of dispensing justice both criminal and civil to those in his neighbourhood. In the most ordinary lawsuit one party was thus constituted the judge in his own cause.[48]

The abolition of this prerogative in 1748 directly stimulated progress and the rise of the legal and commercial middle classes: 'when the abolition of heritable jurisdictions and the unity and impulse given to the country by the annihilation of domestic faction began to open new views to industry, and

comparative opulence became attended with fresh wants
and with the usual demand for increasing accommodations'.[49]
There is a very obvious relation here to *Waverley*: it is Bradwardine and McWheeble we are reading about. The Baron's
scraps of law Latin, his *adscripti glebae* (an oppressive and
uneconomic survival), his rights of regalities with pit and
gallows, his concern over the details of his feudal tenure are
no mere humours. They are part of a whole socio-political
complex, which also contains his Jacobitism, his aversion to
the Union and the poverty of his estates and tenants. *Waverley*
is indeed – quite differently from any other novels of the series –
very much an illustration of academically constructed types.
Fergus MacIvor is another telling example: he is exactly the
type of man Adam Smith imagined in his account of the
destruction of the feudal system by commerce.

I shall summarise Smith's arguments briefly. The power of
the barons was in part a consequence of the economic organisation of society. Rent was paid in kind, and had to be spent on
the maintenance of men – the retinue. Thus the anarchy of
feudalism was self-perpetuating.

In a country which has neither foreign commerce nor any of the
finer manufactures, a great proprietor having nothing for which he
can exchange the greatest part of the produce of his lands which is
over and above the maintenance of the cultivators, consumes the
whole in rustic hospitality . . . He is at all times surrounded with a
multitude of retainers and dependants who, having no equivalent
to give him in return for their maintenance but being fed entirely
by his bounty, must obey him for the reason that soldiers must
obey the prince who pays them.

And then follows the famous passage that begins

But what all the violence of the feudal institutions could never
have effected, the silent and insensible operation of foreign commerce
and manufactures gradually brought about . . .[50]

As soon as the proprietors could find a way of spending their
entire revenue on themselves, even on the most trivial items
of personal adornment, they parted with the maintenance of a
thousand men, and with it the whole of their authority. 'To

gratify the most childlike vanity was the sole motive of most of the great proprietors.' There is, of course, more than this in *Waverley*. The emotions, the mutual love and trust between Fergus and his clansmen, are not the less real because they are economically determined. And Fergus does not in fact squander his men's maintenance on clothes, jewels or carriages. For the clan system was not ended insensibly – it was brought to a close by violence. Nevertheless, we are made to feel constantly that Fergus' main characteristic is vanity; to use one of Scott's typical formulations, he loved them because they were his. We know that when the clansmen cannot be sold for an earldom, they will be replaced by sheep. And this is what happens in the next novel – *Guy Mannering*. Scot puts it directly in his *Tales of a Grandfather*: the chiefs of the next generation learned to 'value themselves less on their solitary and patriarchal power than on the articles of personal expenditure and display which gave distinction'.[51] Yet however much a text-book figure Fergus is, we should note that superficially similar characters in later novels – Herries and Ravenswood – are not involved in this version of the decline of feudalism. Neither indulges in personal display, neither squanders his birth-right. Herries lives a life that is plain and austere; he is driven by motives that are rationally inexplicable. Edgar's dispossession is the thing of interest itself, the process by which he becomes dispossessed unimportant. Deprived of his heritable jurisdictions by 1748, Herries should be without power over those resident on his old estates: but as we know, the opposite is true. Once again, it is not that Scott is denying the truth of a piece of history he has previously asserted – he is writing about something else.

THE ENLIGHTENMENT AND CONTEMPORARY POLITICS

Although Scott's position as a practical and party politician will be addressed in a separate chapter, many misapprehensions about his place in the cross-currents of the early nineteenth-century political world may be avoided if I give a brief exposition of the theoretical bases for his treatment of the really major issues: the French Revolution and the democratic or Reform movement in England.

There is a passage in *The Antiquary* where Oldbuck, a Whig, defends the French Revolution. It has occasioned a good deal of critical surprise and been adduced as evidence of 'Scott's dualism'. But Oldbuck's views are no different from Scott's own stated comments on the French Revolution in his *Life of Napoleon*. He treated it as part of the general constitutional history of Europe, linked to constitutional changes in other states and to the transition from a 'feudal' to a 'commercial' civilisation. 'The French Revolution, the original movements of which so far as they went to secure to the people the restoration of their natural liberty and the abolition of the usurpations of the crown . . . [was] . . . peremptorily necessary and inevitable.'[52] Scott explains why the Revolution was violent and not peaceful, insensible, as it should have been according to the model of the Scottish school. To begin with, the French king had engrossed so much power in his own person that he was held responsible for all wrongs.[53] The nobility, who had once been the military arm of the kingdom and so excused taxes, were no longer an effective power, with their military duties assumed by mercenaries, but their privileges had survived. And the middle classes, who had risen to considerable real – or financial – power, had no corresponding weight in the constitution. Scott's account of the rise of the middle classes of Paris is less observation than the fleshing-out of a theoretical skeleton long since committed to memory. It is worth comparing it with the passage from *The Wealth of Nations* quoted above on p. 68.

There was . . . the influence which many plebeians possessed as creditors over these needy nobles whom they had supplied with money, while another portion of the same class rose into wealth and consideration at the expense of the more opulent patricians who were ruining themselves. Paris had increased to an enormous extent and her citizens had risen to a corresponding degree of consideration; and while they profited by the luxury and dissipation both of the court and courtiers, had become rich in proportion as the government and privileged classes grew poor. Thus the Third Estate seemed to increase in extent, number and strength like a waxing inundation, threatening with every increasing wave to overwhelm the ancient and decayed barriers of exclusions and immunities behind which the privileged ranks still fortified themselves.[54]

Scott's treatment of the slogans of the Revolution and of the post-revolutionary period – liberty, equality, the republic, the Code – were also derived from the Scots and not, it is important to add, from Burke. Bagehot claimed that Scott's objections to radical politics were that they would 'level prince and pauper in a common égalité – substitute a scientific rigidity for the irregular and picturesque growth of centuries – replace an abounding and genial life by a symmetrical but lifeless mechanism'.[55] This is Burkean. But it was Scott's purpose to show not that the Revolution was dull and unlovely but rather that it was the reverse of scientific. According to the Scottish school, progress moves society away from the primitive and simple to the artificial and complex.

By such gradual advances in rendering their situation more comfortable, the most important alterations are produced in the state and conditions of a people; their numbers are increased; the connections of society are extended; and men being less oppressed by their own wants are more at liberty to cultivate the feelings of humanity; property, the great source of distinction among individuals, is established and the various rights of mankind arising from their multiplied connections are recognised and protected; the laws of a country are thereby rendered more numerous, and a more complex form of government becomes necessary for distributing justice and preventing the disorders which proceed from the jarring passions and interests of a large and opulent community.[56]

Law is the expression and guarantee of such a complexity, the recognition of rights that have actually come to be established. These rights have been historically defined and recognised, from numerous conflicts and a succession of separate and individual contracts that constitute a series of unconscious but binding precedents. A registration of the 'development of

71

rights', closely combining law and ethics, in the development from primitive to modern societies, is the substance of Bruce's *Elements*, which, as we have seen, probably had a considerable influence on Scott.

It is in their handling of the law that the Scottish school come closest to Burke. Law can only change with the life of a society or nation and is only a consequence, and not an agent or cause, of social change. Law is of slow growth. It is built upon experience, observation and the desire to meet the challenge of particular relationships. Its growth is linked to the expansion of knowledge, of prosperity and of the 'division of labour'. Great legislators are looked upon with scepticism.[57]

Scott's account of the Code Napoléon drew J. S. Mill's most bitter criticism of the *Life*,[58] for both were aware that the principles involved had a wider application. Scott dismissed the Code, and by implication a great deal of reform based upon ideals or theory, on the grounds that individual human understandings are incapable of grasping the vast complexity of a modern society.

It is therefore a vulgar though a natural and pleasing error to prefer the simplicity of an ingenious and philosophical code of jurisprudence to a system which has grown up with a nation, augmented with its wants, extended according to its civilisation and only become cumbrous and complicated because the state of society to which it applies has itself given rise to complexity of relative situations to all of which the law is under the necessity of adapting itself. In this point of view, the Code of France may be compared to a warehouse, built with much attention to architectural uniformity, showy in exterior and pleasing from the simplicity of its plan, but too small to hold the quantity of goods necessary to supply the public demands.[59]

Liberty and its relation to a complex society have already been discussed; for the Scottish school, liberty means the rule of constitutional law, the institutionalised guarantee of the rights that a man can expect to have in the society he lives in – of life, property, station and so on. They were deeply sceptical of Rousseau, whose idea of liberty they derided as that of the simple savage who is only free when his existence is materially wretched; with the introduction of property, he will become a slave.[60]

Equality was also defined in relation to the 'progress of society'. Scott's discussion of the limitations to its meaning draws confidently upon all the major topics of the Scottish school: the importance of property, the division of labour, the separation of ranks, the imperative of material progress:

In the proper sense, equality of rights and equality of laws, a constitution which extends like protection to the lowest and the highest, are essential to the existence and enjoyment of freedom. But, to erect a levelling system designed to place the whole mass of the people on the same footing is a gross and ridiculous contradiction of the necessary progress of society . . . The inequalities arising from the natural differences of talent and disposition are multiplied beyond calculation as society increases in civilisation . . . it must be admitted that in every state far advanced in the progress of civilisation, the inequality of ranks is a natural and necessary attribute.[61]

Republicanism received similar treatment: it was inconsistent with the demands of modern society. This looks odd if we think how few monarchies have survived, but the problem is one of definition. Republic was understood, perhaps obtusely, to imply something on the lines of early Rome, or best of all Sparta: republics were small, agrarian, non-expansive and virtuous – meaning that personal ambition was suppressed in the interest of the whole community. Republics and democracies were understood to entail direct participation of all men in the process of government; representative democracy was either misunderstood or looked upon with (not unfounded) scepticism. Ferguson wrote in *Civil Society*:

Whether in small or great states, democracy is preserved with difficulty under the disparities of condition and the unequal cultivation of mind which attend the variety of pursuits and applications that separate mankind in the advanced state of the commercial arts . . . How can he who has confined his views to his own subsistence or preservation be intrusted with the conduct of nations? In the disorder of corrupted democracies the scene has frequently changed from democracy to despotism . . . From amidst the democracy of corrupt men and from a scene of lawless confusion the tyrant ascends a throne with arms reeking in blood.[62]

And if Ferguson's work was too close, chronologically, to the French Revolution to have the ring of objectivity, the works of Hume, particularly the history of the Civil War, were not. The remarkable parallels between the French and the English revolutions, which were rapidly drawn by both sides as first Robespierre and then Buonaparte arose to play Cromwell's role,[63] seemed to underline the justness of Hume's political philosophy.

Just how prophetic and accurate the works of Smith, Hume, Ferguson and the others must have seemed in retrospect can be gathered from a glance at the life and works of Sir James Mackintosh, a pupil of Millar. Mackintosh is best remembered for his eulogy of the Revolution, *Vindiciae Gallicae*. His analysis of the causes of the Revolution is strikingly similar to Scott's. But he scorns all notions of 'feudal freedom' and 'Gothic independence'. The attention of political philosophers ought to be directed towards our present needs and not on the antediluvian formation of our present institutions. His voice is similar to Ferguson's – but with how different an intention:

All the governments that now exist in the world . . . are the produce of chance, not the work of art. They have been altered, impaired, improved or destroyed by accidental circumstances beyond the foresight or control of wisdom . . . A government of *art*, the work of legislative intellect, reared on the immutable basis of natural right and general happiness which should combine the excellencies and exclude the defects of the various constitutions which chance had scattered all over the world was now loudly demanded by the injustice of them all.[64]

But it is a different, and chastened, Mackintosh who writes *A Discourse on the Law of Nature and Nations*. The reign of terror and the Napoleonic wars have brought about a complete reorientation of his political rhetoric. Now we hear of the importance of remembering that the outlines of liberty were first sketched in by the hands of those noble barbarians the Goths; of the useful and beautiful variety of governments and institutions; of the progressive improvement in property as the keystone of society; of universal anarchy in Rousseau; of liberty as meaning protection against wrong, and, most entertaining of all, a violent about-face from the position of *Vindiciae* quoted above:

Such a body of political laws must in all countries arise out of the character and body of the people; they must grow up with its changes and be incorporated into its habits. Human wisdom cannot form such a constitution by one act, for human wisdom cannot create the materials of which it is composed. The attempt, always ineffectual, to change by violence the ancient habits and the established order of society so as to fit them for a new scheme of government flows from the most presumptuous ignorance, requires the support of the most ferocious tyranny and leads to consequences which its authors can never have foreseen.[65]

That military despotism must result from experiments at democracy was an item of common agreement in the Scottish school. Scott writes in *The Visionary* (1819): ' "Emperor with all our hearts," echoed the assembly, "anything for a quiet life." And so have ended the dreams of radical reform and universal suffrage in all ages, and so ended mine.' Millar was understood to favour republicanism, but his was a very theoretical republicanism based on the premise that the 'progress of society' would eventually bring about a levelling-off of the classes as industry and commerce made the lower classes less dependent on their superiors. Scott, with the effects of the post-war industrial slump before his eyes was entitled to feel sceptical. In *The Visionary* he comments on the continuing subservience of men to master in political as in economic affairs:

The bulk and mass of the population are rendered incapable of the due exercise of an elective franchise by their want of education . . . as well as by their dependent situation which must place their votes at the command of those who pay their wages . . . [at an election] I could observe something like a partial concert. Several bodies of men in paper caps and wearing aprons voted unanimously each for the master manufacturer by whom they were employed.

How close this is to Smith:

But though the interest of the labourer is strictly connected with that of society, he is incapable of comprehending that interest . . . his education and habits are commonly such as to render him unfit to judge . . . his voice is little heard . . . except . . . when his clamour is animated, set on, and supported by his employers.[66]

So close is Scott to the theory that he had learned in his youth that we might suspect him of seeing animated sociological models during the 1818–21 period rather than the events themselves. *The Visionary* professes to believe that the Reform movement intends to overturn the entire constitution and substitute for it a classical democracy composed of 'ten acre men'. His own anxieties endowed the post-war Reform movement with a programme it never entertained. But when his mistake is admitted, his arguments are still consistent with principles that helped him, and others, to offer more constructive comments in less anxious times.

Scott's 'vision' sees a too-simple form being imposed upon the complex structure of modern life, brought by the 'progress of society' to a peak of wealth, complexity and differentiation. The imposition of a new class structure will overturn 'the division of labour' and place society a thousand years back in terms of material wealth. Each man's ten acres will be imperfectly cultivated, for he will have no tools; there will be no carpenters, smiths, ports, ships, because 'each man has his own ten acres to mind and has not time for any one else'. When he wishes to add force and dignity to his arguments, it is significant that it is to Adam Smith that he turns. In the celebrated 'invisible hand' passage, Smith had described the growth of capitalism as the essential factor in freeing men from their dependence on the lords of the soil.

[The rich] are led by an invisible hand to make nearly the same distribution of the necessaries of life which would have been had the earth been divided into equal portions among all its inhabitants . . . all of whom thus derive from [the rich man's] luxury and his caprice that share of the necessaries of life which they would in vain have expected from his humanity or justice.[67]

And this is *The Visionary*:

nor can the selfishness of the capitalist devise any mode of disposing [of money] by which, in his own despite . . . the poor would not be fed, clothed and supported out of his fortune. Let any man sit down and devise an expenditure of capital in such a manner as that it shall not be distributed among the community and he will find he has undertaken a task nearly impossible.

Seldom, in the later novels, does Scott include scenes or characters that plainly dramatise his political philosophy, the philosophy he had learned when young and, he believed, tested by experience. But every so often such scenes and characters will occur as striking presences in the background to the main action. In *Anne*, the first part of the novel is set in republican Switzerland, patriarchal, simple and poor; Scott cannot resist pointing out that their increasing wealth and 'luxury' will strike at the roots of republican virtue. In *The Pirate* the crew of the pirate ship turns into a miniature democracy, which is likely at any moment to erupt into violence, anarchy and tyranny.

CONCLUSION

Scott was thus in far more complete and confident possession of the intellectual currency of his time and place than we might have suspected. Although he did wear his learning lightly, it is probable that our misapprehension of him is the fault of Lockhart, from whose image of him as a mildly eccentric, romantic antiquarian Scott will probably never be extricated. This does not mean that Scott has anything more than a very minor claim to a place in the 'history of ideas'. However, knowledge of his intellectual allegiances will help us to see a far greater coherence in his political life and writings. For a period of over thirty years he applied the lessons he had learned from Bruce, Stewart and Baron Hume unhesitatingly to every major political event, and drew the correct conclusions, sometimes unhappily.

Only in one respect did he challenge the findings of his seniors. In the immediate post-war years, immediately after the writing of *Waverley* that is, he began to have doubts about the value of material progress. This was a doubt so serious that it shaped the course of all his future novel-writing and made it impossible for him to write another novel quite like *Waverley*.

3. SOME POLITICAL TOPICS

As Lukacs remarks, the peacefulness of English history is an illusion; brought into close focus, it resolves into a never-ending series of struggles. Even so, the period 1815–32 must rank as a time characterised by an outstanding degree of conflict and divisiveness. Traditional divisions between Whig and Tory appeared quite minor compared to those between town and country, merchant and landlord, farmer and labourer, and industrial and rural haves and have-nots.

My discussion of *Waverley* and *Redgauntlet* has already suggested that the radical differences between them, of both form and content, may be explained by Scott's changing experience of society. We have already seen what assumptions Scott brought to the political world. We will need to know how these were altered or confirmed over a ten-year period. There are other questions that need to be at least provisionally answered. Which interest-groups did Scott ally himself with? Did he allow his thinking and feeling about social and political topics to be dictated by ideology drawn from outside his own experience and perceptions? How much was he motivated by narrow considerations of personal or group interest? Did he make any attempt to equip himself with the technical information necessary for the conscientious formation of opinions? Or was he, as implied by hostile critics, prejudiced, reactionary and obtuse?

Answers to these questions have important implications for the novels. If we can answer 'yes' to the last, then we should admit that such a man is unsuited to be a novelist. The dualism theory seems to me on principle unacceptable. It is true that a creative artist may wish to emphasise in his art ironies and

78

ambiguities, even contradictions, that are inconvenient and inappropriate in everyday life. We might expect a writer protected by anonymity and impersonality to be more extreme, in one way or other, than a man daily involved in a complex mesh of social relationships. At one point, Scott admitted that he would be unwilling to write for the *Beacon* anything that would give offence to individuals: 'our circle is so small and we meet together so much I mean people of different politics that nothing but the necessity of the case would incline one to wish a commencement of hostilities which would inevitably become personal'.[1] However, the suggestion, not quite stated but implied, in Lukacs' chapter, that Scott was able to shuffle in and out of wildly conflicting political personae as he passed through the doors of his writing-room is quite out of one's experience of normal humanity. No one has ever suggested that there is anything in Scott's behaviour to point towards a personality disorder of such a magnitude. Fortunately, there is a way to restore unity of character to Scott without losing respect for his novels: to show that his politics had more sanity and centrality than they have usually been given credit for.

This chapter will define his politics in relation to certain topics. (For a detailed, chronological account, a biographical treatment such as Edgar Johnson's *The Great Unknown* is indispensable.) Important areas are reserved for treatment in later chapters if they have a particular relationship to Scottish society or individual novels. And some topics are omitted entirely if they seem to have no interest for either criticism of the novels or the history of Scott's intellectual development. An example is the corruption associated with the management of the unreformed parliament in Scotland. Scott's *Toryism* seemed so much more defined to his contemporaries than it does to us because it was characterised by a great deal of party politics in the old sense: the giving and getting of places and the management of elections. Sir Herbert Grierson found himself unable to include a huge number of letters in the *Centenary* edition: of those that were excluded a very large number show us Scott hard at work directing this two-way traffic with his prose. At one time or another he seems to have tried to find jobs for half of the unemployable gentry of the borders. And it was, no doubt, a major element in his objection to Reform. A whining sense of grievance is the principal thing intelligible in his 'Address to the Electors of Selkirk',[2] apart from a generalised hostility to French influence. The electors had in their votes a property that would be depreciated if the franchise were to be widened or Selkirkshire cease to return a member by itself. On the other hand, this must be placed against Scott's lively understanding of the pre-Reform principle that the *manager* of Scotland was to deliver Scottish votes to the government in exchange for favourable treatment for Scotland. And when Scott thought that this principle was being flouted, he was willing to defy the party organisation and overturn government legislation, as in the small-notes controversy. He took a good deal of melancholy pleasure in his own boldness, as we can see from the Journal passage for 10 March 1826:

I am not made entirely on the same mould of passions like other people. Many men would deeply regret a breach with so old a friend as Lord Melville, and many men would be in despair at losing the good graces of a Minister of State for Scotland, and all my pretty views about what might be done for myself and my sons . . . But I . . . [am like the Jolly Miller and care for nobody].

Some mention should also be made of the particularly Scottish background. In many ways, in spite of the old divisions of Presbyterian and Catholic, Highland and Lowland, Scotland was a less quarrelsome place than England. Although Scott and his friends were deeply suspicious of Glasgow and Paisley, relations between parties and classes were less rancorous than they were south of the Border. This was not necessarily a good thing for all Scots – Cobbett was amazed at what he considered the pusillanimity of the Scottish peasantry. If Scott was afraid of events in England, he was able to draw comfort from Scotland, although he was afraid of English radicalism being transmitted like a disease to the Scots who, he thought, once infected would prove more troublesome patients than their southern neighbours. In addition, a good many of the political topics did not deeply concern Scotsmen when their own practice was different, and frequently better.

ENGLISH LAW REFORM

English Tory opinion frustrated or opposed the Whig Sir Samuel Romilly's attempts to introduce a measure of penal reform into England. As Scott describes it, it is clear that he approves of the proposed reforms because he considers that the law has lagged behind the 'progress of society' and needs to be brought into phase with it:

This eminent lawyer has greatly distinguished himself, as the reader must be aware, by the repeated efforts which he has made to infuse into the more antiquated and barbarous parts of the English code some portion of the science and refinement which characterises the present age. The criminal laws of a rude people are generally framed rather from the impulses of passion than the dictates of understanding, and have reference not so much to the promotion of public welfare as the gratification of revenge . . . The obstinate and in some respects undiscriminating attachment of the English has left ample room for the judicious interference of the hand of reform.[3]

Scott approves of Romilly's bill to remove 'corruption of the blood' for treason and felony, for they were survivals of feudalism. He enumerates the absurdities of the English laws relating to debtors in connection with the same member's Freehold Estates Bill. He describes Bennet's bill to abolish gaol fees as 'benevolent and salutary' and regrets that reactionary influences have excepted the courts of King's Bench, Admiralty and Common Pleas from the competence of the bill. He approved of the bill to abolish the pillory, an instrument he found both inefficient and brutalising, and ascribed opposition to the bill to interest and prejudice on the part of the 'high law authorities'. However much support of such reforms might seem a matter of course, it was far from *de rigueur* among the Tories. Scott was in favour of the abolition of two of the statutes of Elizabeth: that for the relief of the poor, and the Statute of Artificers and Apprentices, which regulated relations between employer and employed. His approval of this amendment to the laws, which makes it inconvenient to present him as a paternalist or philanthropic Tory, is consistent with his adherence to Smithian laws. The second law was 'The ignorant policy of a barbarous age which favours so much restrictions on commerce and manufactures and encourages a dangerous interference with the pursuits of individuals . . . the reign of Queen Elizabeth, though glorious in other respects, was not one in which sound principles of commerce were understood.'[4]

THE CORN LAWS

As part of his chronicle of the year 1815, he included a chapter called 'Observations on the Policy of the Corn Bill'.[5] It is clear from the opening paragraph that he dealt with the topic unwillingly. This is not, however, because he despised anything so mundane; it is more the expression of a genuine dilemma. We shall see that he went to some lengths to understand the technicalities of the problem.

In the chronicle for 1814, he seems to have been much closer to the Whig line on the Corn Laws. The repeal of the Statute of Artificers drew this comment from him: 'so little was political economy understood in these times that the notion never seems to have occurred that agriculture is best promoted by the prosperity of commerce and manufactures; and that restraints upon either defeat the end at which they aim'.[6] This was clearly meant to be of significance to the Corn Bill: he had mentioned the same principle in a brief discussion of an earlier draft of it. He remarked that it was only the apparent interest of the landowner to keep the price of corn as high as possible and the apparent interest of the manufacturer to keep it as low as possible.[7] In this year (1816 that is, the year in which Scott wrote the 1814 account) the conduct of the landed interest is criticised in terms that Whig opponents of the bill had employed in 1815 – that farmers had over-speculated on marginal lands so that what 'nature had intended for pasture was permanently injured by such acts of agricultural violence'.[8] The farmers had forsaken the 'parsimonious and humble mode of life pursued by their fathers',[9] diverting capital from production to consumption and maintaining a way of life above their stations.[10]

However, in the following year (1817 for 1815) he was willing to acquit both landowners and farmers of both charges. The increase in production was necessary during the war, especially in 1812; and the new wealth of the farmers had made them into an enlightened and progressive middle class, whereas they had been obstinate and backward because of their poverty and ignorance. Their improvement was a real addition to the nation as a whole.

In the meantime, Scott has been diligently reading political economy and has come under the influence of Malthus. In introducing his 1815 remarks, Scott says that he is the more confident because his opinions are supported by the best economists of the day.[11] In Malthus, Scott found an economist who – as he thought of himself – did not neglect the subtler aspects of economics. For example, Ricardo thought that if the tax on imports were lowered or abolished, then the price of corn would fall and wages with it, allowing an expansion of industry and a rise in profits. Scott countered:

Economists reckon too much as if all the springs and counterpoises of the political machine wrought mechanically and without human volition. The moral effects are left out of view entirely and because it is reasonable that plenty of subsistence should produce cheap labour it is held to have that instant effect. But it is not so. At the first burst of plenty the labourer becomes indifferent about labour (as all men do) on finding that he can for a time subsist without it; and the farmer is obliged to bribe him with a continuance of high wages for a time at least, though his own means of affording them have diminished.[12]

Scott is very selective in his borrowings from Malthus, a number of whose arguments are not heard of in the 1815 account: the desire for self-sufficiency in grain, the need to achieve a balance between agriculture and industry. Malthus has enabled Scott to reconcile the protective nature of the bill, which favoured the landed interest, with the *laissez-faire* theories of Smith. In Malthus' words:

It is not of course meant to be asserted that the high price of raw produce is, separately taken, advantageous to the consumer; but that it is the necessary concomitant of superior and increasing wealth, and that the one cannot be had without the other.[13]

And Scott:

when a country is increasing rapidly in its wealth, commerce and manufactures, and population, the increase in the demand for corn will tend much more to raise the price than the other causes will tend to keep it down. In a rapidly advancing country, therefore, the price of corn, as well as the rent of land, will continue in a constant state of advancement.[14]

Scott claims he would deprecate any lowering of rents because while not lowering the price of corn it would represent a backward step. However, he was not satisfied with this position: letters written during the agricultural crisis of 1822 state that rents must be lowered, that people cannot expect to live as well as they did when the war was on.[15]

SCOTTISH LAW REFORM

Approval of English law reform did not challenge Scott's prejudices: when they were deeply involved, he showed himself bitterly opposed to any sort of reform. This is how Scott's opposition to the changes in the Court of Session, which was outlined in his 'A View of the Changes Proposed and Adopted in the Administration of Justice in Scotland', has been described. The details of the essay need careful examination, for Scott's views, and their tendency, have been misrepresented by the few writers who have mentioned this essay.

Scott's criticism of the final bill was, as it happens, not very hostile, and expressed the wish that as 'The prevailing sentiment is that this mode of procedure is of evident utility in certain descriptions of causes . . . in deference to the public opinion, the experiment ought to be tried.'[16] Privately, to his Journal, he wrote that although he had originally been against the changes, he now respected both the Lord Chief Commissioner and the Jury Court over which he presided although 'this is high treason among the Tories'.[17] In public he wrote:

The act of parliament extending the trial by jury to civil causes to Scotland was passed during the present session; a measure which may be considered as far the most important and it is hardly to be doubted the most beneficial alteration in the jurisprudence of Scotland which has taken place for a long course of years.[18]

It is true that Scott's prejudices had been aroused: but these were national, not social or political. The bill had been introduced without proper regard for Scottish opinion; no one with an intimate concern in, or knowledge of, Scottish law had been asked to help frame the bill, and it had been introduced in defiance of the Act of Union, imposing laws on Scotland as if on a colony. In short

too little attention was given to the genius and the characteristics of the law of Scotland; and too little deference paid to the unalterable habits of the people. An established system is not to be tried by those tests which may with perfect correctness be applied to a new theory . . . the people have by degrees moulded their habits to the laws they are compelled to obey . . . Let us not be understood that a superstitious regard to antiquity ought to stay the hand of temperate reform. But the task is delicate and full of danger.[19]

He describes the intermingling of law and custom and national character in terms of a living organism – 'usages that have struck their roots deep and wide . . . It is only in its natural soil where it has long been planted that the tree can be expected to flourish.'

This part of Scott's argument has attracted a good deal of comment and has been cited to show his allegiance to Burkean conservatism: 'In style and sentiment the inspiration of this is Burke. Such is the judgement of men of the world (and scholars in the law) like Burke and Scott upon the abstractions of a recluse like Bentham who thinks of life as a mathematical problem.'[20] Leaving aside the unfairness to Bentham, if Burke

is the inspiration of this, then we should logically credit him
with a much wider influence than is usually supposed:

In the elastic frame of artificial society it is hard to say what vibra-
tions may be excited or to what extent they may be propagated by a
mere local impulse. It is a great living body and animated by sympathetic nerves of which no anatomist has yet demonstrated the
course or connection; and we may paralyse the hand or tongue while
seeking to remove a blemish from the eye ... The judicial institutions
of a nation are parts of its living body. They have been developed
together from one radical germ; and have modified each other in
the course of their expansion. The same blood circulates through
them all. [21]

The similarities between this and the citations from Scott are
immediate and obvious, and yet this was written by Francis
Jeffrey. Was he a serious and convinced Tory? [22] There are
many such passages in Scott: *Malachi Malagrowther* frequently
uses images that compare Scotland to a living body. We need
only go, not to Burke, but to the academic and legal background
that Scott and Jeffrey shared, to find the origins of this type
of thinking.

The proposed changes in the Court of Sessions comprised
two main parts: the rearrangement of the various chambers,
and the introduction of jury trial for matters of fact in civil
cases. It is to the latter that the remarks of Jeffrey and Scott
refer. Jury trial was used in all cases that involved the Crown.
But it was felt that jury trial, in causes that were comparatively
trivial and would not compel really responsible behaviour from
the jurymen, promised to agree very ill with the habits of the
Scots. Scott and Jeffrey both thought that the English had
very inflated ideas of its value:

We can listen to the cabalistic sound of Trial by Jury ... and retain
the entire possession of our form and sentiments.
We have doubts as to the expediency of such a measure.
Jury trial is one of the objects of English idolatry, and we are not
partial to idols. [23]

Jury trials are criticised on grounds of expediency and utility.
Scott thinks that jury trials, involving greater tediousness and

expense, would prove to be a 'formidable engine of oppression . . . in the hands of the rich'. And Jeffrey quotes Bentham's opinion that jury trial is 'admirable in barbarous times but not for an enlightened time'.

Bentham wrote, in 1811, an attack on the proposed changes that makes Scott's seem very mild. Bentham expressed the hope that he would as soon see Scotland introduce jury trial as 'open the port of Leith for the importation of a pack of mad dogs'. He thought that the possibility that fairer decisions would be arrived at would be greatly outweighed by 'the probable mischief, in the shape of the increase of delay, vexation and expense'.[24] 'Bentham's juristic utilitarianism and Scott's consequent indignation are representative of the whole struggle between philosophic radicalism and romantic conservatism.' Things are not quite as conveniently simple as Kirk suggests.[25] In the discussions of the alterations of the structure of the Court of Sessions, Scott's intentions are obviously 'utilitarian' and not significantly different from Bentham's. Both of them cite, in their accounts of the defects of the existing system, the expense and delay caused by a system of written pleadings; the effects of the lack of opportunity for cross-examination of witnesses; the ability of *mala fide* suitors to delay proceedings; the evil results of prolonged and indefinite reviews of suits and passage from the Outer to the Inner House; and the inability of one court to deal with the increasing pressure of business.[26]

Bentham and Scott were equally in agreement when they considered the proposed remedies. Three courts of session would be one too many. As the divided chambers were to meet separately and not concurrently there would be no effective difference as far as the volume of work was concerned. They objected to the proposed Court of Review, for it would really be nothing more than the old Inner Chamber with a new name.

This is a highly technical subject, and one that has little or no inherent interest for today. Yet it is only by condescending to such trifles that we can see how confused and inadequate is the conventional estimate of Scott's attitude to legal reform, and by extension to reform *per se*. His criticisms were practical and highly informed. Lockhart seems less than candid in ascribing Scott's opposition to the changes to 'his habitual and deep-rooted dread of change in matters affecting the whole machinery of social existence'.[27] However, as usual, Lockhart's opinion has been decisively influential.

MALACHI MALAGROWTHER

It was the financial and mercantile crisis of 1825, through which Scott was himself brought to bankruptcy, that precipitated the various financial reforms of which the abolition of small notes was to be a part. Ever since the report of the Bullion Committee (1810) Ricardian economists had been urging that inflation caused by an excessive issue of paper money was the root cause of the country's economic troubles. Scott had opposed this, not very convincingly, by ascribing inflation rather to a shortage of gold, in the *Edinburgh Annual Register* for 1815.

Scott himself frequently denounced the authors of the early boom–slump cycles. After a journey through Lancashire (where the crisis started) he wrote: 'Gods justice is requiting and will yet further requite those who have blown up the country into a state of unsubstantial opulence at the expense of the health and morals of the lower classes.'[28] And in a letter: 'The banks and monied men should use their influence which is omnipotent with the manufacturers to inforce these resolutions so necessary for the general quiet.'[29] Was there no contradiction then when Scott defended the Scottish banks, with their issues of paper and their readiness to extend credit? Croker thought there was, and that Scott was repaying the banks for personal favours he had received at the time of his own personal crash.[30]

He defends himself, and the banks, by remarking that it is impossible in Scottish conditions to over-issue small notes. He discounts the theory that small notes increase the likelihood of a panic by claiming that the holders of these notes tend to be people of small incomes who are very careful of what they have: 'the apprehended runs on the Scotch banks by the holders of small notes have never taken place and [are] never likely to'.[31] This was borne out by a number of the witnesses before the subsequent House of Commons Select Committee.

As far as small notes are concerned, the immediate occasion of the controversy, there is no doubt that they could have had no connection with the precipitation of the commercial crisis. The entire small-note circulation in Scotland was no more than £1.8 million, far too small to have permitted over-trading on the scale of the 1825 disaster.[32] However, the system of cash credits with which small notes were intimately connected constituted an additional capital of some £6 million.[33] It was suggested that the 'building mania' in Glasgow was based on cash credits. However, it is doubtful if the banks could have checked speculation. There was in Scotland a capital of about £20 million in bank deposits and all of this was 'seeking employment'. The crisis was the result of the extremely rapid commercial and industrial development of the previous fifty years, which had produced, and had been accelerated by, a process of capital accumulation, immense by comparison with the £400,000 that had been invested in the Darien disaster and was estimated to represent about half the total capital of Scotland. The banks had if anything acted as a check on the spirit of speculation, as compared with private capitalists.

On purely technical grounds, Scott was probably right to defend the Scottish small notes. And if he were not, we can still be grateful to *Malachi* for showing us a Scott who was both vigorously independent of the party line and also in full and autonomous possession of the facts. He was the first to mention the banks' role in the formation of a rural middle class, and the importance of the 'credit and branch' system to the poorest and most under-developed of the northern communities, which would otherwise have been starved of the capital they needed. Whether it was a tribute to his personality or to his technical knowledge, all the discussions of the bill that subsequently took place in the Houses of Parliament and in the Committee centred on points that Scott had raised, and verified them.

PETERLOO

I have already cited Lukacs' view of English history as 'a resultant made up of the components of ceaseless class struggles and their bloody resolution in great or small, successful or abortive uprisings'. Lukacs' view is that 'the relative stability of England at this period' enabled Scott and others to see the struggle objectively and yet not lose sight of the middle way that arose from class struggles. He adds that Scott's objectivity was heightened by his being tied to those 'sections of society which had been precipitated into ruin by the industrial revolution and the rapid growth of capitalism'. In spite of the suggestiveness of Lukacs' wider critical statements, it is hard to say whether he displays a hazier grasp of the details of Scott's life or of English history or of the Waverley novels. Lukacs was doubtless right to stress the importance of 1848 – in continental Europe and in the Austrian Empire particularly. In England, however, the year had less significance, while others, which Lukacs ignores, were perhaps just as traumatic. 1848 was the year in which bourgeois writers had to either recognise and accept the new epoch that was dawning, or else be doomed to the role of apologists of a declining era. Scott, I believe, experienced a similar crisis in 1819, the year of Peterloo.

The class struggle, or, as Scott called it, the constitutional question, was of course the single most important 'event' between 1815 and 1832; most of the individual political crises can be subsumed into it. On the whole, even in the period leading up to the Reform Bill, Scott looked on matters with a fair degree of calm and objectivity and seldom failed to engage with the technical problems behind the rhetoric. Yet for a brief period, at the end of 1819 and the beginning of 1820, he lost his political nerve.

This did not endure long. By 8 February Scott was already

demobilising the Melrose sharpshooters (see below, chapter 5). And some time in the early spring he wrote a political article that attempted to mediate between the parties.[34] In effect, he recants his own violence:

I have waited till some more qualified persons should propose to treat of these frightful signs of the times with which we have been visited in something like a liberal and independent manner. I have waited in vain. The spread of faction has possessed us all and the more important moral phenomena are treated only as worthy of consideration only [sic] in so far as they affect the paltry interest of the existing parties. The Manchester affair was only considered by the Whigs as a good opportunity for getting the popular cry on their side for a season, and many a staunch Tory regards the conspiracy of Thistlewood as a d–d lucky hit for advancing the ministerial interest at the coming elections.

A Tory who refers popular discontent to

the impious sedition and rebellious doctrines so zealously promugated among the lower classes

mistakes the effect for the cause:

these men have indeed been the bellows which blew up the flame and but that [sic] their efforts would have been to little purpose had there not previously existed a smouldering fire around which lay a quantity of fuel ready to catch the blaze. The truth is that the profligate and abandoned characters who have placed themselves at the head of these dissentions have, with the single exception of Cobbet, shown so very little talent that we can no more attach to their agency the power of creating so much disturbance than we can ascribe to the porpoises the command of the storm because they are seen to gambol and tumble as the waves begin to rise.

The body of this article has been lost. A hint as to what it might have contained can be found in Scott's introduction: 'Whatever I say concerning the faults of the higher classes is dictated with the earnest desire that they may be amended.' Slightly later he wrote to the young Duke of Buccleuch:

fashionable young men . . . lose sight of real power and real importance the foundation of which must be laid even selfishly considered in contributing to the general welfare and like those who have thrown their bread upon the waters expecting and surely receiving after many days its return in gratitude attachment and support of every kind . . . I cannot look forward to these as settled times.[35]

My guess is that even at this period Scott wanted an income tax, as the moralising contrast of selfishness and enlightened self-interest suggests (see pp. 95–9).

The period under consideration lasted from September 1819 to January 1820. It included two major pieces of political writing: *The Visionary* and the 'Letter on Peterloo', published below as the appendix. This long letter, which Scott clearly considered to be something like a statement of editorial policy, underlines the seriousness with which he regarded the situation and the confusion and panic into which it threw his thoughts. He is anxious at all costs to justify the actions of the magistrates and condemn those of the populace (how unlike the author of *Guy Mannering* and *The Heart of Midlothian*) and to play down accounts of fatalities. There is none of Scott's customary prosaic attention to detail, especially of the economic background of discontent. Instead there are rhetorical fantasies about atheist demagogues engaged in awful plots to subvert the entire noble fabric of the constitution – exactly the sort of thing Scott ridiculed only six months later. The letter was signed L. T. – Lawrence Templeton, the persona he adopted for the publication of *Ivanhoe*. This, and the date, suggest that there is a connection between the political events of 1819 and the writing of group IV novels: *Ivanhoe, Monastery* and *Abbot*. There is another shred of evidence for such a link: the men of Darnick had been particularly keen on Scott's sharpshooters; out of gratitude, Lockhart informs us, Scott's imagination began to dwell more and more on the old peelhouse at Darnick, which was the germ of *Monastery*.[36]

The Visionary (the title is significant) is a similar (unconscious) attempt to withdraw attention from real events and causes and to substitute fantasies based on theory. Vision I pilloried the Whigs for their dangerous flirtation with the Radicals. Vision II implied that the Reform programme, which was understood to involve a sort of agrarian communism, would result in the decay of civilisation and the destruction of agri-

culture, industry, commerce, the Church and the administration
of justice. Vision III envisaged the confounding of Radical
hopes for a just society in the failure of manhood suffrage, the
rise of a brutal new élite of orators and mobs ('beggars on
horseback') and the eventual adoption of military despotism.
In all three visions the Radical movement is described in
metaphors that identify it with violence, destruction, drink,
theft, cynicism and idleness.

Interpretation of this episode is not very easy. My understanding of these few months is not shared by Edgar Johnson,
who believes Scott not to have seriously thought there would
be a revolution.[37] Then there is the question of Peterloo itself.
Was it just one of a series of incidents in provincial England's
response to high prices and unemployment, or did it mark the
formal espousal by the country as a whole of the Reform
programme, as R. J. White suggests?[38] Scott quickly became
re-convinced that the root cause of the Radical discontents was
economic (which was true) and that they could be settled by
economic measures alone (which ignored political realities).
Thus his earlier, panicky conviction that Peterloo heralded
sweeping political changes was possibly more firmly founded
than his later moderation. He had little choice. His interests
and his education combined to make him see Reform as both
unthinkable and literally impossible. Thus he was restricted
to either joining in whole-heartedly with repression, or attempting to cut the ground from under the reformers' feet by meeting
the economic challenge within the unreformed constitution.

'MALACHI MALAGROWTHER IV'

This is the name I shall apply to certain MS fragments in the
National Library of Scotland.[39] The background to the writing
of this piece can be found, not very trustworthily presented, in
Lockhart. Tired of writing *Count Robert of Paris*, and gloomy
about the Reform Bill and the disruption of the Tories, Scott
put the novel aside and refreshed himself with a political essay.
Cadell and Ballantyne heard the article through and persuaded

Scott to drop it, as likely to have a bad effect on the sales of the Magnum Opus. The MS and proof sheets were then burned and that was the end.

I believe no one ever saw this performance but the bookseller, the printer and William Laidlaw; and I cannot pretend to have gathered any clear notion of its contents except that the panacea was the reimposition of the income tax; and that after much reasoning in support of this measure, Sir Walter attacked the principle of parliamentary reform *in toto*.

Actually, at least a third of the article survives, partly in proof and partly in MS. Lockhart implies that the whole thing was abandoned, both plans to publish it separately under the name 'Malachi Malagrowther' and plans to include it in the *Edinburgh Weekly Journal*, very soon after the original meeting on 17 December 1830. Yet it was not until 14 February 1831 that Scott resolved to abandon publication.[40]

The article was divided into three sections: a survey of the present ills of the country, a review of measures proposed to remedy them, and the announcement of the cure – the income tax. Only the first section survives.

The argument starts with an explanation of the real causes of the national distress – 'the derangement of the finances'. This is a theme that had occurred frequently in his account of the French Revolution: 'It is indeed on the subject of finance and taxation that almost all revolutions among civilised nations have been found to hinge.'[41] He cited the examples of Switzerland, Holland, Austria and America. Similar generalisations and examples are to be found in *MM* IV.

Such a crisis as has fallen to these countries . . . has unfortunately become at present the fate of Britain; and while to a casual observer the country seems to contain all the means not of maintenance only but of luxury and superfluity, there is a secret malady prevailing among all classes of men which makes the rich man fear for his hoards and the poor man for the necessaries which are essential for his sustenance.

Scott thought it was irrelevant to ask whose fault it was; what was needed was a 'gallant and generous resolution on the part of the nation at large . . . *Lest all should destroy all.*' Scott is studiously moderate: although he regrets the conduct of the working men, he concludes that it is 'not to be wondered at'. Various proposals for allaying the storm are touched on, with the caveat that 'now when a servile war is well nigh commenced, . . . it is no time to trust to remedies totally inadequate for preventing the mischief'. The traditional parliamentary cries of Retrenchment and Reform are remedies he has in mind. He would not quarrel with retrenchment were it effective but thinks it could only be a 'placebo'. As for Reform, he would be prepared to accept a moderate bill, as the Tories expected Earl Grey's Bill to be:

a plan of national reform of which . . . I neither can nor will express any other sentiments than those of respect for their intentions and a belief that it is not the purpose of the proposers to destroy or deface the constitution of Britain but on the contrary to bring it back to that model on which it was originally constructed and render it both in theory and practice that perfect system which it has often been represented.

However, he cannot believe that Reform will redress the national grievances. Firstly, he does not believe the Tories will persist in their split long enough for the bill to be passed. And even if it did become law, it would not meet the demands of the Radicals. 'I am convinced that so able a man as Lord Grey [would not] impose upon the public any system of reform which he might now propose as calculated to meet and satisfy the wishes of the country as far as the dissensions are occasioned by the more democratical influence in the constitution.' Then Scott proceeds to examine the relations between rich and poor, as expressed in the workings of the poor-laws, and concludes by naming his panacea, the income tax. The article ends here but the remainder can be guessed at.

Scott's over-riding interest in political and social questions in the post-war years was in the 'poor' problem. At one stage, late in 1819, he wrote to Laidlaw: 'I am glad you have got some provision for the poor. They are the minors of the state, and especially to be looked after.'[42] This looks like Tory paternalism. However, if one looks more closely into the letters and occasional writings, there are suggestions and comments to be found much more reminiscent of the hard school. His 1816 comments on proposed reforms in the structure of poor-law administration give us once again the student of Malthus:

The principle on which the poor laws are founded is confessedly erroneous, and the practice is not only imperfect but so deep have the roots of this pernicious system struck into the whole frame of society that extreme temerity alone would propose the sudden application of a cure which would go to the very foundation of these mischievous establishments. Yet nothing short of this will permanently avail . . . [These laws] had their origin in the most fatal error that was ever committed – an error which proposed to avert by the weak instrumentality of human institutions the penalties which the inflexible laws of nature have affixed to human indiscretion and profligacy. To improve the machinery of the poor laws is only to communicate new force to an engine already too powerful for the welfare of the state.[43]

Letters of the immediate post-war years are full of remarks of a similar root-and-branch tendency. The poor-laws are 'an old and inveterate cancer',[44] an 'Augean stable',[45] a 'sad quagmire'[46] and a 'Slough of Despond'.[47]

By the test of the 'public works' controversy, Scott is shown to be nearer Malthus than to the Ricardians. Ricardo thought that employing men on public works – roads and so on – would merely throw an equal number out of work somewhere else by withdrawing capital. Malthus thought there was an excess of capital, which could be made to provide employment through public works and the improvement and beautifying of estates.[48] Scott is continually giving his correspondents details about the correct way of employing the poor on public works so as to keep them from starving and at the same time to preserve their independence. He wanted to keep the work economic and disliked the notion of charity creeping in; he liked schemes that included piece-work. He frequently justified the Abbotsford extensions and plantations in these terms.[49]

In talking of the abolition of poor-rates, he tended to be

thinking about rural areas. In cities, he thought, rates were inevitable. He recognised that such notions as prudence and forethought were meaningless in an urban context. He felt that legislation ought to provide a substitute for patterns of behaviour that urban, industrial life had broken down.

There would perhaps be no means so effectual as that (which will never be listened to) of taxing the manufacture[r]s according to the number of hands which they employ on average and applying the produce in maintaining the manufacturing poor . . . I cannot but think that the necessity of making some fund before hand for the provision of those whom they debauch and render only fit for the alms-house in prosecution of their own adventures though it operated as a check on the increase of manufactures would be a measure just in itself and beneficial to the community.[50]

Moreover, Scott's local (or national) experience intervened. English Toryism may have favoured an easygoing paternalism and encouraged the old poor-law, but this had little relevance in Scotland. Most contemporary observers felt that the Scottish system was more satisfactory than that of England.[51] The law of settlement was unknown and litigation between parishes avoided; the management of poor-relief was supervised by Kirk and landlords and not delegated to corruptible officials; there were no assessments as poor-relief was conducted entirely on a voluntary basis. Scott frequently suggested that the English law should be amended and made more like the Scottish practice.[52] He was not alone in this – it was frequently suggested in the House of Commons.[53]

MM IV, after discounting retrenchment and Reform, suggests that there is 'another remedy . . . I mean an amendment to the poor laws, the constant cause of discord between those who receive and those who pay charity'. Yet Scott merely disliked the working of the poor-law: he was not against poor-relief as such.

the foundation of the English poor laws is laid in the laws of nature . . . the claim of property in the earth and its possessions is not more competent to the rich than that of the poor to have subsistence not merely to preserve their lives but to something resembling comfort, out of the funds of industry on manufactured labour, to which the pauper has contributed his might [sic] . . . But the artificial rules of society in imposing on the rich the support of the poor as a literal tax and obligation has occasioned so much cause of dispute and dissension . . . the workhouse with all its miseries and degradations . . . and his daily bread granted him on such terms as are likely to make him loathe it . . . the poor man learns that his dependence is not on his own providence, industry or honourable spirit of exertion – he is separated from the ties of his family and sent to debauch at the ale house where he learns the 'metaphysics of murder and despair'.

Yet how is this related to income tax? For in Scott's view, it is such a tax that is to bring back the poor to that 'relative place in society from which they have been so [forcibly?] depressed'. Income tax was a measure associated pre-eminently with the old Pitt party, to which Scott's sympathies leaned above all, and which had been a progressive force in economic affairs in the early years of the century. In 1816 it was obvious that revenues that had been adequate before the war would be insufficient. Ministers decided to repeal the war malt tax and impose a new income tax of 5% instead of the war income tax of 10%. But pressure of public opinion led by Brougham (the character of Whigham in *The Visionary* reflects Scott's intense dislike of him) resulted in the total repeal of both income and malt taxes. Thus the fiscal system was 'shattered . . . to pieces'.[54] The piecemeal imposition of indirect taxation had to be resorted to. Lockhart tries to suggest that Scott had fallen behind the times with regard to income tax – that his views had already been 'triumphantly answered by the organs of the Liberal Party'.[55] In fact, the Liberals – or Whigs – had merely won a cheap popularity in 1816 and were afraid to change their views. Lord Althorp, who was to be Liberal Chancellor in Grey's cabinet, declared that 'to grant relief to the productive classes by a reduction of taxation and make up the deficiency by imposing a property tax would be a very good plan'.[56]

At this time, Peel opposed the plan; but Althorp also lost his nerve when it was his turn to present a budget in 1831. And then it was not old-fashioned Tories who wanted an income tax,

as Lockhart snidely suggests, but liberal Ricardian Tories
such as Huskisson, Parnell and Liverpool. Parnell had been
chairman of the finance committee, which had been broken
up because it was suspected of being about to recommend an
income or property tax. The fruits of its labours appeared in
Parnell's *On Financial Reform*. He was in favour of abolishing
many indirect taxes, especially excise and the taxes on raw
materials, as being counter-productive as regards the export
trade, and replacing them with a new tax: 'Persons who hold
the most opposite doctrines on the subject of our financial
and commercial difficulties have made an income tax part of
them . . . [Falling chiefly on] rent, tithes, interest, money and
dividends, the large revenue it would yield from the moment
when it was imposed would not be accompanied by any shock
to industry.'[57] The *Westminster Review* also declared for the
income tax and recommended the abolition of excise.[58] This
is the burden of the 'Fragment of Excise', with Scott calling
for the abolition of a 'whole army of Jan Gallusers who are
supported at great expense'. Scott had not just caught up with
Tory opinion: he had regretted the abolition of the tax in
1816 and had been recommending it at intervals ever since –
in 1819, 1822, 1829.[59]

And so the outlines of Scott's plan can be seen. National
discontent is caused by financial troubles and exacerbated by
the workings of the poor-law system. The poor should be sent
out of the workhouses and encouraged to work, and work
should be provided for them. It was clear that demand would
be slack in the current financial climate, so something had to be
done to stimulate production. Excise, as a tax ultimately on
exports, had to be abolished and the revenue made up through
an income tax. The poor would no longer be a 'burden' and
would regain their independence, their honoured place in
society. Agitation would finish and the assemblage of large
groups of the discontented be avoided.

In fact, his whole line of reasoning was justified by Peel's
1842 budget, which introduced an income tax to replace import
taxes in an attempt to cope with a severe economic depression

and popular discontent. The measure was held to be very successful and was renewed at the end of four years.

CONCLUSION

As a politician, Scott was well-informed, consistent and sincere, even technically competent. I find much to admire in his courage in sticking to his faith in something as mundane and unspectacular as an income tax. Yet his politics were designed for implementation in a social order that was to remain the same, if more justly the same. He never accepted the need for more than a token attempt at Reform. Peterloo shocked him not because it convinced him that Reform would come but because he thought he discerned among the people a determination to push through a political programme that could only result, as he thought, in disaster, economic, social, political. For a time, he was prepared to take part in any military action necessary to oppose the rising tide of Radical demands. When the crisis was past, he found a way of taking part in politics that neither accepted nor directly confronted the Radical programme. He restricted himself to tinkering with the given components of the system while imaginatively blocking the entrance of any new terms. In other words, he side-stepped the problems of time, change and progress.

I will argue in more detail in part III of this book that the results on the novels were profound. Time, and so history, become quite unimportant in the later novels, the structures of which are closed, circular and repetitive, quite without the linear flow of *Waverley*. If the novels of groups II and III also exhibit this structural tendency, the 'Manchester affair' brought one important change: it removed from Scott the easy assumption that there was any automatic congruence between the necessitarian, gradualist doctrines of political economy, the logic of current events, and his own experience and perception of society.

4. SCOTTISH SOCIETY 1770-1832

As well as constituting Scott's life-span, this period has a good claim to be treated as a unit. Many observers considered the year 1770 as the one that marked Scotland's appearance as a modern and progressive nation. The year 1832 is a natural limit too in that the political arrangements of the nation, which had been stable since the Union, were transformed by the Reform Act.

This period of very great social changes may be temporally sub-divided according to the way in which these changes were perceived. The first period, of about thirty years, until the beginning of the Napoleonic era, was one of optimism, of singleminded enthusiasm for economic rationalism and productivity and, to a certain extent, of a complementary radicalism in politics. The war years themselves limit the second period, in which the previous economic trends were more fully realised but opinion was less securely on the side of economic rationalism and when, of course, radicalism evaporated. It was still a period of strenuous economic progress, yet the goals of increased productivity could be reached only by an ever more costly input, and the human costs were more easily visible. The third period was initiated by the post-war depression and downward turn of prices, wages and rents; circumstances that seemed to be beyond the control of the government, let alone that of the ordinary individual, however progressive and prudent his policy, whatever the scope of his economic ambitions. With this comparative failure came a renewed look at the losses and sacrifices. Interestingly, these periods correspond closely to stages in Scott's life: of his education and apprenticeship, of his poems, of his novels.

This chapter will be more concerned with the way in which

these changes are reported and interpreted contemporarily than with what 'really happened'. The sources used are opinionative and ideological rather than factual and statistical. The justification for this must be partly that the Waverley novels exist within a context of opinion and ideology and partly that Scottish social historiography is regrettably somewhat under-developed.[1]

At this time, articulate Scotsmen tended to see a great gulf between their society and those of the past. Thanks to the 'Scottish school' they were able to transcend the barbarous-past/enlightened-present polarity typical of the eighteenth century and see the changes in their historical context as the outcome of inevitable trends.

If by 1770 the society can be really seen to be taking shape, Scotsmen of the age dated their era from 1745 or 1748. David Craig argues that the '45 could hardly be a serious theme 'for an intelligent novelist of the contemporary'.[2] Yet other students of society, whether their interests were legal, political or agricultural, seriously thought of it as an event rivalled in importance only by the Union. They were little interested in the causes of the revolt, and it was vital to their beliefs that only a tiny minority of Scots were Jacobites. Scott wrote: 'A handful of men had disturbed the tranquillity of a peaceful people who were demanding no change of their condition.'[3] Its importance was as a symbol of changes that had taken place and a herald of those to come. It was felt that without the military pacification of the Highlands and the Heritable Jurisdictions Act, the economic rationalism that was transforming society could never have taken root. Scott must have grown up with this sense of the importance of the '45. Walter Scott W.S. provided information to Robert Douglas, Minister of Galashiels, who wrote the County Agricultural Report for Roxburghshire, in a pair of letters. There is no doubt in his mind about the connection between improvement and the '45 – and this in a southern county, not in the Highlands:

Is it not worthy of remark that altho' the act of parlt. for dividing runrigg [strip cultivation] lands past in the 1695 yet no division took place for it for about 50 years thereafter . . . while that mode of possession continued, and which took its origin from mutual defence, the hands of the proprietors were tied up which often caused strife law suits and disorders.[4]

Here is the unprofitable patchwork of Tully-Veolan.

Improvers, who regarded a rise in rent as the surest index of 'advancing civilisation', made their vision of the '45 the common and accepted one. Thomas Guthrie recalled how difficult it had been between 1688 and 1745 to encourage anyone 'in these precarious times to invest money in the cultivation of the soil'. Leases were long but rent low.[5] However, when cattle became a safer type of property, the price of grass rose ten times between 1748 and 1808.[6] According to the minister of Elgin the consequences of the civil war caused his parishioners to become civilised and their industry to be 'directed by intelligence'.[7] Archibald Campbell of North Knapdale emphasised the effects of 1748: 'The effect of the reformation was astonishing. No sooner were men emancipated from their fetters than they began to improve their properties.'[8]

The old-fashioned rural equilibrium was destroyed. However, the improving spirit that was admired in the south-east was complemented by a trend in the north-west that gradually came to seem more and more disruptive – the dismissal of a rural population that a changing agrarian economy could not absorb. The apologists of the new order were quite frank in admitting that social affections were not to be trusted to; only self-interest offered a secure base for planning. Before the '45, the Highland lairds counted their estates in terms of men; afterwards, they were not slow to discover that their money rents were much smaller than those of comparably sized properties in other parts of the kingdom. Sentiment slowed down the rate of change, but 'Gradually, however, men educated under different circumstances came forward, and feeling more remotely the influence of ancient connections with their dependants, were not inclined to sacrifice for a shadow the substantial advantage of a productive property. The more necessitous, or less generous, set the example.'[9] From tenderness or vanity, some clung to the old ways; but Selkirk expected that soon 'this must change (and the point of balance is now): the Highlands in general must soon fall into that state of occupancy and cultivation which is most conducive to the pecuniary interests of its individual proprietors'.[10] One must be careful not to generalise too freely from purely Highland affairs: there were Highland problems arising from the topographical and geographical peculiarities of the area that had no counterpart in the south. But these were not usually the objects of contention: throughout the country, the main challenge of response and adjustment was over the disappearance of a society whose relationships were determined by use, status and tradition, and its replacement by one in which social relationships were understood to be contracts between (apparently) free individuals. The Highlands are interesting because they exhibit the paradoxes of the situation with unusual clarity. Of course, there was no obvious division between old and new, and in the whole country, even in quite small areas, they continued to interpenetrate for as long as a hundred years.

The leading aims of the 'new' in the countryside may be defined as 'productivity' and 'freedom of the individual from the direct control of others'. These objectives were understood to be mutually reinforcing.

It may seem a truism that farming methods should tend to increase, or at the very least maintain, the soil's productivity, but at this time it was advanced as something of a novelty. Improvers were fond of quoting Swift's remark that the greatest benefactors were those who succeeded in making two blades of grass grow where only one grew before. 'The object of agriculture is to increase the soil's produce; and the purpose of all institutions and directions respecting the treatment of ground is to facilitate the means of accomplishing that end.'[11] Not only did this ideology bring an exciting new logic into the transactions of society, it seemed to fulfil the austerest demands of Calvinist theology that man should arrange his works to meet the providential design.

Since the influence of Malthus was as yet unfelt, one of the aims of government, according to the prevailing political economy, ought to be to increase population absolutely. If this could best be achieved by a more rational division of labour, there should be no regrets for the loss of unproductive small tenants. The minister of one parish in Argyll justified the changes he saw taking place around him. Normally it would be unwise to turn people off good arable land and fill it with sheep but

the complaint does not seem to apply to this country. The strength of a nation surely cannot consist in the number of idle people which it maintains. That the inhabitants of this part of the country were formerly sunk in indolence and contributed very little to the wealth or support of the state cannot be denied. The produce of this parish, since sheep have become the principal commodity, is at least double the intrinsic value of what it was formerly; so that half the number of hands produce more than double the quantity of provisions for the support of our manufactures; and the system by which land returns the most valuable produce and in the greatest abundance, seems to be the most beneficial to the country at large.[12]

In this optimistic phase the intercourse between town and country was felt to be more purely advantageous than at a later stage. The same minister, Dougal M'Dugal, was glad to think of his ex-parishioners becoming 'industrious hands in bleachfields, printfields and many other branches of manufacture'. The stimulus that the rise of Glasgow gave to agriculture and the introduction of a more progressive and comfortable life-style from the town was something to be rejoiced at in the small rural parish of Cambuslang.[13]

Scott did not personally enjoy practical farming, but from a sense of duty he encouraged his tenants to improve their holdings;[14] he was a member of the Selkirk Farmers' Club and took the chair on occasion;[15] and in Roxburghshire he was the 'first mover' of a scheme to drain a piece of common ground, sell it improved, and buy off all claims on the common at the rate of £30 sterling a head.[16] It was as a planter that Scott was most energetic and enthusiastic. Here the importance of the juncture of a variety of motives can be seen: utility, aesthetics, profitability, benevolence. In a letter written to the young Duke of Buccleuch Scott describes his own experience:

There is scarce a farmer of common sense but who is aware of the vast advantage which plantations afford the pastoral farmer in the single article of shelter. I have myself planted on half a small farm chiefly grass and spoke lately with the farmer who had last possessed it. I expected to hear him say I had destroyed the farm – on the contrary he offered me for the half which remained unplanted the same rent which he had formerly paid for the whole considering as he himself said that the advantage afforded by shelter and inclosing amply compensated the diminished extent of the ground . . .
. . . I can conceive few things more agreeable . . . than the power . . . of thus regulating the future productions of Nature . . . to complete a landscape which at first exists only in the planter's imagination . . . in fact you put the pencil in Nature's hand and compel her to paint a landscape according to your pleasure but on her own magnificent scale and with her own inimitable materials.[17]

Great planters like Sir Archibald Grant of Monymusk became legendary in the countryside for creating wealth merely by assisting nature's work. George Robertson's imagination was strongly fired by one Barclay of Ury who transformed his estate by two complementary operations, of removing stones and of draining: 'perhaps 100,000 cart loads of stones were removed, and went to fill up the drainage'.[18] Great hopes were entertained that sheep would be the economic salvation of the Highlands. It was argued that sheep could graze on land that would otherwise be unproductive, without touching the arable portions of the land. Sheep would suit the Scottish conditions far better than black cattle; the ground would produce a greater weight of meat, and there would be the addition of wool; sheep would free Scotland from the dependence on the droving trade and the English market, since local manufactures for wool could be established: 'emigration would cease, independence and manliness would ensue, the population would increase'. In addition to all this, the fertility of the soil would be increased.[19]

The evil consequences of sheep farming seem to have been

exaggerated by history and popular tradition. Malcolm Gray argues that a great deal of the land going over to sheep had never been occupied.[20] He adds that save for the great Sutherland clearances, only the edges of the old arable land were taken over by sheep. Southey, no friend to Highland lairds, was able to write of one clearance: 'When Lord Breadlane turned his mountains into sheep farms, he removed his Highlanders to [Taymouth]. The evil of the migration, if it were so mismanaged as to produce any, is at an end, and a wonderful improvement it has been, both for them and for the country.'[21]

But the ordinary Highlander, and indeed many a small tenant elsewhere, was unable or unwilling to make much of a contribution to the growth of the GNP. One of the principal agents of productivity and perhaps the most pregnant with social implications was the revolution that produced the capitalist farmer of the great sheep walks of the Borders and Highlands, the sprawling arable farms of the Lothians and Berwickshire. These farms and their holders were widely and bitterly resented, but they seem to have been inevitable given two conditions that developed at the same time. One was the lapse of claims of traditional occupancy: 'the whole transaction betwixt landlord and tenant is purely a matter of paction'.[22] Since the demand for land was so great, neighbours began to bid against one another instead of remaining in their traditional holdings; and, competition being once established, strangers were emboldened to put in bids. Rents offered were so high that landlords could hardly refuse the temptation[23] and because rents were high tenants worked on very small profit margins, making only very large farms economic. Secondly, so much could be offered because of the great rise in the price of produce; and in a large measure because of the revolution in banking – the rise of the cash credit and branch system. No farmer could begin farming in the Lothians without a stock of £2,000 and as the rent for a year might be as much as £3,000 for 900 acres, the banks alone averted a crisis of capital in Scottish farming.[24] We should remember that it was this capitalisation of agriculture that Scott defended in *Malachi Malagrowther*.

Farming was carried on as a business, highly mechanised and disciplined. Cobbett was disgusted by Berwickshire 'high farming' with its discipline of labourers, lack of cottages and substitution of bothies or barracks, and the resemblance of farms, with their steam threshing-machines, to factories.[25] In the old-fashioned, 'but and ben' farm houses, the family – that is, farmer and wife, children, maids and ploughmen – would live communally in two rooms of a house that was very much part of the farm.[26] Gradually, the houses became larger; there was more separation of rooms from offices, the children and servants had separate rooms; there was a greater division between family and servants and between farm and dwelling-house. Towards the end of the period there were still more severe disturbances in the old pattern: farmers were not content to have their labourers living in cottages on the farm lands, since they were a permanent responsibility. Instead they had to live in villages and towns, probably at some distance from their place of work, sometimes so far that the labourer would leave his family during the week.[27]

This whole process, which transformed the life of the entire agricultural population of the southern counties, may be compared to the development in Elizabethan England of a more rigid class system, expressed in the division of the hall into separate apartments; yet, compared with the criticism that this produced, the Scottish revolution went almost unopposed. The rural manners Scott touches on in *The Heart of Midlothian* and *Guy Mannering* had almost disappeared by the time he wrote. There is a brief connection with the previous paragraph when Ailie does not offer Brown a *separate* chamber at Charlie's Hope, an action nostalgically approved by Scott. My argument that the past/present confrontation does not enter imaginatively into the narrative structure of the novels, on the whole, still does not invalidate the traditional assumption that Scott wrote partly to register the passing of a traditional way of life.

There was criticism of these changes in Scotland; but there were few men of this generation who were able to resist the logic of improvement. The great store farmers were welcomed as an important and independent middle class:

Now a most comfortable change for the better has taken place. Of the present farmers, some no doubt still exhibit that sort formerly known by the appelation of *gude men*, the toiling and struggling cultivators on small farms; but a second sort occupy large territories and, intimately acquainted with the theory, the practice and the commerce of farming, shrewd and sensible, in easy and some in affluent circumstances, independent of either lairds or factors; they live in a most neat, handsome and hospitable manner, and give their children a very extensive education.[28]

Some objected to large farmers on grounds that were ultimately political: 'it is very improper to elevate men too high above their station. As many of our farmers have got a very narrow education, riches have often the unhappy effect of making them proud and leading them to treat their superiors [the minister?] with insolence and contempt.'[29] There was a pronounced trend to upward mobility among the farmers. The *Political Account of Scotland* has this note about one Thomas Johnston who had purchased a vote: 'Rich. Made money as a farmer, and purchased his estate. A son Writer to the signet.'

This was clearly a development to arouse the hostility of the established gentry, their retainers and apologists. But Scott was not prepared to regret it, at least publicly. There is an article in *Blackwood's*, April 1818, entitled 'Effects of Farm Overseers on Farm Labourers', which is of quite extraordinary interest for the study of Scott's opinions about society. Nominally by William Laidlaw, the piece was in all likelihood written by Scott himself.[30] The country minister who purportedly writes the article has met an old sheep farmer from the districts of high farming where farms have increased in size from perhaps 100 to 1,000 acres. Inevitably, the farmer argues, a large gulf appears between master and servant, and so a grieve [steward] is appointed. He is likely to run the farm in his own way and corrupt the labourers with his own idleness and indifference. The result is alienation – from the work, from the employer: '[In the old days] the whole household also constituted one family which looked to the gudeman as their natural and patriarchal head, and considered his interest as in some degree connected with their own. The words *our har'st* and *our crops* were commonly used to express those of their masters . . . All this kindly communication is cut off.' It is not that the author of the article could have been concerned with the *political* consequences of this, for high farming, with its discipline, produced not riotous discontent but demoralised acquiescence.

Critical of the current pattern of rural relations, he has no remedy to suggest to reverse the trend and to reimpose a substitute for old patterns of paternalism and dependence. Rather, he expects the social revolution to issue in fuller independence for the mass of the rural population, and regards the distresses as a mere temporary period of adjustment between two phases of society. In the society of the future, neither direction nor protection will be significant features: its members will be much more surely individuals. The following passage is remarkably apt to novels of groups III and V:

The evil, like all other evils, will work its own cure, or it will be productive of good in some way or other, that we had not yet foreseen . . . perhaps we may be assisted in our conjecture by attending to an analogy. The old feudal state of society has been compared to a tree; the old connexions of master and servant, that we have seen broken asunder before our eyes, were the terminating branches; they had ceased to shoot and grow, but they still continue to bear leaves and sometimes a little fruit. The filial affection, generosity and self-devotion of the clans are no more; but neither is their individual helplessness, ignorance and servility. Men value themselves more as individuals . . . the rural labourers will learn to disdain to be compelled to work and to be over looked like slaves . . . Those who have most industry will begin to prefer piece work.[31]

The fundamental change from feudal to modern society is seen here, not as primarily a surrender of colourful old manners in exchange for peace and plenty, but as an ineluctable passage from tribal to non-tribal, from a community in which status and tradition were all, to one composed of individuals whose relations with the other members of the society were more and more of the nature of free contracts.

John Anderson, Prize Essayist of the Highland Society, wrote: 'it is only by eradicating every trace of feudal dependence that the sense of individual importance which can fit him [the Highlander is meant] to be the associate of free men can be imparted to the emancipated serf'.[32] Anderson rejoiced that useful sheep and cattle had taken the place of the idle parasites of former times and hoped that more of them would take themselves off to be minders of shuttles in Glasgow. Many others, of whom Scott was one, however much they believed in individualism and progress, found it hard to acquiesce in the dismissal of the clansmen as mere caterpillars of the commonwealth. This is why so much stress came to be placed on their *martial* spirit, for here was one area in which they were inarguably *useful*:

Does the state owe no paternal regard to these men? Is it not a debt of gratitude due by their country to cherish them? Is it not the soundest policy to nurse and rear that race of people? Are all our wars at an end?[33]

[it cannot be] for the welfare of any state to deteriorate the character of, or wholly to extirpate, a brave, loyal and moral people – its best support in war.[34]

If the hour of need should come – and it may not perhaps be far distant – the pibroch will remain unanswered.[35]

Undoubtedly a public relations exercise whose unwitting clients were the clansmen was just as much the *raison d'être* of the martial scenes in some of the Waverley novels as Scott's predilection for military fun and games.

Hard though it is at this distance to distinguish fact from propaganda, it is clear that there was no simple division in Scottish society between either enlightened moderns and feudal despots or between rapacious exploiters and benevolent paternalists. There were few who did not see the truth on both sides. And, it seemed, there were few social relations in which good economics and good faith were bound to part company.

THE POWER OF THE LANDLORDS

The landed gentry of Scotland, the lairds, taking the class as a whole, suffered no diminution of its power and influence during these years. Cockburn remarks that during the war years the landed gentry was at the height of its power and prestige, while the merchant class had very little of either.[36] He perhaps exaggerates the impotence of the other wealthy classes, but it is true that the position of the lairds was very strong, that their ability to control the lives of their social subordinates remained immense, though more in some areas than in others. In matters of estate management, in causes between tenants, recourse was often made to the baron baillie, for the authority of the baron court had been only curtailed in 1748, not abolished. It was still competent to deal with everyday country affairs. The larger lairds were likely to be JPs and everyone whose estate was worth £100 Scots was entitled to act as a Commissioner of Supply. Most important of all, those whose estates were valued at £400 or more were entitled to vote in the county elections – a very important connection with the sources of power and patronage.

Even apart from their legal powers, lairds had many ways of influencing the lives of their tenants, for good or evil, especially in the north-west:

In every country where leases are from year to year . . . much of the character of the people must depend on either the virtue or caprice of their superiors; for though local jurisdictions be abolished, there is still a species of despotism remaining, by which the displeasure of the superior is equivalent, in its effects, to the punishments of the law.[37]

This was not quite the same in the south-east; Scott wrote to Maria Edgeworth: 'In our country the presence of the proprietors is of very little consequence to the tenants, who are wealthy and independent and generally get the better bargains in proportion to the neglect of the landlords.'[38] Yet in all areas, within the broad limitations imposed by the economic framework, it was very noticeable to observers, particularly

in the earlier phase, that the conditions of tenants and workpeople on similar and adjacent estates would differ significantly
according to the characters and dispositions of the landlords.
Later on, even with the best of intentions and the most efficient
management, the lairds were powerless to the extent they
depended on markets and financial frameworks beyond their
control.

To the small farmer however, the laird was the very type of
authority. Except in regions of enlightenment, long leases or
any formal contract but the yearly traditional bargains were
unknown, and the tenant was tenant-at-will for all practical
purposes. And since it was becoming obvious that tradition
was not sufficient to temper lairdly greed, the tenants were
reckoned to have no incentive to invest either capital or labour
in their farms beyond that required for mere subsistence.
Leases of nineteen years were thought to be the minimum
required to encourage improvement, but better 'two lives'
(that is the death of the son of the lessee). With a lease the
farmer was secure in his tenure and certain of his profits;
but the laird did not on that account seem any the less powerful. If he were an improving landlord his power would seem
the greater, for he would bind his tenants to perform wide-
ranging improvements meticulously detailed in the leases.
For years to come the laird would be reminded of his
own importance as he saw the countryside changing at his
will.[39]

The transmutation of servitudes and thirlages into fixed
money payments is interesting because it marks a very clear
division between feudal and modern ideas of return for land.
In spite of the obsolescence of feudal servitudes it was difficult
to change them because they were linked so closely to the
Scottish system of landholding, which preserved the forms of
feudal tenure. One grievous survival was 'thirlage', which
obliged tenants to grind corn at specified mills and was of
course attended with all kinds of oppression and dishonesty.
In 1808 Scott had to judge an action brought by a landlord
and a miller against a farmer for 'abstracted multures' and

had to find for the plaintiffs while plainly disliking the law.[40] Labour services were obnoxious, as they stood in the way of farmers' becoming efficient and because they savoured of feudalism. All over Scotland individual landlords were giving up these rights, influenced by both the liberal and the economic argument. It was difficult, however, to accede to the logic of these arguments and to say no to the emptying of the Highland straths.

Could the style and sentiment of the ancient relations between high and low be retained in the new economy? This was a question frequently asked at the time. If it was impossible, were there good grounds for supposing otherwise? Is it a mistake to look for continuity and tradition in social relations at all?

In the Highlands at least, it was expected that the ancient ties would soften the acerbity of change; yet the proprietors were expected to promote and encourage and not hinder the economic transformation. It was hoped the spirit of clanship might be revived on a modern basis so that the Highland proprietors might 'have found in the voluntary attachment of their tenants a grateful substitute for the loyal obedience of their clans. Amid the gradual changes and improvements of the age might not the recollections and most approved virtues and traits of chivalrous times have been retained?'[41] 'Kind' proprietors (the word used in the old sense) knew that the surest way to improve their land was to begin with the people. The concepts of clanship and chieftainship became subtly idealised and sentimentalised, fit for an urban market. 'What greater influence ought a liberal minded landlord to desire over his tenantry than what arises from the reciprocal exercise of good offices; such as condescension, humanity, beneficence and a desire to see them and their families happy and prosperous on his part; and on theirs, punctuality in paying their rents.'[42] Again, we can sense the figures of Waverley and Colonel Gardiner here, although we should not suppose that Scott was not fully aware of the differences between the MacIvor and the friend of the MacIvor. His was no mere unconscious expression of the *zeitgeist* but a full and critical comprehension of it.

Quite frequently, the lairds and chiefs connected by the oldest ties of blood turned out to be the least responsive to the new duties of a liberal landlordship, and the most rapacious. But what could have been expected, even from a kindly, liberal and economically enlightened chief or laird who was determined that his own and his dependents' prosperity should grow together? His two principal aims had to be to increase agricultural productivity and develop industry to pay for imports. The agricultural aim never had a chance, for increased productivity was more than balanced by an increased population. The dilemma of the landlord is succinctly stated by Scott in his lighthouse-yacht diary:

To have good farming you must have a considerable farm, upon which capital may be laid out to advantage. But to introduce this change would turn adrift perhaps twenty families, who now occupy small farms *pro indiviso*, cultivating by patches, or *rundale* and *runrig*, what part of the property is arable, and stocking the pasture as common upon which each family turns out such stock as they can rear, without observing any proportion as to the number which it can support.[43]

On Lord Armadale's estate, the number of tenantry amounts to 300, and the average rent is seven pounds each. What can be expected from such a distribution, without the greatest immediate distress and hardship to these poor creatures? It is the hardest chapter in Economicks; and if I were an Orcadian lord, I feel I should shuffle on with the useless old creatures, in contradiction to my better judgement.[44]

Demographic problems were exacerbated by social traditions. The Duke of Argyll, an active and liberal landlord, instructed his chamberlain of Tiree that the farms on the island must not be too small – not less than 'Four-mail'.[45] Although he felt that there was far less rent coming to him from the island than he would have expected, he would accept rent in kind and undertake to do the tenants' marketing. He repeated his demand for four-mail lands in 1802; the chamberlain replied that it was impossible owing to the excess of population and the inability of any single tenant to stock such a farm. Highland society made room for extra mouths by constantly narrowing its own standard of living, which, in spite of the potato, was brought ever closer to starvation. The new model of economic man, acquisitive and independent, was not accepted by Highland society. There was little hope for the creation of a rising middle class in such a society, for the lower class felt itself bound together as one community. The duke complained bitterly at the frustration of his plans to encourage self-sufficiency among his tenants:

When I am doing all I can to raise emulation and industry among these people by making every man independent of his neighbours, I find you pointing out a measure which must counteract all that I am doing. I mean taking men bound not only for their own rents, but for the rents of their neighbours. That must not be. Every man must be bound for his own rent only.[46]

The populations of North Uist, Tiree and Eigg doubled during the last half of the eighteenth century. The dilemma of the landlord was very real, for any attempt to avoid the iron laws meant a long-term deterioration of the system and a future disaster; a rigid system of accounting meant immediate misery. Very few lairds were in fact willing to countenance strict adherence to book-keeping: 'The proprietors in question never drive away their people but in cases of extreme necessity. These cases are frequently so urgent that it would be the height of cruelty to continue the people in their possessions in the way they themselves would wish.'[47] All over the Highlands, the crofting movement was an attempt to foster individualism. Runrig farms were divided into a number of single holdings, each just large enough to enable a single tenant to wrest a living from the soil. This change was brought about in Skye and parts of Inverness in 1811, but by 1840 the system was in ruins. Family loyalties were so strong that the crofts were subdivided three or four times. Few now held out any hope of finding a solution. 'It is . . . perfectly evident that no liberality on the part of the proprietor can render the present immense surplus in any measure comfortable. And there is, humanly speaking, no other way to provide for them than by emigration.'[48] Those lairds who were severest with their tenants, even to the extent of forcing them into emigration, may have been kindest in the long run.

In retrospect it seems to have been a vain hope, but prior to 1815 it seemed possible that all the disadvantages might have been offset by close attention to certain export industries – kelp, cattle and fish. Scott regarded his friend Macdonald of Staffa as an 'excellent example of Highland chieftainship' for 'by dint of minute attention to his property, and particularly to his kelp . . . he has at once trebled his income and doubled his population'.[49] He had improved his estate 'with the prudence and wisdom of a Scottish farmer, combined with that love of his people and desire to render them happy which was the finest feature in the character of an ancient Celtic chief'.[50] This was in 1809; but in 1828 Scott had to report: 'One great cause of the destruction of many highland lairds and their people has been the fall of Kelp since the war. Before that I knew one Laird make £20,000 a year his poor tenants having a like sum for manufacturing it. Now since Barilla can be purchased instead, Kelp has fallen immensely.'[51] The fisheries brought practically no income to the Highlands, and the price of cattle fell at the same time as that of kelp.

But the sentiment of landlordship was strong and growing outside the Highlands. Staffa's patriarchalism was not purely traditional but fostered by philosophy and sentiment: this Macdonald was, as it happens, by education and training an Englishman. In the south and east, the ideology of chieftainship was restated in terms of the eighteenth-century feeling morality, as well as in the more practical terms of the economists so that the whole ideology was just as much a new creation as it was an affirmation or restatement of tradition.

It is no contradiction to assert this and to maintain that this society was characterised by a movement towards a greater freedom and a greater separation between classes. The progressive relationships between classes were impersonal and mediated through calculated economic arrangements.

Scott at one stage thought the post-war crisis might bring landlords back to the realisation that a tenant was more than a creature that paid rent. But he thought that close personal relationships were impossible, and this was one of the reasons for his enthusiasm for the Yeomanry and the sharp-shooters.

Many of the leading exponents of this landlordship spent much time away from their estates. This was more or less a *sine qua non* for success, since it gave them the appropriate experience and information and the capital that could not be raised on the estate itself. Lord Gardenstone, one of the Lords of Session, purchased the estate of Johnston in 1765. At this time a population of 54 inhabited the village. Gardenstone built a new village, which had 550 inhabitants by 1800. He also provided local government in the form of a baron baillie, established a library and a school and was responsible for the development of a bleachfield.[52] Sir William Forbes engaged in the usual agricultural improvements of enclosing, planting, road- and bridge-building; in addition he built on his estate the village of New Pitsligo, where he spent £1,000 on a bleachfield and on weaving machinery.[53] These examples are really typical of the way in which enlightened capitalists were transforming the countryside and its life at this period. They did *not* go to the country for the pleasures of rural retirement; their bustle of improvement, with its concomitants of cottagers, industry, agricultural improvements and education, was at once a source of profit and a social and religious duty. A lone quietist like Joshua Geddes was not of their number.

We have seen how the spirit and attitude of the established landed gentry was undergoing remarkable changes. How far was the composition of the class changing, and was its character altered by the passing of land into the hands of the newly wealthy, and was it easy for new proprietors to make their way in county society and the political hierarchy?

There is little precise information about the amount of land changing hands; what there is, is on the whole regional. In Argyll for instance, there were over 200 landlords in the middle of the eighteenth century and only 156 by 1800. But much of the land that changed hands must have gone to established proprietors.[54] One indication that the situation was serious for the old proprietors was the amount of land under entail, a device increasingly resorted to by the gentry to forestall social change. The practice was anathematised by improvers, since it limited the ability of the occupier to ameliorate the estate, and kept it out of the hands of those who could.[55] It was also held to be responsible for a good deal of friction between father and son and for the genteel beggary that unmarried gentlewomen might find themselves in.[56] It was argued that landed families had special duties in society, but that the families did not need to be ancient: people who came into the possession of land acquired landlordly feelings soon enough.[57] This seems to have been true: the new proprietors were as good landowners as the old, from a social point of view; if anything, they were less ruthless exploiters of their inferiors, but not more notable for rational and humane estate management. Generally speaking, new men fell easily into the mould of county society. If any one class can be termed outstanding, it would be the returned émigrés or 'nabobs'. These were among the most vigorous and improving of landlords, and they seemed to present an ideal combination of traditional belongingness (most of them were lairdly younger sons) and commercial competence.[58]

It would be convenient with respect to certain of the novels, *The Bride of Lammermoor* for instance, to suggest that there was a rapidly developing gap in Scott's time between the old landed class, economically inefficient but involved in an irreplaceable mesh of interpersonal relationships, and a new moneyed class, efficient, but socially disruptive. Harry Levin writes: 'If history did not teach us that the old farms were dying out, and that the country estates were being mortgaged, we should know from reading *Castle Rackrent*, *The Bride of Lammermoor* or *Wuthering Heights*.'[59] R. C. Gordon's account of *The Bride* is based on the (unsupported) assumption that there was such a change.[60] However, although individual families did lose their estates in this as in any period, for a variety of reasons, it was by no means so general as to alarm even the most reactionary supporters of the aristocracy and if there was a good degree of mobility in the landed class, it was not accompanied by any new ideology that the old proprietors were unable to participate in or were openly hostile to. Neither Scott nor anyone else had any reason to be pessimistic about the future of the lairds at this time, unless he were frightened of outright revolution.

TOWN AND COUNTRY

Cockburn's contention that the 'merchants' had no political power is exaggerated because it ignores the strength of their connection with county politics. Mercantile was closely connected by blood with gentle society[61] and there was no clear distinction between the interests and ideology of the two groups. The county franchise gave the merchants the political power that was denied them by the archaic constitution of the boroughs, or that they frequently did not want.[62] The county system was apparently just as exclusive as the burgh, but the ability to create fictitious votes made the county electorate far more responsive to the realities of changing power. A prosperous merchant would find himself eagerly courted if he did possess a vote and asked to accept a fictitious one if he did not. Since votes were scarce, it would be completely impossible for any new laird to be cold-shouldered by neighbours who had any interest in party politics, and since economic well-being was so closely connected with patronage, all *were* interested in party politics.

Furthermore, the situation that obtained in England, where a country gentleman could be securely wealthy by merely sitting on his estates and avoiding vice, was very rare in Scotland. A good deal of the awfulness of Mrs Elton can be accounted for by her dubious mercantile background (Bristol, not Bath). There is something more than mere snobbery about it; the English novel in the nineteenth century drew a good deal from a pastoral vision of a normative gentry untainted by dark Satanic mills. But in Scotland, not only did modern economics and urban personnel penetrate county society, the reverse was also true. The gentry were involved in industrialisation in towns and villages, and sentiments of landlordship were carried over into the relations between master and men in some of the great industrial communities. To a novelist like Trollope there was something distasteful when the landed gentry made, as they at times did, a great deal of money out of industry. In *Mr Scarborough's Children* old man Scarborough's industrial profiteering is in key with his testamentary chicanery. David Craig comments that Scottish novelists saw nothing remarkable in the changes brought about by industrialisation, while Cockburn, on the other hand, entered many comments about factory life in his Journal. Scotland not only had no Dickens but had no Disraeli. However, Cockburn himself was without interest in factory conditions *until the late 1830s*. Earlier, in the age of Scott, he had been absorbed, like others, by the political crisis. And there was no class of men that had a vested interest in opposing industrialisation, for the other educated classes were all implicated in it. There was thus no economic basis for a Disraelian blend of radicalism and old-fogeyism. Gentry and clergy alike saw industry as an economic salve, as a source of labour for light hands. Sometimes this good will was more than exhortation: the lairds would lend their countenance, influence and support – in feuing lands for factories, mills and villages, and in providing economic backing. Scott's kinsman, Scott of Gala, was the most active laird behind the successful Galashiels wool industry, while his factor, George Craig, was the town's banker.[63] The minister, Dr Douglas, was another source of credit.[64] Sir Walter used his influence with the Board of Manufacturers on behalf of Galashiels men. In 1820 he wrote to them in favour of James Patterson, the inventor of a new cropping-machine. The manufacturers of Gala received for a new drying-house the sum of £50 and a certificate from 'Mr Walter Scott of Abbotsford testifying to its great usefulness'.[65] More rarely, heritors would be active entrepreneurs. Sir James Johnstone founded the village of James Town to house antimony miners working in an industry he had himself developed. Nor was a sort of social responsibility forgotten: the wages and conditions of the workpeople were modelled on the conditions of well-off rural labourers; they each had a cow and a piece of ground, and the company would buy grain when it was cheap and sell it to employees in times of scarcity. It also provided a library and a school for the children of the employees. Such an enterprise was not uncommon, and exhibits the bond between the small industrial communities and the social traditions of the countryside.[66]

Industrial enclaves were not – in the beginning – alarming to political orthodoxy. Except in times of recession, the work force was not radically inclined and even at times of severe social unrest the existing social controls – gentry, employers – were usually sufficient to overawe them. When the military had to be called in, as it was in Glasgow and Paisley in 1819, to subdue popular discontents, it was a sign that existing and traditional controls had become inadequate. But industrialisation had not always been so ruthless and exploitive in Scotland as to produce riotous discontent. The managers and owners of the great mills of Deanston, Catrine, Ballindalloch and Blantyre had exercised a certain amount of discipline over their operatives outside the factory walls; the sale of spirits had been forbidden in the villages; and some of the institutions of the rural parish – schools and poor's rolls – had been reproduced. These companies maintained their standards, yet the total picture was much more gloomy by 1830, for these industrial new towns were now of much less importance.[67] It is not necessary to blame a decline of tradition for this: there were changes in the pattern of industrial distribution, which had important consequences. Scott gives one of the earliest and soundest explanations of it, one that speaks a good deal for his capacity for unprejudiced analysis.

The actual Radicals in Scotland are only to be found in the large manufacturing towns where a certain number always entertain those sentiments which are always more or less widely extended amongst the giddy multitude according to the pressure of the times, the price of provisions the plenty or want of work and so forth. The situation and habits of the Scottish manufacturers, considered as a part of the community, have been powerfully affected, and much for the worse, by the general introduction of steam for driving engines. Since I remember Scotland manufactures were usually situated within the vicinity of waterfalls for convenience of driving the machinery – this drove the undertaker into remote and solitary places where they erected their cotton mills while their workmen formed a little village round them. . . In hard times a man was obliged to maintain his workpeople till work came round, and was usually assisted on such occasions by the country gentlemen. In short, the employer possessed the natural influence over the employed which go [sic] so far to strengthen the bonds of society. But where the engines are driven by steam there is and can be nothing of this – the buildings are erected nearly as possible if not in the actual precincts of Glasgow or Paisley – when a manufacturer wishes to do a particular job he gets some two hundred weavers from lanes, streets and garrets without the slightest attention to character or circumstances or to anything but that they have ten fingers and can work a shuttle. These men are employed for perhaps a fortnight and are then turned off, the employer knowing no more than if they were so many old pirns or shuttles. [68]

It was these conditions that first drove a wedge between gentry and industrialists. Scott is moved by two considerations: the misery, indeed the alienation, of life in the great cities, and the possibility that the cities will explode.

Urban life was, and became increasingly, important in Scott's novels, but his awareness of contemporary problems was, like that of other Scots of his generation, blinkered by the rural traditions of Scottish society. Some signs of the struggles of adjustment can be seen in their attitudes to the poor. To traditional Presbyterian austerity was added, in the early nineteenth century, a Malthusian pessimism, the unchecked effects of which would have been to throw the working-people upon their own, ever more slender resources. The first forty years of the nineteenth century saw the Scottish system of poor-relief crumble and collapse. Originally similar to that developed in England under Elizabeth, it had gone in a different direction. Poor-relief in Scotland was still a very personal matter, with the parish authorities administering limited funds and caring for a few parish paupers. The existence of large numbers of destitute and friendless was not envisaged by the system. Destitution might well be regarded as a disgrace, and it was a shame to allow neighbours or family to come upon the parish. The officially administered charity was in fact very small and represented only a small fraction of the help and assistance the Scottish people gave each other. In the Orkneys, for example, there was a 'roundsman' system in existence at the end of the eighteenth century by which the poor were given bed and board by all the families of the parish in turn. In Sutherland one parson claimed that there was almost no work for the sessions to do since blood ties were felt so strongly that people would never allow their connections to receive parish relief.[69] Tolerance was extended all the way to the poorest of wandering beggars or 'sorners' who 'used to lodge by turns and for many days and even weeks at a time at the houses of their acquaintance and were treated with as much attention and generosity as if they had been capable of making a return'.[70] Robertson reported that the old-style beggars had all the virtues of their society: honesty, thrift and 'respectability'.[71]

In the nineteenth century much of this must have been mere memory – and one wonders how much romanticised. But just as it was becoming apparent that the Scottish system was crumbling under pressure, the awful example of England enhanced its attractiveness. In Scotland there was no law of settlement, no army of beadles, and only a very modest outlay. The English disease spread from the border; compulsory assessments started in the high-farming region of Berwickshire. Assessments were related to a new and hostile tone in social relations, typical of which was the new attitude to begging. In Berwickshire officers were employed to go to fairs and public meetings and take up all 'gypsies, tinkers, beggars and disorderly persons who cannot give a proper account of themselves' and conduct them to 'the extremity of the county'.[72] A cheerful Podsnap of a farmer, one Thomas Oliver, said in 1833 that there was no mendicity in his county because police regulations forbade it. Asked where the beggars went, he replied that he did not know, and was merely content they were not in evidence.[73] In Edinburgh in 1813 a society for the 'suppression of public begging' was established.

Many of the destitute poor wandered in consequence to England to live off the rates, or to the Highlands, for the hospitality of those hardly better off than themselves. And although critics suggested that the rise of dissenting groups and the non-attendance of heritors at Kirk was diminishing funds that the sessions could administer, there is no evidence that this was so. There was in fact an explosion of foundations of charitable societies in the early post-war years.[74] The heritors would lay a voluntary assessment on themselves to make up any deficiency in parish funds. Scott wrote to Laidlaw: 'A voluntary assessment is the best mode of raising money to procure work for the present sufferers because I see no other way of making this necessary tax fall equally on the heritors.'[75] Many of the best-intentioned men fought the introduction of compulsory assessments. Scott was adamant in refusing to use his right to countermand Kirk Sessions decisions about poor-relief. But, when all traditional sources had been tapped, when the landowners and the traditional bourgeoisie had responded with a worried generosity, there was still a huge surplus of demand for relief.

The real question was – were the towns to set the pattern for the country, or vice-versa? The latter alternative was by far the most attractive, especially as set forth in the vigorous and influential work of Chalmers. He expressed and put into practice the view that the old system merely needed overhauling. He found nothing irreconcilable between nineteenth-century industrialism and eighteenth-century agrarianism. With smaller parish boundaries in towns, with parishes responsible for their own poor only, and with a conscientious clergy backed up by a large committee of lay welfare workers and moral policemen, he thought that the trends towards impersonality might be halted. 'We think that the same moral regimen which under the parochial and ecclesiastical system

of Scotland has been set up, and with so much effect, in her
country parishes, may, by a few simple and attainable processes,
be introduced into the most crowded of her cities.'[76] Chalmers'
ideas, and the St John's, Glasgow, experiment, which drew a
lot of enthusiastic response from ministers eager to serve in
the mission carrying the gospel of self-help from country to
town, only perhaps served to delay the arrival of officially
regulated poor-relief, which could alone have alleviated the
misery of the city poor and saved them from the epidemics.
It was the closeness of outbreaks of disease upon the heels of
economic crises that convinced Chalmers' principal critic,
Dr W. P. Allison, of the necessity for a radical change in the
whole system.[77] Point by point, Allison answered Chalmers'
account of the advantages of the old system. His problem was
the city, and while 517 rural parishes remained unassessed,
the cities would always support the country.

His analysis of city life was not dissimilar to Scott's; but
the industrial city was familiar to him, and not an object of
dread. Compare Scott's 'The high state of civilisation to which
we have arrived is perhaps scarcely a national blessing since
while the few are improved to the highest point, the many are
in proportion brutalised and degraded'[78] and Allison's 'While
the higher ranks in Glasgow have been advancing in wealth
and luxury, a large proportion of the lower ranks have been,
at least as rapidly, receding towards barbarism.'[79] While
Chalmers regarded poor-relief and the problems of poverty
as moral questions, Allison, and Scott more hesitantly, came
to think that traditional morality was irrelevant in the new
conditions. Scott was genuinely one of the first to see that
cycles of boom and slump in the textile industry, with periods
of high wages followed by destitution, mocked any talk of
the virtues of a stable agrarian society, like thrift and prudence.
In the cities, a legal provision was necessary on both political
and humanitarian grounds.[80]

5. QUEEN CAROLINE AND
KING CHARLES

The argument has been implicit in previous chapters that the Waverley novels have as their subject matter more the world of post-war Britain than the historical periods they are set in, or any themes extracted from these epochs, such as the value of chivalry or the merging of polarities. However, since the connection between the historical epoch and the contemporary world is only visible in metaphors developed within the novel, metaphors that do not arise inevitably from the contexts of either world and are indeed transferrable from one epoch to another, then my conclusions rest heavily on interpretation and assertion. It would be convenient if a place could be found where the relationship is more like that found in parable or allegory, where more authorial signposts could be read. If even one such novel can be found, then the general principle that the novels *may* refer primarily to Scott's own age is established.

There are at least two candidates. One is *Woodstock*. It would be possible, and not even very novel, to demonstrate that this work is heavily influenced by Scott's reflections on the causes, progress and consequences of the French Revolution, for *Woodstock* and the *Life of Napoleon* were composed simultaneously. Other commentators have noted the way in which the figure of Cromwell seems to hark back to that of Napoleon. In the *Life* there are dozens of comparisons between the two men, as there are between Louis and Charles, and between the two Restorations. Of course, Scott is frequently mindful to point out that the comparisons are not complete. In the way of character drawing, there seems to be half a parallel made between the three commissioners of the novel, Harrison, Bletson and Desborough (very different from the anonymous 'captains' of Scott's source) and the triumvirate of the revolution, whom Scott describes in the *Life* very much as a novelist. The terms of the comparison are: that they are three; that Desborough is like Danton (both are principally described as being coarse, brutal and strong); that Harrison is like Robespierre (both are cruel, cold-blooded and fanatical); and that Bletson is like Marat (cowardly). Some terms are missing: Harrison does not seem to have Robespierre's 'vanity' nor Bletson Marat's 'bloodthirstiness'.

Throughout the two works, there is a considerable amount of statement of political principle, or theory. Republicanism and democracy are condemned in terms that I have stated in chapters 2 and 3. There are also scenes, particularly crowd scenes, that seek to demonstrate the disorderliness of democracies. Thus in *Woodstock*, chapter 1, the lower orders discuss theology (always a 'substitute' for politics with Scott): 'many of them unwashed artificers . . . the presumption of these learned Thebans being in exact proportion to their ignorance, the last was total and the first boundless. Their behaviour in church was anything but reverential or edifying.' The scene culminates in the brutal ejection of the minister from the pulpit by Tompkins and the latter's delivering an impromptu harangue. This can easily be compared with one of the manias of revolutionary France: 'The revolution appeared to have turned the heads of the whole lower classes, and those who had hitherto thought least of political rights, were now seized with the fury of deliberating, debating and legislating, in all possible times and places.'[1]

In the novel, the palace of Woodstock, in which almost the whole of the action takes place, becomes something like a symbol of England (memories of *Richard II* are at work). Within this, the Tower of Rosamond and Love's Ladder become associated with the expression of the King's will, with abuse of power and the corruption of the court. This is reinforced in the novel by Charles II's attempt to revive feudal iniquity by seducing Alice (he offers her a form of marriage similar to that undergone by George IV with Mrs F.). When the tower is blown up, it is the monarchy that is demolished, morally if not physically (Charles manages to escape through the cellars at the last moment). It is such a strong – and long-awaited and signposted – image in the novel that there must be some connection with this passage from *Napoleon*: describing the French monarchy before the Revolution he says: 'it might be compared to some ancient tower swayed from its base by the lapse of time, and waiting for the first blast of a hurricane, or shock of an earthquake to be prostrated in the dust'.[2] In *Woodstock* and in *Napoleon*, disorder, and so democracy and radicalism, thrive when the upper classes, represented conveniently by the monarch, turn their backs on their responsibilities (see Scott's account of the Revolution as discussed above in chapter 2) and merely claim their selfish privileges – symbolised in the novel by Charles Stuart's lechery. Here is the connection with Scott's 1820s. The same sort of linking can be found in a slightly earlier novel, but more precisely and emphatically, and better, if not satisfactorily, integrated into the entire action. This novel is *Peveril of the Peak*.

Scott had no very great opinion of *Peveril*; yet he thought the third volume 'much superior to the two first'.[3] Dickens commented favourably on the work in a letter of 1839.[4] And in 1839, he was working on *Barnaby Rudge*; although Dickens does not say so, it is significant that he should have commended a novel that, like his own, concerned anti-Catholicism, mass hysteria, mob violence and imprisonment. Some scenes may have had an even longer influence: 'Morning dawns on Newgate as well as on the freest mountain turf which Welshman or wild goat ever trode; but in so different a fashion that the very beams of heaven's precious sun, when they penetrate into the recesses of a prison house, have the air of being committed to jail' (chapter 35). Dickens would not have dissipated his effect by embedding the fantastic image in this matrix of poetic diction, weakening generality ('a prison house') and co-ordination and subordination in the syntax; yet the kernel sentence is pure *Little Dorrit*: the very sun had the air of having been committed to jail.

Dickens, it is well known, drew on Radical and Chartist agitation to fill out his picture of the Gordon riots, or, more simply, manifested his apprehension of the violence in his age under cover of a historical novel. There is a secret connection here with *Peveril*, for it too is inspired by political happenings of the 1820s, and Scott also discovered a resemblance between his own times and those of the Gordon riots, as well as with the 1680s and with 1710:

But Lord, what a stupid monster John Bull is . . . that is driven frantic at the sight of a red flag, would run bellowing mad on such subject as the popish plot of 1682 or more lately on such worthy topics as John Wilkes, Net Currency, Lord George Gordon or Queen Caroline.[5]

I suppose the first week of parliament will put to rest the question of the Queen which considering the row it has raised and the rational view which will one day be taken of the grounds of the commotion has been unmatched since the days of Sacheverel.[6]

Although the Catholic question was being raised again at the same time, Scott remarks that it has 'lost all public interest and importance'[7] and 'Nobody here cares much about it.' If Scott was interested in 'opposing fanaticisms' (F. R. Hart's term) then the interest must have been political rather than religious.

The Queen Caroline affair began to lose its interest in April or May of 1821 and Scott is quiet about it, occupied with *Kenilworth, Pirate* and *Nigel*. In February 1822, he was planning *Peveril*: 'I am turning my thoughts to that tumultuary and agitated period of Charles 2nds reign which was disturbed by the popish plot.'[8] In other words, it was the plot itself, and the violence and agitation that it called forth, in which the novel originated, and not in, say, an exploration of varieties of religious enthusiasm. And since Scott has previously compared the Caroline riots with the Popish Plot, I think it well worth reversing the comparison.

A bare two or three months before this letter, Scott had raised the whole question of historical parallels in a letter to his son Charles, saying: 'our eye is enabled to look back on the past to improve on our ancestors' improvements and avoid their errors. This can only be done by studying history and comparing it with passing events.'[9] Before the outbreak of rioting associated with the Pains and Penalties Bill, Scott had drawn a parallel between Charles II's court and George IV's:

No man of experience will ever expect the breath of a court to be favourable to morals . . . One half of the mischief is done by the publicity of the evil which corrupts those who are near its influence and fills with disgust and apprehension those to whom it does not directly extend. Honest old Evelyn's account of Charles II's court presses on ones recollections and prepares the mind for anxious apprehensions.[10]

Trivial though it seems today, the quarrel between the king and queen excited public opinion to an enormous degree and it was this – 'the publicity of the evil' – that engaged Scott's attention. Scott had been in favour with the Princess of Wales during the early days of her marriage; as the Whigs and Radicals took her up, Scott turned against her, although it could hardly be said that he was much in favour of the king. Caroline is mistaken, he writes, in thinking that even the mob seriously approves of her: 'I believe the ground of the huzzas is rather hatred of the King.'[11]

A piece of occasional journalism called 'The History of John Bull' gives a very good insight into the workings of Scott's mind at this moment.[12] The vagaries of public opinion, rather than king or queen, are the subject of the article. Significantly, Scott finds it necessary to devote the first portion of the article to the French Revolution (a burlesque account that ends with Napoleon's exile). There is no very immediate or obvious connection between those events in France and the Pains and Penalties Bill: yet Scott needs that framework to place it against – just as later he will need the Civil War and its aftermath of comparative quiet, which is in turn succeeded by a revolutionary situation. Then comes an account of Peterloo/1819:

Chapter 31. How John [England] was sick of the quiet and had thought of murdering his steward and officers that he might reform the abuses of his household and how he came to his senses again in some measure.

Then comes the divorce scandal:

And of a lady who durst not sleep in her bed without someone to hold her in.

And then the Radical disturbances:

Chapter 34. How in other times the witnesses stoned the accused but how in Bullock's Hatch [Great Britain] the friends of the accused stoned the witnesses in order to get at the truth. Of the advantages of keeping such a family of utter reprobates that no word can be believed that comes out of the mouth of e'er a rogue or jade amongst them because in such a case their tongue can be no slander. How John Bull danced in his shirt for very joy because his oldest wife had pronounced a certain Great Lady to be no better than she should be and how he threatened to beat all his friends who advised him to put on his clothes.

Interestingly, the Queen affair is imaged as primarily judicial proceedings with a mob in attendance. This is the image to which the narrative in *Peveril* also leads: the trial of the Peverils, their acquittal and their bad treatment by the mob are the structural centre of the book.

More and more Caroline had allowed her speeches, which were written by Cobbett, to ally her cause with that of the Radicals. In a letter to the *EWJ* of 7 February 1821, Scott sarcastically links the two:

the Cato Street conspiracy was a scheme entirely devised and got up by the ministers themselves . . . Ing's carving knife was supplied to him by Lord Castlereagh's butler, and . . . the unhappy Thistlewood was bribed to submit to the gallows by the promise of an annuity for life . . . What do you say to the recent case of Colonel Brown who has obviously been assassinated by Ministerial hirelings to throw the odium of the attempt upon the friends of the Queen?

This was probably never considered either witty or profound. But it does show that at this time – when the events referred to were no longer quite topical – Scott's mind is going over an order of events in which mob violence, royal profligacy, political instability and a sense of grotesque absurdity are all

mixed. Without trying to fit these things into any more system-
atic account of the plotting and significance of *Peveril*, a couple
of verbal similarities may be adduced. The seeming desire of
the ministers to take their own lives with the Cato Street
conspiracy might be compared to Charles II's complaint:
'I can scarce escape suspicion of the Plot myself, though the
principal object of it is to take away my own life' (chapter 31).
And could Ing's carving knife be remembered when Oates
accuses the Countess of Derby of drawing 'from her bosom a
broad, sharp-pointed knife, such as butchers kill sheep with'
(chapter 41), and giving it to him for the King's murder? There
is the same playing with incongruity, with a disregard for
propriety and likelihood so great that it amounts to an abuse
of language.

More obviously relevant to the contemporary situation is
the pseudo-authorial comment that Scott puts into the mouth
of the young Earl of Derby:

'It seems,' said the Earl of Derby, 'that Old England, who takes a
frolicsome brain-fever once every two or three years for the benefit
of her doctors and the purification of the torpid lethargy brought
on by peace and prosperity, is now gone stark staring mad on the
subject of a real or supposed Popish Plot . . . and the nation *like a
bull* at Tutbury running, is persecuted with so many *inflammatory
rumours* and pestilent pamphlets, that she has cocked her tail, flung
up her heels, taken the bit between her teeth and is as furiously
unmanageable as in the year 1642' (chapter 15; my italics).

There are obvious verbal parallels with 'John Bull'. There is
also a repetition of one of Scott's favourite comments, that the
troubles of the post-war years were the result of a surfeit of
peace and plenty: 'We are still agitated here by the consequences of the transition from a state of war to a state of peace
and are very near arriving at the uncomfortable conviction that
the latter with all its old adjunct of Plenty is one [of] the most
ruinous matters that can befall us.'[13] The 'doctors' whom the
Earl of Derby mentions are of course politicians. In 'John Bull'
we hear how 'the Hoaxites and the Hittites [i.e. Whigs and
Tories] contended for the honour of physicking John Bull out

of the fever he had got from dancing in his shirt'. The Earl of Derby's comments are called pseudo-authorial because they are almost indistinguishable from comments made by the omniscient author throughout the novel; there is perhaps a variation in tone. Both speakers purport to give a general and objective view about what always or usually happens in England. It is associated with the use of the simple present and with adverbs like 'always', 'as usual', 'often'.

The Puritanical party . . . had enjoyed power for several years, and, of course, became unpopular among the common people, never at any time attached to those who, being in the immediate possession of authority, are often obliged to employ it in controlling their humours (chapter 4).

the people were fickle as usual (chapter 4).

a woman's brain is sometimes as inconstant as a popular assembly (chapter 5).

the rude herd acted but according to their kind (chapter 5).

rumour took care to make the usual additions to reality (chapter 8).

it [the plot] is received by the credulous people of England with the most undoubting belief (chapter 17).

when did Englishmen . . . remember anything when hurried away by the violence of party feeling (chapter 18).

zeal, amongst the lower orders at least, is often in an inverse ratio to knowledge (chapter 20).

These comments are selected from the first third of the novel; by their tone, anti-popular, and by their intrusiveness, outside the normal narrative mode of the novel, we are made to feel that the author has some over-riding purpose, or, if not that, a particular preoccupation with party, mob violence and prejudice. It should also be admitted that the feeling that the media are to blame for exaggerating things in a crisis that is not half as severe as they make out is a very typical conservative response.

However, Scott certainly wants to make us think that there is an over-riding purpose. The epigraph runs: 'If my readers should at any time remark that I am particularly dull, they may be assured that there is a design under it.'

On the face of it there is little similarity between the Popish Plot and the Queen Caroline affair. In the one the sympathy was with the witnesses and against the accused, and in the other vice versa. Scott could not have made of *Peveril* a precise parable of current events even if he had wanted to. The figure of Mary Stuart would have been much more suitable. Lady Louisa Stuart wrote that Scott was, in fact, contemporarily suspected of defending Caroline through the portrait of Mary in *Abbot*.[14] But Mary was, in that novel, an austere, Puritanical figure, not a figure of sexual licence, as Caroline was, nor was her entourage Radical or anti-authoritarian. I suspect that Scott could never have compared the Scottish queen with Caroline; it is indeed doubtful whether he would have been able to run a comparison between Caroline and any woman. Charles II is, however, here as in *Woodstock*, a useful figure on whom to cast contempt. The strategy of *Peveril* is to avoid these logical difficulties by stressing those features of the Popish Plot that – to Scott – have a relevance to the contemporary situation.

He emphasises and repeats a number of words like 'madness', 'frenzy', 'Mania', 'delirium', 'fever', 'possession', to characterise the state of the country:

the nation is in a scarlet fever

those trembled under the apprehension of some strange and sudden convulsion of empire who were formerly only occupied by the fear of going to bed supperless

the circumstances which have thrown the country into a ferment general delirium.

England at the time of the plot, then, is represented as being afflicted by a species of mass hysteria, a special sort of insanity. This again is a very convenient hypothesis for conservative writers, and if this were all, we certainly would not need to bother with the novel. One of the reasons Scott gives for the fever is that the people are 'tired' with quiet.

Even if this were acceptable about the Popish Plot riots, it would hardly be adequate to account for the discontents of Scott's own times. Absurd though the mob's support for Caroline was, few people contemporarily, including Scott, doubted that she was little more than a convenient peg. There certainly were deeper causes of discontent, which could not be passed off as hysteria. Scott does want to emphasise the credulousness and absurdity of the London mob that besieges the courts (chapter 42) but there is something else in the novel too – a sort of general sourness at social relations, with the intractability of the 'people'. The retreat of the Earl and Countess to their stoutest fortress is occasioned by the plot, but their flight is prompted by their fear of the people of the Isle of Man who are resentful of (significantly) taxation. The Isle is no primitive Eden, like the Shetland Isles of *The Pirate*: 'Party spirit had come among these simple people and destroyed their good humour while it left them their ignorance' (chapter 11).

Then there is the affair of the attack by the miners on Bridgenorth's house. In a sense, this is gratuitous, for it is not required by the plot, and its consequences are nil. The miners have no other part to play except to rebel. The scene is here because it is dragged in to mirror some of Scott's fears and fantasies about mob violence – it is related then to the deep, rather than the surface, structure of the novel. Mob violence in the great cities was, of course, for Scott an index of the unavoidable depravity of great centres of population; but in the rural north, things cannot be so simply explained. In *Peveril*, there are vague hints of economic motives; the miners are discontented with Sir Geoffrey for not paying their wages, but even more so with Bridgenorth who threatens to close the mine: 'The rogues were mutinying for their wages but yesterday; they will be all ready for good or bad' (chapter 25). The miners then attack and well-nigh burn down a gentleman's house.

Only a year or two earlier Scott had lived in fear of a 'servile rising' with '50,000 blackguards . . . ready to rise between

Tyne and Wear'. [15] There was even a rumour circulated by the press that Abbotsford had been attacked at the time of the Queen Caroline riots. [16] To see Scott even contemplating an attack by a mob on a gentleman's house is a little confusing. But then, they were fighting for one gentleman against another (and rather a dubious one). As Scott went over these troubles in his mind, he often comforted himself with the thought that many of the 'decent' country people were behind him and his class. At the moments of the greatest outrage, he dallied with the idea of fighting the Radicals at the head of his loyal yeomanry. Without too much violence to critical probability, this episode could be seen as the fusing into one image of Scott's hopes and fears during the disturbances of 1820–2. On 8 February 1820 Scott issued a broadside for local distribution called 'To those inhabitants of the Regality of Melrose, who offered or proposed to offer, their services to form a Corps of Marksmen under Mr Walter Scott of Abbotsford'. [17] At this time the greatest danger had passed, and Scott was able to write:

We are not at present, and I trust will never again be placed, under the painful necessity of assuming arms . . . for the . . painful task of combating the misguided violence of our fellow subjects . . . For myself, I can only say, that the feelings of gratitude towards those individuals who have on this momentous crisis offered me their support, are in proportion to the confidence they have shown themselves willing to repose in me . . . this distinguished proof of your kindness and confidence encourages me to hope that if an emergency similar to the late crisis should occur, while I am able to get on horseback, I will not want the backing of my neighbours.

Is this the origin of Lance Outram's faithfulness, the miners' rescue of Julian? Scott felt that he ('offered *me* their support', 'repose in *me*') was both beleaguered and supported, and that the Radicals were crazily misguided and corrupted, and yet justified.

Still more to the point, as regards structure and origin, are the constant and denigratory references to London. Among Tories and Radicals alike distrust and hatred of London in the Romantic period is so well known as hardly to require addi-

tional comment. Scott distrusted London partly as Radical
and partly as corrupting, disturbing and an engrosser of wealth.
The theme of the corrupting influence of London has already
been raised in *Nigel*. A letter of Scott's deplores the improvement in communications in as far as it makes public opinion
much more dependent on London.

It must make the public feeling and sentiment of London, whatever
that may chance to be, much more readily and emphatically
influential upon the rest of the kingdom . . . Formerly in Edinburgh
and other towns the impulse received from any strong popular
feeling in London was comparatively slow and gradual, and had to
contend with opposite feelings and prejudices of a national or
provincial character; the matter underwent a reconsideration –
and the cry which was raised in the great mart of halloo and humbug
was not instantly echoed back.[18]

A few years later, he was to write in *Malachi Malagrowther*:
'Is any real power derived by centering the immediate and
direct control of everything in London? Far from it. On the
contrary, that great metropolis is already a head too bulky
for the empire and should it take a vertigo the limbs would be
unable to support it.'[19] The novel is structured in stages that
are defined by their closeness to London: the deep provinces
of the Isle of Man and the Peak; Julian's journey to the city;
his penetration of the recesses of the court and justiciary; the
reader's awareness of other corrupt urban scenes.

It would be convenient to be able to characterise the passages
in the Isle of Man and the Peak as scenes of primitive virtue.
Although the novel has the familiar journey shape, through
scenes that represent moral deterioration, there is no geographically located base of virtue to sustain the hero's identity.
The moral positives to which he can turn are the vaguely
sentimental and heroic figures of his mother and of the Countess
of Derby. The Isle of Man and the Peak are simply vacua where
a young man can spend years without coming into contact
with the court, or London, thus preserving the naivety that
the novelist wants to contrast with urban sophistication.

The novel really begins when Julian decides to set out for

London. On his journey, the city sends out tentacles of its corruption to meet him in the figures of Chiffinch, Chaubert and Christian. There is a sort of emblemism in the meals that Julian eats: the good English mess of bacon and eggs at the inn, the ragouts that he is treated to by Chaubert – provincial virtue and metropolitan luxury respectively. Scott is very open about the shape of his plot – as open as this symbolism is unsubtle. Chapter 30 begins:

LONDON, the grand central point of intrigues of every description, had now attracted within its dark and shadowy region the greater number of the personages whom we have had occasion to mention.

Julian Peveril . . . had arrived, and taken up his abode in a remote inn in the suburbs.

But Julian soon leaves the relative safety of the suburbs to experience in quick order the Park, Chiffinch's, Newgate, the Tower, the Court of King's Bench, the court.

At the same time, we follow the fortunes of Fenella and Alice through the domains of the Duke of Buckingham. He is an emblem of the courtier or politician, and his house, 'which bore a strange analogy to the irregular mind of its noble owner', is also an image for the mazy complexities of London itself: 'his Grace found it convenient to surround himself with this ruinous area, into which officers of justice could not penetrate without some difficulty and hazard' (chapter 37). At the centre of all this is Buckingham's harem where Alice is kept. Her journey to some extent parallels Julian's – all the time she gets closer to the centre of the maze, and finds more and more corruption there. Buckingham's retreat is paralleled by Charles' court and pander's house: both are guarded and difficult of access. And both remind us of the palace of *Woodstock*, which Henry II surrounded by a literal maze to prevent his wife's authority reaching his mistress. As in that novel, corruption is expressed in terms of sexual licence. Although it is incidental to the everyday amours of the Restoration court, this licence is principally located in the plot to debauch country virginity (Alice) to the King's aging lusts. The plotters are Bridgenorth, Christian, Chiffinch and Buckingham. The same plotters are also made in the novel to be behind the winding-up of the Popish Plot. When the story is abstracted it looks somewhat unlikely: fanatical Puritans and dissolute courtiers work together, are supported by the mob and pander to the King. In other words, Scott worked fairly hard to join sides that were usually opposed. And the combination of Caroline, Whigs and Radicals was not more unlikely, and equally opposed to what Scott considered the solid conservative sense of the provinces.

The Radical side is represented in *Peveril* by the pair Bridgenorth/Christian. By creating two characters, Scott is able to suggest deep and convinced fanaticism coexisting with unscrupulous opportunism. Bridgenorth is associated with the plot against his daughter, but his good faith is retained.

The connection between Puritan fanatics and latterday political Radicals is obvious enough, and had been implicit in the novels since *Old Mortality*. Scott draws attention to this comparison in:

I shall expect much news of your campaign [against Radicals in 1820] which puts one in mind of the chaces after the covenanters. But the radicals are not half such honest enthusiasts.[20]

did you observe how easy it would be for a good historian to run a parallel betwixt the Great Rebellion and the French Revolution, just substituting the spirit of fanaticism for that of soi disant philosophy.[21]

Bridgenorth's language would be very appropriate to later Radicals (not even slightly caricatured): 'the rapacity of power . . . shadow of liberty . . . a tyrannical government . . . aristocratical pride . . . oppressed and deluded country'.

This discussion has largely been conducted in terms of superficial and extractable elements. It has been an attempt to read the signposts to Scott's intention. But is this anything more than a matter of intention and the occasional local effect? We have seen that Scott sensed a similarity between a moment of English history, and some contemporary events, and that some time later he wrote a novel dealing with that period, and that much of the language and some of the design of the novel have some relevance to this original intention. But what of the novel as a whole? Is it a mere whimsical plaything? Or does it have anything to say about the experience of living in a time when discontent is rife, disorder is rampant and authority shaken? We might ask it to show the causes and/or the effects of the mild anarchy that Scott depicts. Ideas about the intention of the novel must be checked against its successes and failures. My opinion about *Redgauntlet* was that as the Jacobite scenes were relatively dull and perfunctory, the novel cannot really have been about Jacobitism, whatever Scott's intention. The test was really a critical intuition: where the novel seemed to be most alive, it was there that the meaning had to be and nowhere else. In *Redgauntlet* I suggested that the meaning resided in the delineation of 'psycho-social' conditions and interactions by a variety of literary means – none of them very deducible from the bare outline of the plot. Applying the test to *Peveril* I would want to confirm Scott's judgement that the third volume is much better than the preceding two. The novel lumbers into life at about the moment Julian lands in Liverpool (chapter 20), is at its best between Julian's meeting with Fenella in London (chapter 30) and his and his father's acquittal (chapter 42) and fades away again with the exposure of the Buckingham–Christian plot against Charles. Here it should be admitted that contemporary critics who mention *Peveril* do not, on the whole, agree with this judgement. Edgar Johnson,[22] A. O. J. Cockshutt[23] and perhaps F. R. Hart[24] all admire the earlier volumes more, particularly the portrait of Bridgenorth and the feast at Martindale Castle.

This latter *is* a fine scene and is linked by its absurd humour to the latter portions of the novel. And, I would urge, to the politics of 1821. In 1821, Whigs and Tories who, according to Scott, had managed to settle a good many of their differences, were at each other's throats over the Queen affair:

Whig and Tory . . . is reviving with great violence[25]

parties running higher than they have been this twenty years[26]

And on 12 January 1821 the Foxites (500 of them) and the Pittites (800, including WS) held competitive formal banquets in honour of C. J. Fox – or the reverse. Scott took part, and vociferously, yet he sensed the absurdity in it, as he wrote to Lord Montagu: 'The next frolic is to be eating and drinking in opposition to each other.'[27] However, this rather exuberant sense of folly darkens and becomes in *Peveril* a tragi-comic image of the disruption by human vanity of all the social pieties represented by national holidays and communal feasting: because the occasion should be a ritual, its perversion is so much the more potent. Nevertheless, the first two volumes fail to sustain this high level of creativeness. Reading them, it is difficult not to come to the conclusion that Scott – with all his facility – was simply allowing himself to fill up pages. There is much in these first 200 pages of political history and of the adumbration of a theme of the folly of party feeling. A critic who felt that Scott's main purpose was the reconciliation of opposites would find a lot to comment on, if not to admire, in these pages. At the end, Roundhead and Tory are united in the symbolic marriage of Julian and Alice. This is a possible way of reading the novel, and Scott has idly filled his pages with enough mechanical passages of this nature. After all, what easier way to write a novel than to retell *Romeo and Juliet*? Yet when his imagination seems to be engaged – when his metaphoric powers are drawn into action – this theme altogether disappears. Whenever metaphor replaces metonymy as the principal mode of the novel,[28] this is the place to try to find its real significance. Following the analysis of *Redgauntlet*, we could expect to find fantasy, doubling, simile, literary allusion – and, in the story and characters, a delineation of states of anxiety.

Such a scene is chapter 33 where Julian is introduced to Newgate, and the half-a-chapter preceding it in which he is examined by the Newgate magistrate. The grotesque absurdities in this section distinguish it from the previous part of the novel. There is the magistrate who, under the combined influence of an exaggerated idea of his own importance and a hysterical belief in the Plot, provides for himself layer after layer of protection, locks, doors, grilles, and then attires himself in quilted armour. The scene ends farcically when the magistrate hits out with a flail at Julian but only manages to knock himself down. The scene in which the hero is examined by an incompetent magistrate is one of the staples of the *Waverley* novels. Here we can feel an added significance in the fantastic detailing of the scene.

Julian is hurried on to Newgate, and as he enters he sees:

a number of debtors . . . employed in playing at hand-ball, pitch-and-toss, hustle-cap, and other games; for which relaxations the rigour of their creditors allowed them full leisure, while it debarred them the means of pursuing the honest labour by which they might have redeemed their affairs and maintained their starving and beggared families.

Comparisons with Dickens again spring to mind. Yet Julian curtly passes by this 'careless and desperate group' ('desperate' is an important word, as will be shown in chapter 6 below). Scott's mind is little attracted by this kind of social criticism. He has mentioned the anomalies of English debt laws in his non-fiction; this episode is present in order to make us, with Julian, experience a diminution of respect for a law that was still, as Scott wrote, a part of English life.

Julian is conducted through Newgate, which is presented as a maze, a 'labyrinth', a 'spider's web', guarded by thick doors, steel, locks, nails, metal plates. At the end of it is a jailer, 'fat and bloated', 'like a toad', 'a huge bloated and bottled spider', an 'overgrown man of authority'. The distortion of authority and humanity that he represents is obviously related to Maulstatute, similarly swollen and immobile. Authority, in their persons, comes to seem both absurd and repulsive.

This image is broadened when we find that it also applies to Buckingham. His mansion is situated in the middle of a maze, surrounded by old buildings; he refers to his prisoner Alice as a bird in a cage, just as Julian's jailer calls him; and there is a repetition of the spider image in Buckingham's bombast to Jerningham (*à propos* the plot): 'I must be in the midst of the most varied and counteracting machinery . . . directing and controlling a hundred combined powers' (chapter 38). As Julian goes on into the prison he learns two more things. First there is the corruption in the administration associated with the demand for 'Garnish' (related to the bill for the abolition of jail fees) and the misuse of language that is a feature of maze-prison life. Julian is told that he will be brought the 'darbies'; he asks for 'The Earl or Countess', having understood 'the Derbies'. What is really meant is 'fetters'. In prison, language has a special significance, or it disappears altogether, to be replaced by 'looks and expressive signs'. Language is something that deceives.

As we might expect, this theme is taken up in other parts of the novel. Fenella is one important part of it: her silence and not her size is the main point about her. Julian wonders at the 'passion of a being so unfortunately circumstanced, cut off, as it were, from the rest of mankind, and incapable of receiving in childhood that moral discipline which teaches us mastery of our wayward passions'. The socialising power of language is rather assumed in the novel: mainly perversions of linguistic power are imagined. Julian in the jail is like the whole of the nation vis-à-vis the lies, rumours and deceits broadcast by the authors of the plot. Oates, the principal witness, reminds us of magistrate and jailer, and his very speech is described as a deformity.

Oates was by nature choleric; and the credit he had acquired made him insolent and conceited. Even his exterior was portentous. A fleece of white periwig showed, on a most uncouth visage of great length, having the mouth, as the organ by the use of which he was to rise to eminence, placed in the very centre of the countenance, and exhibiting to the astonished spectator as much chin below as there was nose and brow above the aperture. His pronunciation, too, was after a conceited fashion of his own, in which he accented the vowels in a manner altogether peculiar to himself (chapter 41).

'Theay are stoifling the Plaat!' (chapter 42).

I cannot recall a single other character in Scott whose individual speech characteristics are so described and criticised.

What is the effect of such abuses? Let us follow Julian in the prison a little while longer. He says: 'Take five [guineas] and place me with Sir Geoffrey.' The jailer places him with Sir Geoffrey Hudson. When he gets over his surprise, Julian is able to understand the jailer's equivocation. However, as we follow Julian, before the trick is explained, we share his surprise at meeting Sir Geoffrey. Expecting to be reunited with his father, Julian enters the cell and sees

something rolled up in a dark corner, which rather resembled a small bundle of crimson cloth than any living creature . . . Julian, at the first glance, imagined from the size that he saw a child of five years old; but a shrill and peculiar tone of voice soon assured him of his mistake.

. . . 'I sought Sir Geoffrey' –

'And you have him before you, young man.'

Well, mistaken identity, an occasion for comedy. But fantasy has been given the rein; do we not wonder for an instant if Sir G. Peveril has not been reduced? And was not Julian uneasy at seeing his father dwarfed, or dead? – for this is the impression given first of all by a small bundle of crimson cloth. Could Scott have used a situation so full of mythical overtones without having a use for them?

In the following chapter, the little Sir Geoffrey's claims to know his namesake, his duelling, his Civil War swagger, his imitation of Peveril, all stir in us some kind of suspicion that he is a kind of anti-masque whose function is to ridicule the big Sir Geoffrey. If this is the case, the symbolic function of the episode becomes clear: authority is being questioned, cut down: of the state, the law, the father. Sir G. Hudson is Sir G. Peveril castrated. Notice how Buckingham's revolt against his master Charles is imaged as partly a desire to supplant him in the bed of his mistress (or mistress-to-be).

There has already been an anticipation of this interesting passage where Julian, arriving in the vicinity of Martindale Castle, sees that the 'Polar Star of Peveril' – the castle beacon, which symbolises the life of his father – has been extinguished. Soon after, he hears an insolent song in which his father is mentioned and infers that 'some strange revolution has taken place'. A couple of pages earlier, Ganlesse, the mysterious stranger on horseback, has paid farewell to Julian in this way:

'Fare well, then, Sir Julian of the Peak – that soon may be . . .'
'How mean you by that phrase?' said Julian, 'and why apply such a title to me?'

The memory of *Macbeth* contained here is very meaningful. Julian has talked to the stranger for some time; he is highly ambiguous – a man of many names (and, in fact, Christian); he has learned to tempt and disturb Julian so much that at one stage a comment of his makes Julian 'start like a guilty thing' (cf. *Hamlet*). Julian is led to think that his father is dead. The revolution and the extinguishing of the beacon reinforce these suspicions. We know that Julian is a loving son and Sir Peveril lives to a ripe old age. Yet, with him, we wonder if he will be Sir Julian. The echo of *Macbeth* compares Julian to Macbeth, it makes him kill the king–father and take his place. And that he does not do so makes us resign this possibility only to the realm of unconscious and suppressed desires.

In this version of Oedipus, Scott's conscious stress is not so much on intimate psychic disturbances as on social disorder. Julian's disturbing feelings about his father, never admitted or described so much as externalised through symbol, doubling and literary allusion, are paralleled by the riots and the various types of insubordination that take place in the state.

In the moralising part of the novel (the less important part) the blame for this state of affairs is apportioned to the authority-centres in the kingdom, particularly to Charles II. There is a general movement in the book that describes how Charles behaves in such a way as to alienate all those on whose affection and trust he depends. A parallel is provided by the Earl of Derby – king in the Isle of Man – a king distinguished by his levity and disregard of his subjects. Charles's lenience with people like Buckingham and Colonel Blood (who tried to steal his crown – another castration image) makes us wonder whether more to admire his generosity or his laxity. We feel that he is belittled by not protesting when Chiffinch calls him 'old Rowley' in his hearing. Then there is the Buckingham–Alice sub-plot.

Julian's suppressed fantasies about his father are no more than a way of imaging the ambiguity of all men's feelings about authority, in the historical world of the novel, and in the real world of Scott's own time.

If *Peveril of the Peak* is a message in code, it is not hard to decipher. As in his letters of 1820–2, Scott criticises the wealthy and higher classes for their immorality and selfishness, which, combined with a wilful cultivation of factiousness, lead to a breakdown of order and morality in the kingdom. In the symbolic layer of the novel, this is translated into the degradation or assassination of the father, which in turn changes the world into a strange unfamiliar place for the hero (and for the 'people'/'jury'), one in which he cannot find his way (the pole star is extinguished) or trust any of his senses (seeing or hearing: the magic 'poisoned' banquet, Fenella's tricks, little Sir G., Oates' language, the voice in the cell).

The fundamental story in the novel is another version of *The Bride of Lammermoor*: the literal children, and the 'minors of the state', are betrayed by their fathers and turn against them. Alice is prostituted (unconsciously or vicariously) by her father; she does not kill him, as Lucy does hers (again by proxy) but he is exiled. Scott cannot fully express these myths – for him, they are almost unthinkable. A literal parricide would be indefensible, and he had no twentieth-century psychoanalysts to help him control these images by making them more 'natural' in their universality. Nevertheless, they remain powerful images of his sense of social dislocation. In the parts of the novel that matter, Scott made a highly complex and multi-layered social drama, which transcends its origins in a trivial cause of the 1820s and makes any simple statement of the novel's message problematic.

PART III

6. DEVELOPMENT

A SKETCH OF THE DEVELOPMENT

The Waverley novels move away from realism towards fantasy, allegory and symbolism. Realism in the novel must be the response either of a man who is by and large satisfied with his world or is prepared to channel his dissatisfactions into a thorough-going negative critique or of one who can feel both sides simultaneously and combine a fundamental personal commitment to the larger social tendencies with an enthusiastic damnation of all that was unjust and inhuman, like Balzac and the early Dickens. But Scott was just the opposite; as we can see from an examination of his life and thought, he was not satisfied – in later years – with any part of his society but was not prepared to attack it openly. The optimism, the belief in progressive improvement, which he had assumed to be his own, began to disappear by about 1816; and by the end of 1818, the disillusionment was complete. The more completely disillusionment took over, the more Scott deserted realist modes of novel-writing; and the more completely he faced that collapse of his hopes, the better novels he wrote. But, like Dickens of later years, Scott was inextricably a part of his society and was unable to distance himself from it, nor was he forced by worldly failure to the periphery. The final possible realist mode, that of retaining a personal aloofness from society while participating fully as artist–observer – the ironic modes of Austen and James – was not a possibility for Scott, any more than it was for Dickens.

If such a division, into 'optimistic' and 'pessimistic' does over-simplify, it still offers a better way of seeing a shape and logic in Scott's oeuvre, as long as the optimism and pessimism are understood to comprise far more than the two terms –

fear of change as such and an angry dislike of any form of social mobility – that are usually offered. Furthermore, it permits a division of the novels into groups more useful than the usual Scotland-versus-the-rest-of-the-world dichotomy because it allows for a sharper distinction of the individual modes and topics, and shows that the Scottish novels frequently overlap with non-Scottish novels. I would distinguish five groups, taking 1814 and 1819 as pivotal years:

Group I: *Waverley*; entirely optimistic and realist.

Group II: *Guy Mannering* and *The Antiquary*; residual optimism with irruptions of pessimism, realism adhered to, but with symbolic/allegoric modes showing signs of being about to take control.

Group III: *The Black Dwarf* to *The Bride of Lammermoor*; the break is now complete, society is fragmented, realism disappears, fantasy and symbol show the pain experienced by individuals and the destruction of community.

Group IV: *Ivanhoe* to *Abbot*; because the vision of group III has become actual in Scott's real-life society and not merely a fearful potential, the mode of the novels retreats to pseudo-realism; fantasy and allegory are abandoned; social change and civil violence are examined in a largely discursive mode.

Group V: Novels that take up and develop from group III; metaphorical modes return; sometimes the novels imagine an idealised society; sometimes they centre on the destructive forces inside society – pride, greed, corruption; sometimes they imagine the plight of individuals within corrupted societies – the alienation of the defeated; the limited, small securities that can be gained by those whose instinct commits them to the mainstream of life; sometimes they imagine a totally destructive process in which society and individuals destroy each other, a process associated with Scott's despair at progress, at the defeat of 'organic' by 'artificial' society. This group includes all the novels written after and including *Kenilworth*.

GROUP II

These immediate successors of *Waverley* are linked by tone, character, action and theme. The communities described in both novels are further attempts to capture the ethos of Tully Veolan.

But what the themes of the novels are is a question that has elicited a number of answers. One tempting possibility is to look forward to *Lammermoor* and *St Ronan's*, and to link the declining fortunes of the houses of Bertram and Wardour with those of the Mowbrays and the Ravenswoods. A serious elaboration of this link tends to make of the novels a conservative, or reactionary, lament for the destruction of ancient families, for the loss of power of the old aristocracy and gentry of Scotland, and for their replacement by upstarts unconnected by birth or tradition with the local community.

The persistence with which Scott depicts declining old families is certainly worthy of remark; but there is no evidence that he had any emotional bias in favour of the old-fashioned landed gentry as a whole. Furthermore, there was in fact no reason to lament their decline, for the landowners (and Tories) were at the height of their power in these years. If new men were buying their way into the countryside, they did not represent a threat to Tory supremacy or initiate a hostile and alien ideology in the countryside. The manufacturers, nabobs and writers who made the most inroads into rural society were largely connected by ties of blood, interest and ideology to the old ruling classes. What external reality would the novels then reflect if they are assumed to be an elegy for the old gentry?

In fact, a distinguishing feature of both the novels is the vein of satire that tends to make us sceptical about the value of 'artificial distinction of ranks'. Sir Robert Hazlewood in *Guy Mannering* is a Jonsonian humour whose entire character is based on pride of rank. Like Jonson, Scott uses exaggeration as the vehicle of his satire:

[the King's advocate will view] the mere fact of having wounded young Hazlewood of Hazlewood, even by inadvertency, to take the manner in its mildest and gentlest, and in its most favourable and improbable light, as a crime which will be too easily atoned by imprisonment, and as more deserving of deportation.

These are dreadful days indeed – days when the bulwarks of society are shaken to their mighty base and that rank which forms, as it were, its highest grace and ornament, is mingled and confused with viler parts of the architecture (chapter 42).

Parallel to this are Sir Arthur Wardour's snobberies in *The Antiquary* (chapters 5 and 6), his assumption of the role of Sir Epicure Mammon (*The Alchemist* is referred to several times in the novel), dreaming of the wealth he will receive (chapter 41):

his language and carriage were those of a man who had acquired the philosopher's stone.

In this mood, if anyone endeavoured to bring Sir Arthur down to the regions of common life, his replies were in the vein of the Ancient Pistol –

> A fico for the world, and worldlings base!
> I speak of Africa and golden joys.

Jenny Rintherout's commentary is humorous folk morality: 'He'll be grander than ever now, he'll no can haud down his head to sneeze for fear o' seeing his shoon' (chapter 26). Sir Arthur's pride is no mere individual humour; it is caught up and generalised in the figures of the Countess/Earl of Glenallan and Hector M'Intyre. Rank is not the only target of satire; a mild irony undercuts lawyers, historians, fearful property owners and Volunteers.

The common denominator is human pride and ambition. There is in fact a medieval or balladic strain of moralising in *The Antiquary*, medieval in that pride, power and ambition, in quite obvious personifications, are constantly challenged by the presence of death. Death is almost as omnipresent in this novel as it is in *The Pardoner's Tale*, and the chance of pointing ironic contrasts is never passed up. There is the death of the old Countess:

'Dead! are ye no imposing upon me? has she left a' at last, lands and lordships and lineages?'

'All, all,' said the Earl, 'as mortals must leave all human vanities' (chapter 32).

The scene at Glenallan insists on this contrast; over the gateway is

a huge scutcheon, in which the herald and undertaker had mingled,

as usual, the emblems of human pride and human nothingness –
the Countess's hereditary coat-of-arms, with all its numerous
quarterings, disposed in a lozenge, and surrounded by the separate
shields of her paternal and maternal ancestry, intermingled with
scythes, hour-glasses, skulls, and other symbols of that mortality
which levels all distinctions (chapter 27).

As Edie meets the nobleman, Scott points out how the ill
health of the Earl

showed how little wealth, power and even the advantages of youth,
have to do with that which gives repose to the mind, and firmness
to the frame (chapter 28).

The pride that sends Lovel and M'Intyre to their duel is
sharply rebuked by Ochiltree in medieval terms ('he was
like a grey palmer or eremite preacher'):

'are ye come amongst the most lovely works of God to break His
laws? Have ye left the works of man, the houses and the cities
that are but clay and dust, like those that built them – and are ye
come among the peaceful hills and by the quiet waters, that will last
whiles aught earthly shall endure, to destroy each others lives,
that will have but an unco' short time by the course of nature to
make up a lang account at the close o't?' (chapter 20)[1]

Pride, death and the power of nature are taken up in the
powerful and exciting scene of the Wardours' escape from
death on the sea shore (chapters 7–8). This scene, if not actually
forced or obtrusive, is hardly necessary for what plot there is
in the novel. It is there for the opportunity it gives to reinforce
these moral lessons. The scene is deeply considered, with Scott
lavishing as much verbal art on it as he knew how. The great
vividness of the passages of adventure-excitement and natural
description is a rhetorical framework for the simplicity of the
moral reflections:

'Good man,' said Sir Arthur, 'can you think of nothing? Of no help ?–
I'll make you rich – I'll give you a farm – I'll –'
    'Our riches will soon be equal,' said the beggar, looking out upon
the strife of the waters; 'they are sae already; for I hae nae land,
and you would give your fair bounds and barony for a square yard
of rock that would be dry for twal hours.'

'a pedigree of a hundred links is hanging on a tenpenny tow; the whole barony of Knockwinnock depends on three plies of hemp.'

Above all there is the sense of humility required by the pathetic dignity of Steenie's death and funeral, which is set in ironic contrast to Hector's comic worsting by the seal. Hector is on his way to the funeral at the time; the episode on the beach reminds us of the Wardours' walk, which also began light-heartedly but almost ended tragically; the sea beast stands for the power of nature, which Hector frivolously offends; it reminds us of his equally frivolous duel with Lovel. Hector lives to hear the tale told again, and with the contrast between him and Steenie, Scott offers a commentary about social relations, ranks and distinctions. It is linked with the conversation in which Monkbarns endeavours to show his haggling skills and is rebuked by the fishwife:

And div ye think . . . that my man and my sons are to gae to the sea in weather like yestreen and the day – sic a sea as it's yet outby – and get naething for their fish, and be misca'd into the bargain, Monkbarns? It's no fish ye're buying – it's men's lives.

Here is the balladic element – is not the imagery, tone and morality drawn from *Sir Patrick Spens*? The ironic contrast between the home-keeping gentry and the sea-going poor is brought into a directly contemporary context when Monkbarns attempts a sermon on temperance. One of the greatest occasions of scandal for moralists of the time was what they called 'dram drinking', which was variously estimated to be 'greatly on the increase' or 'greatly on the decline'. Monkbarns tells Maggie that he hopes the distilleries will never work again, and her reply is a marvellous rebuke to him – again balladic with its rhythms, half rhymes, short lines, alliteration:

Aye, aye, it's easy for your honour, and the like of you gentlefolks to say sae, that hae stouth and routh, and fire and fending, and meat and claith, and sit dry and canny by the fireside . . . wadna ye be glad to buy a dram wi't, to be eilding and claise, and a supper and heart's ease into the bargain, till the morn's morning?

Then there is the story of Martin Waldeck, which has a strong medieval-morality taste to it, built around the contrast of wealth and death. Nowhere does this large-scale reference to no-longer current literary modes seem inappropriate. It is always a part of the living speech of the characters, a crystal-lisation of their attitudes, and suggests that the vanity, folly and avarice are universal, an eternal topic of literature. It implies acceptance and tolerance. It also implies a large con-fidence in society. In spite of the satire, which is like that of *The Alchemist* and *Bartholomew Fair*, the overall tone of the novels and their drawn-out happy endings suggest that there is to be no root-and-branch social criticism.

But criticism there is, of a more anxious, though less obvious, nature than satire on aristocratic pride. Indeed, Scott's very indulgence to, and lack of satirical rigour with, his old fools of family is an important rhetorical device. The attitude of the reader is supposed to be of indulgent acceptance; this attitude is both aim and subject matter of the two novels. It has been remarked that the communities gathered around Fairport and Kippletringan bear a family resemblance to that of Tully Veolan. The resemblance lies above all in the flexibility and undemandingness of these pre-industrial, pre-work-ethic socie-ties. The difference between *Waverley* and group II novels is that the attitude is more precariously maintained later. Whereas Bradwardine maintains his economically useless tenants out of pride and kindliness, there is now a suggestion that the kindliness of the old Scottish society is in danger. In both *Guy Mannering* and *The Antiquary*, traditional kindliness is upset by acts of arbitrary authority. The changes that were transforming Scottish society, as outlined in chapter 4 above, required the elimination of anomalies like Ochiltree and Merrilies.

Begging, work and poor-relief made up one of the prime topics for writers on the Scottish social revolution. Scott's own attitude has been described above. There can be no doubt that he knew the gravity of the situation and the inability of the old system to deal with massive numbers of paupers in times dominated by the pattern of industrial slump and boom.

The introduction to *The Antiquary* (written a decade and a half after the novel) makes it clear that Edie is 'by no means to be confused with the utterly degraded class of beings who now practise that wandering trade'. Beggars like Ochiltree had been licensed and allowed. But even by 1790, the time of the action of the tale, the advanced thinkers of the age were beginning to protest against this feature of eighteenth-century society. As Scott wrote the novel, old-fashioned tolerance was becoming a thing of the past, and both author and reader must have known this. The novel makes a passing reference to both the old practice and to the new institutions that were to destroy it, but presents them humorously, as ineffective and impotent. Monkbarns, after his defeat over the *praetorian*, says 'I have always been against poor's rates and a workhouse – I think I'll vote for them now, to have that scoundrel shut up' (chapter 4). Sir Arthur says that he has 'directed the constables to take up that scoundrelly old beggar, Edie Ochiltree' (chapter 7). The role of the old-fashioned beggar is defined in Wordsworthian terms. Edie cannot be assimilated by the new ethic:

I downa be bound down to hours o' eating and sleeping.

His function in society is as an index of its kindliness:

And then what wad a' the country about for want o' auld Edie Ochiltree, that brings news and country cracks frae ae farm steading to anither, and gingerbread to the lasses, and helps the lads to mend their fiddles, and the gudewives to clout their pans, and plaits rush-swords and grenadier caps for the weans (chapter 12).

Anything that threatens Edie threatens the cohesiveness of Scottish society.

The gypsies of *Guy Mannering* are more interesting and complicated. They really were gypsies, an actual feature of life in Scotland. The writer of the *NSA* account of Roxburghshire might almost have been bearing witness to the reality of Scott's picture when he wrote:

At home they are usually quiet and peaceable . . . Numerous instances can be referred to of the grateful sense they entertain of

favours bestowed on them . . . most of the savage features of the
gipsy character may be referred to their loose, wandering and disorderly life; to their lamentable ignorance of the duties which they
owe to God and man.[2]

Scott was disturbed by attempts to eradicate them by force,
attempts that paralleled attacks on the old-fashioned beggars.
He wrote an essay for *Blackwood's* called 'The Gypsies of
Hesse-Darmstadt in Germany' in which his attitude is made
clear:

I have dwelt longer on these dreadful scenes than you or your
readers may approve; yet they contain an important illustration of
the great doctrine, that cruel and sanguinary laws usually overshoot
their own purpose, drive to desperation these [sic] against whom
they are levelled, and, by making man an object of chase, convert
him into a savage beast of prey . . . [this] may serve to stimulate
the exertions of those humane persons who have formed the project
of reserving this degraded portion of society from mendicity,
ignorance and guilt.[3]

The 'great doctrine' was indeed a preoccupation of his, especially at the time of this article (1818): that it is the duty of
society to look after its own, and all of its own, and not to
drive any of its members, or groups of them, to despair or
outlawry, by savage laws; that is, repression, or oppression,
will lead to the fragmentation of society and the exclusion of
individuals from its processes. The theme is continued in all
group III novels.

Chapter 6 of *Guy Mannering* displays Godfrey Bertram, who
is moved only by a sort of vanity, in the act of offending
against all those liberalities of society that he had previously
encouraged, or perhaps connived at. Poachers, beggars and the
village idiot all feel the weight of his hand together with the
gypsies. The expulsion of the gypsies stands for something
more general; why else is it framed by these other examples of
rural injustice? Once again the loss to country society is presented in terms that recall Wordsworth:

These things did not pass without notice and censure. We are not
made of wood or stone, and the things which connect themselves

with our hearts and habits cannot, like bark or lichen, be rent away without our missing them. The farmer's dame lacked her usual share of intelligence, perhaps also the self applause which she had felt while distributing the *awmous* (alms) in the shape of a *gowpen* (handful) of oatmeal to the mendicant who brought the news. The cottage felt inconvenience from interruption of the petty trade carried on by these itinerant dealers. The children . . . (chapter 6).

There is however a possibility that Scott intended something here beyond the general unwillingness of Scottish society to put up any longer with its old parasites. Some of the phrases he uses seem to betray an intention to make the gypsies symbolise some other, more settled and permanent, groups.

They had been such long occupants, that they were considered in some degree as proprietors of the wretched shealings which they inhabited. This protection they were said anciently to have repaid by service to the laird in war (chapter 7).

Certain qualms of feeling had deterred Ellangowan from attending in person to see his tenants expelled (chapter 8).

A strong posse of peace officers, sufficient to render all resistance vain, charged the inhabitants to depart by noon; and, as they did not obey, the officers, in terms of their warrant, proceeded to unroof the cottages, and pull down the wretched doors and windows – a summary and effectual mode of ejection, still practised in some remote parts of Scotland, when a tenant proves refractory (chapter 8).

The last phrases tend to distance the whole action, and the gypsies seem to have been presented rather as squatters than tenants. Yet the first paragraph quoted is an almost perfect description of what was known as the 'customary' or 'kindly' tenant, particularly of the tenants of the Highland straths, who had also paid for their holdings by military service. Chapter 5 above has shown that Scott was capable of disguising contemporary events in his fictions, and the ejection of the gypsies of Derncleuch bears a very strong resemblance to a famous trial of the time. Patrick Sellar was tried for brutalities in connection with the Sutherland clearances. This account shows how closely the real and the fictional events resemble each other:

The first witness to be called was William Chisholm, for whom the Sheriff-Substitute of Ross-shire was sworn as an interpreter, since Chisholm spoke no English. The witness described how Sellar had come to his home in June 1814, nearly two years before, with twenty men besides four sheriff officers, who had pulled down and set fire to the house and its barns. His mother-in-law, Margaret MacKay, was still in the house when it was set on fire, for she was a hundred years old and bed ridden though she was not ill. It was Sellar himself who ordered the house to be fired.[4]

Chisholm further stated that he had lost the roof timbers of his house; but he was not believed because he was 'disreputable looking'. Land at the other end of the strath had been offered to other tenants who had been ejected, but not to Chisholm, a tinker, 'because of two years back complaints had been made against him as a worthless character'.[5]

The points of resemblance are: the gypsies too were tinkers; the woman in the case was Meg M.; in both cases economic oppression was justified by the supposed bad character of the victim; the mode of eviction is identical. It is at least arguable that this very trial was the origin of the episode in *Guy Mannering*. The dates do not quite fit, for although the incident took place in 1814, the trial, when it was most public, did not occur until 1816, after the novel had been written. However, there can be no doubt that Scott, as Clerk of the Court of Sessions, must have known of the affair before it came to trial.

If this was the case, the scope and significance of *Guy Mannering* are wider than has been thought. The novel is not a nostalgic account of Scott's boyhood but a parable of contemporary events. One cannot say that it is radical, reforming literature; yet its very uncontroversiality may have enhanced its effectiveness. If this is so, why was it not mentioned in contemporary notices? One answer might be that the reviewers were not observant enough, for one writer outside the literary mainstream did notice – David Stewart of Garth. His *Sketches* contain the following:

The author of *Guy Mannering* has alluded to this 'summary and effectual mode of ejectment still practised in the north of Scotland when a tenant proves refractory' in his admirable description of the colony of Derncleugh. When this picture of fictitious distress, of which such a lawless race were the supposed objects, has created a powerful sensation where ever our language is understood; what heart shall withold its sympathy from real distress, when faithful, blameless and industrious beings are treated in the same manner, without the same provocations and where, instead of 'thirty hearts that would hae wanted breed before ye wanted sunkets' more than twice thirty thousand have been turned adrift in different parts of the north.[6]

This is exactly the reaction a novelist could wish for. It must be added that for many contemporary observers of the social scene, the Highland tenants were neither blameless nor industrious, and were little better than gypsies. It is also worth noting that part of Meg Merrilies' 'speech' is couched in language that was traditionally used by the peasantry to describe the evictions associated with sheep farming – which Scott himself imitated on numerous occasions; compare 'This day ye have quenched seven smoking hearths' (*Guy Mannering*, chapter 8) and 'Within the memory of man I could name many farms where the old people remember twenty smoking chimneys and where there are now not two.'[7]

These novels were written at a time when the euphoria that had greeted Waterloo was dying away and the economic situation of Britain was beginning to be disquieting. The price of grain had fallen and many country people were experiencing real distress. It was not yet a social crisis however. Letters that Scott writes at this time are on the whole optimistic; he is prepared to see the change as an inevitable but temporary dislocation, and hopes that there will be real social gains from this period of distress:

It will check that inordinate and unbecoming spirit of expence or rather extravagance which was poisoning all classes and bring us back to the sober virtues of our ancestors. It will also have the effect of teaching the landed interest that their connection with their farmers should be of a nature more intimate that that of mere payment and receipt for rent and that the largest offerer for a farm is often the person least fit to be preferred as a tenant.[8]

The last part of this has a detailed connection with *Guy Mannering*: thrifty, honest, neighbourly Dandie Dinmont is asked if he could not take another farm to occupy his surplus capital, to which he replies: 'I dinna ken, the Deuke's no that fond o' led farms, and he canna bide to put away the auld tenantry; and then I wadna like, mysell, to gang about whistling and raising the rent on my neighbours' (chapter 50). The reference in the letter to 'extravagance' throws light on the figure of Sir Arthur Wardour, although we can see how far Scott is from even that sort of realism which Maria Edgeworth used in the depiction of ruined extravagant landlords in *The Absentee* and *Castle Rackrent*. If the proposition about landlords and tenants is expanded and understood to refer to all classes of rural relations, then the two novels make sense as an attempt to convey, if not the precise nature of the bond, which must be presented in non-economic terms, then its power and importance. Scott would like to present a vision of the strength of the communal bond unmediated through economic gains: to create a realistic novel that centred on readily understandable ideas about economic justice would have been to have either opposed or accepted, say, Scottish economic rationalism, neither of which Scott wanted to do.

The Antiquary and *Guy Mannering* are both romances of community, to use the word adopted by Donald Davie.[9] Both novels assert that no class (as no individual) can consider its fortunes independent of those of any other class. In *Guy Mannering* the redemptive power of society is heavily stressed, while in *The Antiquary* Scott is more interested in showing the inability of man to exist as a solitary being divorced from society.

The concept of redemption will appear below in connection with *The Pirate*, and will be linked with the use made in that novel of *The Tempest*. In *Guy Mannering* a similar sort of use is made of *The Winter's Tale*. Superficially, this is indicated by the repetition of the common theme of the last plays, 'that which was lost is found'; by the presence of Leontes' jealousy in Mannering's (otherwise an inexplicable element in the novel);

by the occurrence of quotations from the play; and by the chronological break in the middle of the novel. More central however is the abstraction of the idea of winter and the deliberateness of the 'seasonal' imagery. The novel is divided into three phases: Harry Bertram's birth; his abduction; the events leading to his restoration. Each part takes place in winter – in November. The wintry aspects of the scene are emphasised. The natural bareness of the Dumfries landscape is pointed up. When Mannering returns to Kippletringan it is 'a cold and stormy night' (chapter 11). The journey of Brown, which is a Romance-type quest, is barer and bleaker as he nears his native regions; first through the moors of Cumberland (chapter 23), then from Charlie's Hope to Woodbourne ('To add to the inconvenience of the journey the snow began to fall pretty quickly': chapter 27); the cold night spent in the Kaim of Derncleugh, then the attempt to reach an understanding with Julia Mannering on the frozen lake, where he shoots young Hazlewood. The theme of winter and barrenness is repeated in Mannering's attempt to secure for Lucy a portion of her inheritance: Lucy 'touched on her regret that at such a season of the year he should have made, upon her account, a journey so fruitless' (chapter 46). Winter symbolises the nature of social relations as they exist in this community. Everything is related to the sin of Bertram in expelling the gypsies. The entire community suffers: the house of Ellangowan falls, and the community endures the imposition of the alien king, Glossin. But the community is also resilient and forgiving. It is through Meg Merrilies's agency that Brown is restored to his ancient lands and the 'old' relations are to some extent resumed. In the following passage, Meg acts as a guide, and leads Bertram and Dinmont through a maze to reinstate the young man in his estate – and the seasonal imagery is used very deliberately:

When Meg Merrilies had attained these groves, through which the wintry sea-wind was now whistling hoarse and shrill, she seemed to pause a moment, as if to recollect the way. 'We maun go the precise track,' she said, and continued to go forward, but rather in a zig-zag and involved course, than according to her former steady and direct line of motion. At length she guided them through the mazes of the wood to a little open glade of about a quarter of an acre, surrounded by trees and bushes, which made a wild and irregular boundary. Even in winter it was a sheltered and snugly sequestered spot; but when arrayed in the verdure of spring, the earth sending forth all its wild flowers, the shrubs spreading their waste of blossom around it, and the weeping birches, which towered over the under-wood, drooping their long and leafy fibres to intercept the sun, it must have seemed a place for a youthful poet to study his earliest sonnet, or a pair of lovers to exchange their first mutual avowal of affection (chapter 53).

As Bertram returns to the very place where he was dispossessed, spring returns – not perhaps in fact, but imaginatively. This is the way a poet writes; we should recall that this sort of imagery has already occurred in Scott's verse. In *Marmion* there is an entirely overt comparison of winter to a socio-political era:

> November's sky is chill and drear,
> November's leaf is red and sear:
> . . . To mute and to material things
> New life revolving summer brings;
> The genial call dead Nature hears,
> And in her glory reappears.
> But oh! my country's wintry state
> What second spring shall renovate?
>
> (*Marmion*, Introduction, Canto I)

That winter is not only a guiding motif in the book but con-nected to a theme of class relations is shown by a later passage in which Bertram is recognised and acclaimed by the tenants. Amid shouts like 'I and mine hae been three hundred years here . . . and I sall sell my last cow, but I'll see the young laird placed in his right' (chapter 55) Bertram is restored to the place in society that his father's more than folly lost him, and the restoration scene is rounded off with this image: 'In short it was one of those moments of intense feeling *when the frost of the Scottish people melts like a snow wreath*, and the dissolving torrent carries dam and dyke before it.' There is a similar intensely communal moment in *The Antiquary* (chapter 8) which begins: 'The shout of human voices from above was soon augmented . . .' as Sir Arthur and Miss Wardour are hauled to safety up the cliff. Scott carefully involves almost all the characters of the novel in the rescue, including 'half the country fellows about'. The co-ordinated communal activity is juxtaposed to the isolated fragility of the individual in a series of striking images. The rescue machinery, the fruit of seamanly skill and the trade of the smuggler, 'swung about a yard free of the spot which they occupied, obeying each impulse of the tempest, the empty air all around it, and depending upon the security of a rope, which, in the increasing darkness, had dwindled to an almost imperceptible thread'. The rope is an image of life itself. In the novel, human pride is mocked by death, but death itself is opposed by human solidarity. In this scene, solitary human life, weak and vain, is in danger of being annihilated by the powers of nature; it has to recognise its dependence on the 'two thin links' that connect it with the 'tenderness and care' of human fellowship – the whole community, which hauls away at the top.

The cliff-top rescue looks forward to other scenes in the novel in which Sir Arthur is saved from the consequences of his own actions by nothing less than the concerted actions of the whole community. The death of Steenie Mucklebackitt in the sea from which the Wardours were rescued gives this irony a note of tragic seriousness, and links Wardour's pride with Oldbuck's levity about the price of fish. Yet there is no heroic-sentimental scene in which Steenie gives his life for the Young Leddy. His death is seemingly unconnected with her rescue. The two events are linked poetically.

Yet neither novel is ultimately about the preservation of old families. Sir Arthur is only one figure in *The Antiquary*, and his pride is only one aspect of a condition that involves at least three others: Lovel, Oldbuck, Glenallan. All three are solitary people, alienated from the community half by pride and half by accident. Their separate prides – in soldierly honour, in useless knowledge, in length of ancestry – are rebuked by Ochiltree. Even Oldbuck's comic misogyny is not without a deeper purpose. He himself utters an important statement of the novel's moral theme. Lovel, like Darsie, feels that he is so

detached from all the world, [has] so few in whom [he is] interested . . . that [his] very state of destitution gives [him] independence.

[He asks] nothing of society but the permission of walking innoxiously through the path of life without jostling others or permitting [himself] to be jostled (chapter 14).

This is both a futile sort of hybris (his desire for anonymity causes his duel with M'Intyre) and a sort of immorality. Oldbuck's language is too grave for us to doubt that it carries a weight of authorly approval: 'it is . . . incumbent on you to move steadily in the path of duty, for your active exertions are due not only to society – but in humble gratitude to the Being who made you a member of it, with powers to serve yourself and others' (chapter 14).

Except that they contain no recognisably 'contemporary' features, these two novels are hardly about the past, and if it were not for the novels that they are surrounded by in Scott's oeuvre would never be described as 'historical'. It is difficult to sum up the message they send, but it is something to do with 'keeping faith with the community'. Scott is very aware of the fragility of justice, peace and harmony in communal life in 1815, knows how they are threatened, and hopes, hopes, that they may be preserved.

GROUP III

As we read our way through this group, history seems to take on a much more considerable importance. Yet Scott's attention, it will be argued here, was still on his own time; he was still trying to find symbols and metaphors for 'Britain 181–' but in a climate that, as it is more menacing than ever, calls for a fresh set of metaphors.

The Bride of Lammermoor is frequently presented as the classic example of a 'historical' novel about 'social change' in the real-life historical world of the novel's setting. In practice,

commentary has entailed errors not only of emphasis and interpretation but even of ·fact. R. C. Gordon's representative
essay on the novel is a demonstration of the way in which
'embodiments of ancient virtues' are destroyed by the modern
world. Ravenswood and Balderstone 'define the condition of
Scotland after the union with England (the most important
milestone in Scotland's movement away from feudalism) as one
in which injustice thrives on social change and brings good
men to destruction'.[10] This point about the Union is very
dubious. It conflicts with Scott's known views about the
Union and its effect on law and justice in Scotland. The major
part of Scottish resistance to the Union, he wrote, came from
irresponsible landlords anxious to retain their oppressive
feudal powers (see chapter 2 above). The injustices from which
Ravenswood is suffering are those of pre-Union society. Anti-
Union feeling is shown up for transparent cynicism in Ashton
as he protests 'before men and angels, that if the law of Scotland, as declared in her supreme courts, were to undergo a
reversal in the English House of Lords, the evils which would
thence arise to the public, would inflict a greater wound upon
his heart than any losses he might himself sustain by such
irregular proceedings' (chapter 27). In fact, Ravenswood's
fortunes will be repaired and his estates restored to him by 'this
court of equity'. As the Union helps the hero to prosper, it
emerges in a positive light. Scott's authorly summing-up
seems unambiguous enough: 'The high and unbiassed character
of the English judicial proceedings was then little known in
Scotland; and the extension of them to that country was one
of the most valuable advantages which it gained by the Union'
(chapter 15). Nor can it be said that Edgar is brought to his
destruction by politics. This would be to forget the latter part
of the novel in which, as the wheel of fortune turns, Edgar
stands elegantly dressed, affluent, with a government job,
poised to regain his estates and marry a foreign heiress.

Gordon singles out Blind Alice, dignifying her as a 'female
Tiresias . . . Tory social critic'. She knows that 'the fall of the
Ravenswoods has been due to the sins of the Ashtons and their

ilk, as representatives of a new Scotland without sympathy for the men and traditions of the past'. Is there any reason why we should listen to Alice, and ignore the sexton, from whom in chapter 24 Ravenswood learns some bitter truths about his family?

as for the Ravenwoods, I hae seen three generations of them, and deil ane to mend other.

ye winna persuade me [Edgar's father] did his duty, either to himself or to huz puir dependent creatures, in guiding us the gate he has done.

There are other serious criticisms of the Master's family, some of which will be mentioned below. But it is obvious from this that to represent the tale as a simple contrast between a virtuous, traditional, hierarchical past and a corrupted and commercial present is not even an oversimplification: it is a distortion. Is it possible to call the village of Wolf's Hope a 'centre of moral paralysis'? The fundamental attitudes of the villagers to the Master are set in a perspective of social change very close to the spirit of *The Wealth of Nations*, and presented in language and rhetoric that put them beyond the sort of criticism Gordon proposes.

But it is not to the point to substitute a 'progressive' social-change theory of the novel for an 'anti-progressive' one. The most striking thing about such accounts is how much they leave out. Gordon at one point warns us: 'On its most obvious level *The Bride of Lammermoor* is a tragic love story . . . Scott's use of such powerful material is warning enough against any impulse to interpret the novel as a social tract with suitable anecdotal evidence. Yet . . .' Yet the love story is ignored, and the catastrophe, the bridegroom, Craigengelt, the witches, the bride herself. In spite of the layer of social history, the novel, looked at closely, seems to be very little concerned with process. Its mode of organisation is poetic, and its meaning can best be found by examining the implications of the image that is the fable: the wedding–death or bridal–burial. The tragic paradox of the original fable offered Scott a remarkable opportunity to create an extended work around an image that had been used before, by Blake in *London*, by Coleridge in *The Ancient Mariner*, by Keats, frequently, especially in *Lamia*, and by Scott himself in *Proud Maisie*.

The same image had been used in a novel once before, in a work that must be regarded as an unsuccessful essay at the *Bride* theme: *The Black Dwarf*. It is there in the forced wedding at the end of the novel; in Hobbie Elliot's bride being stolen from the ruins of his farm, and in Hobbie's invitation to Elshie:

'I would take you wi' me man, if ye wad but say it wad divert ye to be at the bridal on Monday. There will be a hundred strapping Elliots to ride the brouze – the like's no been seen sin' the days of auld Martin of the Preakin tower – I wad send the sled for ye wi' a canny powny.'

'Is it to me you propose once more to mix in the society of the common herd?' said the Recluse with an air of deep disgust.

Because the wedding image has no overall organising function in the *Dwarf*, its meaning is perhaps easier to estimate. It is one of a series of images that contrast the life of a community, with its traditions, work, love and hatred, to that of an isolated and excluded individual. Scenes of lonely misanthropy alternate with those of friendship and society. The first vision of the Recluse's hut is contrasted with the pieties of Hobbie's home; his loneliness with the bees who 'filled the air with the murmurs of their industry'; the loves of Earnscliffe and Hobbie are contrasted with Elshie's misogyny (chapter 5). It is not hard to see how themes implicit in *Antiquary* have been amplified in this novel.

The greatest failure of the novel is Scott's inability to carry the story through and to build on the not-inconsiderable interest aroused by the first chapters. But obviously, he had made a mistake with the conception of the dwarf. *The Black Dwarf* initiates a series of novels that deal with ways in which a society fails its members. The images used are imprisonment, outlawry, exile, civil war, proscription; the essential part is that an individual is excluded from the normal social process. The situation itself is Scott's concern: the history, manners, social change, condition of Scotland give a living context for the images. In *The Black Dwarf* Scott attempted to state the images and relationships that troubled him in terms of a literary tradition that gave him ready-made metaphors. In a way, he was trying to deal too directly with his material. The novel is not, after all, about Border customs, or about an abortive Jacobite rising but about Mauley and his exclusion from society. But the story is inadequately contexted and Scott fell easily into the trap of a Gothicism that he, his publishers and the public all rejected. The superiority of *Old Mortality* is to be found in the way in which Scott provides a convincing socio-psychological context for the exclusion theme. For this was the fundamental point about the Covenanters, not their 'fanaticism', as we can see from Scott's non-fiction accounts of them: 'The government . . . drove them altogether from human society. In danger, want and necessity . . . expelled from civil intercourse it is no wonder that we find many of these wanderers avowing principles and doctrines hostile to the government which oppressed them.'[11] They are linked in Scott's work with the gypsies, pirates, MacGregors and other outcasts, and ultimately with the victims of social and economic injustice in post-Waterloo Britain. There is in *Dwarf* a gap between the vileness of the way Mauley is treated and the traditional pieties of the Border community. In *The Heart of Midlothian*, however, it is very convincing that it is just *this* society that isolates Effie.

If the exclusion theme is primary, then social history, and the cultural changes of the novel, are of secondary importance; they are there because Scott's imagination and the taste of his readers insisted that in prose fiction at least a character or psychological condition could not interest without a context that guaranteed some degree of probability. And not only in prose fiction. We may remember the popularity of Crabbe's portraits in verse at this period, and contrast the success that his 'realism' achieved with the bewilderment that greeted some of Wordsworth's poems. Wordsworth said in effect: There was a man like this. The critics replied: But there need not have been;

we are not convinced; this portrait touches our experience at too few points. Jeffrey, whose reactions mirrored public demand for verification, complained of Wordsworth's characters being 'unique specimens of our kind . . . Instead of the men and women of ordinary humanity . . . certain moody and capricious personages made after the poet's own heart and fancy.' Elshie, in spite of his literary conventionality, quite the opposite of Wordsworth's quirky matter-of-factness, represents a similar lack of attention to generalisation, contextualisation. This failure to convince brought Scott to the fundamentally new start of *Old Mortality*. The poet's images are given a context – that of history – which guarantees their objectivity and independence of authorial caprice. And it is *Old Mortality* that initiates the classic form of the Scott novel. *Guy Mannering* and *The Antiquary* had succeeded without a background of history because the images they were built around – of a still largely cohesive society – could be drawn directly from everyday manners. Scott was not willing, however, to use the originals of his images of violence and disruption: he turned first to Gothic, and then to history.

In *The Bride of Lammermoor* this hypothesis may be tested by assuming that Edgar is no Waverley, caught between two worlds of ancient feudalism and modern capitalism, but a redrawing of Elshender. The prehistory of the tale, the fortunes of the Ravenswoods, quickly establishes Edgar as a man cut off from the society of his peers, and indeed from any community. Edgar is in a position very like the dwarf's: he too has a ruinous dwelling and a single servant. The events that bring about his isolation are, however, far more historical, circumstantial and plausible.

One word frequently used to describe the Master's position is 'desperation'. Alice warns Ashton that the Ravenswoods are a fierce house, and that it is dangerous to deal with men 'when they become desperate' and continues 'beware of pressing a desperate man with the hand of authority'. When asked by Bucklaw why he associated with Craigengelt, the Master replies: 'Simply, because I was desperate.' When Ashton considers

Edgar's character, wondering if he has anything to fear from him, he concludes 'not unreasonably, that only desperate circumstances [drive] men to desperate measures'. Finally, towards the end of the tale, Ravenswood repeats the word twice:

I am a desperate man.

Do not urge to further desperation a wretch already desperate (chapter 33).

In Scott's definition, a desperate man is one who has nothing to bind him to the normal community. And it is largely society – and government – that is responsible for desperation. Edgar's position arises from the frailty of justice in Scotland. He voices a position that is very close to Scott's own: 'I hope to see the day when justice shall be open to Whig and Tory . . . men will not always start at these nicknames as at a trumpet-sound. As social life is better protected, its comforts will become too dear to be hazarded without some better reason than speculative politics' (chapter 8). Faction, speculative politics, social and economic discontent all exist at times when society fails to protect its members in the enjoyment of their rights to the comforts of life. *The Bride of Lammermoor* was written in the year in which Scott feared a civil war. And he returned to the idea of desperation in another crisis year, in *Malachi Malagrowther IV*, when he wrote that the working-man, deprived of his right to work and/or to enjoy the fruits of his labour, has nothing to do but to go to the alehouse to learn 'the metaphysics of murder and despair'.

This is not to say that Edgar is a working-man. But that his role has wider imaginative reverberations is borne out by Scott's treatment of the three old women. Lucky Gourlay has the reputation of being a witch: 'for, notwithstanding the dreadful punishments inflicted upon the supposed crime of witchcraft, there wanted not those who, steeled by want and bitterness of spirit, were willing to adopt the hateful and dangerous character' (chapter 31). 'Want and bitterness of spirit', as we see from the three cummers' comments on the bridal

171

procession, are directly linked to the social disorder of the
vanity and selfishness of the upper classes – reminding us of
Scott's comments about upper-class egotism in his letters of
this time. ' "Their gifts," said Ailsie Gourlay, "are dealt for
nae love of us, nor out of respect for whether we feed or starve.
They wad gie us whinstanes for loaves, if it would serve their
own vanity, and yet they expect us to be grateful, as they ca'
it, as if they had served us for true love and liking." ' The
authorly exposure of the hypocrisy of the Marquis and Ashton
lends force and credence to the complaints of Lucky Gourlay.
The catastrophe is fore-ordained; but it also seems to come out
of the bitterness of heart of the three old women, as if they had
the power, as we know they have the will, to harm:

'. . . did ye ever see a mair grand bridal?'
'I winna say that I have,' answered the hag, 'but I think soon to
see as braw a burial.'
'And that wad please me as weel,' said Annie Winnie; 'for there's
as large a dole, and folk are no obliged to girn and laugh and mak
murgeons, and wish joy to these hellicat quality, that lord it ower
us like brute beasts' (chapter 34).

As in *The Antiquary* there is a vein of medieval morality
that appears when the pride of the aristocracy is being criticised: 'There they are that were capering on their prancing
nags four days since, and they are now ganging as dreigh and
sober as oursells the day. They were a' glistening wi' gowd
and silver; they're now as black as the crook' (chapter 35).
But the pride is not that of the Ashtons alone: we are not
entitled to read this as an attack on upstarts. There are important points of resemblance between these scenes and the passage
in which Ravenswood talks to the sexton (chapter 24). Both
contain unexpectedly radical social criticisms mixed with
grim jokes about weddings and funerals:

'I live by twa trades, sir,' replied the blythe old man, 'fiddle, sir,
and spade; filling the world, and emptying of it . . . a likely lass
[Alice Gray] was then, and looked ower her southland nose at a'.
I trow her pride got a downcome . . . I hae heard she married far
below her station; it was very right to let her bite on the bridle

[bridal?] when she was living, and its very right to gie her a decent burial now she's dead.'

The criticism in this dialogue is really centred however on the Ravenswoods. The linking of the 'gravedigger' and 'witches' scenes by tone and imagery would tend to suggest an equivalence – the Ashtons are no worse than the Ravenswoods. The old man's grievances recall the themes of persecution/exile and link them with the bridal/burial image:

'I lost my wind in [old Lord Ravenswood's] service. Ye see I was trumpeter at the castle, and had allowance for blawing at break of day, and at dinner-time, and other whiles when there was company about, and it pleased my lord; and when he raised his militia to caper awa, to Bothwell Brig against the wrang-headed wastland Whigs, I behoved, reason or nane, to munt a horse and caper awa' wi' them.'

'And very reasonable,' said Ravenswood; 'you were his servant and vassal.'

'Servitor, say ye?' replied the sexton; 'and so I was – but it was to blaw folk to their warm dinner, or at the warst to a decent kirkyard, and no to skirl them awa' to a bluidy brae side, where there was deil a bedral but the hooded craw.'

There is an unmistakable symmetry in Scott's imagery which carries moral implications. Ravenswood's plight seems as much his own family's making as, for example, Harry Bertram's was. Bertram's father turned out the gypsies, made them desperate, and Bertram became a wanderer; the Ravenswoods, in lending their hands to the persecution of the Covenanters, turn rituals of life into rituals of death, and their heir is driven from society. These images are poetic; they recur without reference to the process of time. The novel imagines a perversion of moral values that *entirely cuts across the historical progress of events*, thus surely implying that history – the Revolution, the Union, Jacobitism, the end of the feudal order – is there to give solidity to the images of the spiritual condition of the novel's world but has no part in their genesis. This impression is reinforced by the fact that the leading image of bridal–burial is repeated in the legend of the fountain, an event placed long before the historical period of the novel. In the fountain, the pure and

life-giving waters of the spring mingle with the blood of the
dead beloved. The real facts of the legend are kept deliberately
vague: what is certain is that 'from this period the house of
Ravenswood was supposed to have dated its decay'. That
Ravenswood meets Lucy by the fountain suggests an ominous
circularity that eliminates the rationality of history. The
novel is bound up with an imagining of the illness and fatality
represented by the wedding–death theme. Yet it is in no way
imagined as an inexplicable intrusion of metaphysical evil:
the breakdown of human and social values is linked to human
failings: pride, egotism, avarice and injustice. Although the
curse of the well pre-dates the persecution of the Covenanters,
it is really a punishment for that action.

Yet at the beginning of the novel, Edgar's isolation is only
putative; there is still a chance that he might be reintegrated
into his community; the events of the novel make his isolation
complete, even to the extent of denying him the normal ritual
of burial.

The opening of the novel gives us Edgar meditating revenge,
which is born of desperation and will, if accomplished, bring
him to death or exile. The revenge is associated with Malisius
and the black bull's head: when Ravenswood kills the bull that
threatens the Ashtons, he is clearly postponing or renouncing his
revenge. Why? Not, at the moment, for love of Lucy. The reader
is left to infer that Ravenswood's heart is capable of being
touched by instinctive feelings of human solidarity at moments
when there is no time for reflection or reasoning. We have
noticed above that Edgar sought out Craigengelt (neck–money–
guilt) because he was desperate. But he breaks off the connection because, as he explains to Bucklaw, he had changed his
mind. The reader is meant to supply 'Lucy', who is an agent
that binds Ravenswood to the community. There are other
ways in which withdrawal gives way to participation. Ravenswood's retreat into the deserted, monotonous interior of Wolf's
Crag is succeeded by his plunging hotly into 'the headlong
impulse of the chase'; the pathetic disrepair of Caleb's house-
keeping by the miraculous success of the visit of the Lord

Keeper; Ravenswood's hatred and distrust of Ashton is followed by his 'love and gratitude' for him on hearing the Keeper's defence of him before the Privy Council. The rhythm of the novel is one of expansion and contraction. Each of these expansions is followed or accompanied by a deflating irony. Ravenswood impulsively gives himself up to the chase, but his horse is too poor to keep up. Although Edgar is grateful to Ashton, we are constantly aware of the Keeper's hypocrisy. We might describe these movements towards community as the positive of uncorrupted human feelings as against the corruption of human policy and social arrangements. The principal use of this rhythm of action and reaction occurs when Edgar goes to bid Lucy farewell, but instead 'gave his faith to her for ever, and received her troth in return. The whole passed so suddenly, and arose so much out of the immediate impulse of the moment . . .' (chapter 20).

Yet, the novel insists, the corruptions of policy are too strong for individual unsupported goodness of feeling. The turning-point of the work is Lady Ashton's return and Edgar's expulsion. Significantly, the crisis is imagined as a series of social improprieties, the gravest of which – and presented with consummate skill – is Lady Ashton's racing a guest for possession of the front gate. None of the actions seem related to the historical specificity of the period. The symbolism of the coach race could have fitted quite well into any background. Indeed, when the Marquis tells Ravenswood that

the mistress of a first-rate boarding-school could not have rejected with more haughty indifference the suit of a half-pay Irish officer, beseeching permission to wait upon the heiress of a West India planter, than Lady Ashton spurned every proposal of mediation which it could at all become me to offer in behalf of you (chapter 25).

there is an air of downright anachronism: the cultural references are so clearly drawn from the world of Thackeray rather than that of Dryden. It should perhaps be emphasised that Lady Ashton's lack of courtesy is presented as malice, not as *parvenu* uncouthness: Lady Ashton is a Douglas. Yet we are not really interested in her motives, even though they are credible enough. The vital thing is the scene that follows, with Edgar, sitting over the corpse of Alice, reflecting: 'he found himself transferred from the situation of a successful lover of Lucy Ashton, and an honoured and respected friend of her father, into the melancholy and solitary guardian of the abandoned and forsaken corpse of a common pauper' (chapter 25). No longer a wooer, but a wake-keeper; the wedding–death image returns.

If Edgar is man cut off from the society of his peers, Lucy is the type of man betrayed by authority: while Edgar is betrayed by neighbour, colleague, kinsman, Lucy is always seen within the confines of her filial role. And an imaginative link is established between the persecuted girl and the old Covenanters. She is able to get a message out of the castle only through the agency of Bide-the-bent who 'with all the more severe prejudices and principles of his sect . . . possessed a sound judgement, and had learnt sympathy even in that very school of persecution where the heart is so frequently hardened' (chapter 31). It is Lucky Gourlay who is used to deepen Lucy's literal alienation. The isolation theme is stated explicitly twice:

'It is decreed,' she said, 'that every living creature, even those who owe me most kindness, are to shun me, and leave me to those by whom I am beset . . . alone and uncounselled, I must extricate myself or die' (chapter 29).

Lucy was now like the sailor, who, while drifting through a tempestuous ocean, clings for safety to a single plank, his powers of grasping it becoming every moment more feeble (chapter 31).

We are of course entitled to demand that the depiction of Lucy's character, the growth of her madness, should be more than symbolically apt – it ought to be psychologically convincing. Yet the psychological process is what interests Scott least, or perhaps, which might be the same thing, what he is least capable of rendering. He gives us summary where another novelist would dramatise through incident and dialogue. However, the point for Scott is that in the structure of the novel, Lucy and her madness close the circle of correspondences. She is her family's victim; and the peasants, Presbyterians and old people who have been oppressed. The wedding night becomes tragedy; in stabbing her husband surely she is punishing her father, revenging herself upon the whole male–authoritarian world; as we noticed in *Peveril*, the image of castration is not far away. Lucy's revenge is in fact a violent social rebellion. Her whole family is doomed: 'The family of Ashton did not long survive that of Ravenswood.' Symmetry of image and plotting subserves the theme of retribution. Lady Ashton's *unkindness* leads to the end of the family she had wished to aggrandise; that an unjust society cannot endure is perhaps the implication.

One key to the novel's meaning has been found in the contrast of wedding (life, community) and burial (death, oppression) images. Another key might be found in two related *concepts*: justice and kindliness. The society of Lammermoor is one in which feelings of kindliness are all but extinguished. The main focus of this is Lucy's relation with her family. That she could 'feel herself the object of suspicion, of scorn, of dislike at least, if not of hatred, to her own family' is an image of how wrong things are. In the earlier novels Scott had celebrated the instinctual kindliness that bound Scottish society together; here, pride and avarice have thwarted the most intimate of relations – parental and marital.

Tentatively, the novel proposes justice as a refuge in a society devoid of kindliness. The House of Lords will restore to Edgar what his peers have denied him. Lucy hangs onto her engagement to Edgar, as it was 'a binding contract' that she 'neither could nor would resign'. The half piece that symbolises their engagement is 'the link which bound [her] to life'. Her faith to her own word is her only security in an astonishing world. However, only a very token resistance to the prevailing malice of human relationships is offered by the idea of justice, if it is indeed proposed as a value, which cannot be confidently assumed.

The primary effect of the metaphorical structure is to create the image of a society that offers neither sufficiency nor joy to its members. This emphasises the perhaps surprising link with Blake. At the same time the complications of the plot enforce a more limited moral: that a man cannot deny his neighbour's rights to spiritual and material comfort and himself live in ease and plenty.

GROUP IV

As Scott's deepest emotions had welled up in *Lammermoor*, they had been transformed through metaphor, symbol and literary analogue into terms of a complicated poetic drama. This was perhaps the only way they could ever have been manifested. In the three novels of this group, in times of even greater personal and public stress, symbol, image and literary parallel – especially from Shakespeare – almost disappear, or are replaced by evasive surrogates. The spare, controlled power of the supernatural in *Lammermoor* is replaced by the over-written, under-realised figure of the White Lady in *Monastery*. Not only does she derive from an inappropriate literary genre – aristocratic pastoral romance rather than tragedy or folk tale – but she is handled confusingly in her symbolic functions. She is the spirit of Protestantism, and so within the book's own terms an agent of the 'new' society, and yet she also attempts to frustrate one of the essential relationships of the new, the marriage of Mary and Halbert. The 'Euphuism' of Piercie Shafton has some place in the metonymic, historical world of the novel, but no function in the imaginative action.

Monastery is defaced by much reflection on the motives of characters and on the superiority of the Reformed to the Catholic faith. Father Eustace is thus described:

Having finished these meditations, in which there was at once goodness of disposition and narrowness of principle, a considerable portion of self-opinion, and no small degree of self-delusion, the sub-prior commanded the prisoner to be brought into his presence (chapter 31).

Mary Avenel hid her Bible

lamenting only that, for want of a fitting interpreter, much must remain to her a book closed and a fountain sealed. She was unaware

178

of the greater danger she incurred, of putting an imperfect or even false sense upon some of the doctrines which appeared most comprehensible (chapter 31).

the affectionate mother had made preparations for the earthly work which she had most at heart. There were slips of paper inserted in the volume, in which, by an appeal to, and a comparison of, various passages in the Holy Writ, the errors and human inventions with which the Church of Rome had defaced the simple edifice of Christianity, as erected by its Divine Architect, were pointed out. These controversial topics were treated with a spirit of calmness and Christian charity, which might have been an example to the theologians of the period, but they were clearly, fairly and plainly argued and supported by the necessary proofs and references (chapter 30).

This last is a piece of shorthand that tells us plainly what we have suspected: that Scott is not the slightest bit interested in the theological argument. Partisan bigotry would be more acceptable in a novel than this spirit of calm yet biased indifference.

If he was not interested in the doctrinal aspects of the Reformation, why did he write *Monastery*? For the novel consistently avoids myth-making and heads for history. It keeps at a distance from life. There are possibilities of myth: the tower situation, the duel in which both parties flee in guilty terror. And yet all seriousness is dissipated by the involvement of the White Lady. The real theme of the novel is in fact very obvious and, unlike Scott's previous novels, is entirely derivable from a historian's interpretation of the 'background' – social mobility, the rise and fall of ranks, the new men. Halbert is the new man. He does not allow himself to drift with the current, he himself is guide and pilot (chapter 25). He is able to guide Henry Warden (the Reformed Church in person) 'tracing with the utmost accuracy the mazes of the dangerous and intricate morasses and hills which divided the halidome from the Barony of Avenel' (chapter 23). He is not lost without his community, and has never had one. He learns to defy both class and feudal superior. On refusing the job of forester, Halbert is asked by the sub-prior what 'visionary aim' he has before him? 'Visionary' is almost always used pejoratively in Scott, to indicate unreal social ambitions; yet here it is used approvingly. Shafton calls Halbert 'Audacity' and says that his impudence levels the gap between them. Eustace characterises him as one of those men 'whom God raises up among a people when he meaneth that their deliverance shall be wrought out with strength of hand and valour of heart'. The action of the novel draws towards the two marriages, Shafton and Mysie, Halbert and Mary, two symbolic *mesalliances*. Even at the end of the novel Scott is unwilling to refrain from stating his theme a number of times, in a series of aphoristic (and so distanced and manageable) comments:

When I am once more mine own man, I will find a new road to dignity (Shafton, chapter 37).

In times like these we must look to men and not to pedigrees . . . Times of action make princes into peasants, and boors into barons (Murray, chapter 37).

In our days, each man is the son of his own deeds. The glorious light of Reformation hath shone alike on prince and peasant; . . . It is a stirring world, where all may advance themselves who have stout hearts and strong arms (chapter 35).

Of all Scott's novels, *Monastery* is the one that comes down most heavily on the side of change and progress. Its characters most nearly incorporate within themselves the trends of the age in which they live. It is also – bearing in mind that Scott was still at the peak of his powers – the most decided failure.

In *Abbot*, the subject of interest is still narrower: the character of Mary Stuart. As the depiction of historical notables has been until recently the staple of historical fiction, the oddity of this within Scott's work has hardly ever been noticed: never before had he brought a prince so close to the centre of the action. Scott was too polite of course to have given us Mary's point of view, but by circling around her through the viewpoints of a number of males and through the creation of an exceptionally large cast of other – and similarly ambiguous – women, he tried to define an area within which the historical mystery of her character might achieve some sort of resolution. There are other interesting possibilities in the work. Mary seems to be on the verge of symbolising a gayer, more humane and organic, society, which is repressed by a barren, sadistic Protestantism (Lochleven, Lindsay, Ruthven). There is the childlessness of Mary Avenel, the destruction of the Cell of St Cuthbert, the tearing-down of the garlands of flowers and the stopping-up of the spring of healing water. This would have been a theme both truly historical and not obviously related to Scott's own time: yet it is only faintly sketched in, the novel mostly retreating to the hackneyed, literary theme of 'queen or woman', which Scott was to use with similar lack of success in *Kenilworth*.

The inferiority of the three novels, including *Ivanhoe*, to almost anything else in the oeuvre, except for some of the late failures, is widely critically recognised yet has been ascribed to Scott's lack of judgement in choosing an unhelpful 'background' period, while the abandonment of literary modes and the eschewal of social analogues has hardly been noticed. *Monastery* opens promisingly enough with a typical situation from group III: the lonely tower, the orphaned boys, a period of anarchy and injustice. Yet the situation is not developed according to group III logic, which would not allow Halbert to marry Mary or achieve a higher rank in society and would make of Piercie Shafton a far more ruthless and destructive figure of artifice. In terms of 'vulgar sociology', Scott in this novel *is* tending to glorify entrepreneurial capitalism. Yet he cannot do it whole-heartedly: the actual experience of a new man is impossible for him to render even symbolically, which is why he so frequently calls for the White Lady and makes the Catholics into straw men. He did this, I suggest hesitantly, because he could not, in 1819–20, continue dramatising conflict engendered by oppression and injustice when the animosities he sensed in his own society were so perilously close to physical engagement. To disguise his alarm the more thoroughly, Scott turned not to a period of history in which conflict was for a moment in abeyance, but to one in which it had a thoroughly acceptable outcome. Things that seem desperate, he was fond of saying at this time, are often productive of good in ways which we cannot see at the time.

Group v

Upper-class vanity and avarice, which had appeared as a major enemy to community in the earlier novels from *Antiquary* to *Lammermoor*, return in early group v novels – *Kenilworth, The Fortunes of Nigel* and *Peveril of the Peak* – but are seen as both more devastating and more foreign. Located principally in Southern and urban scenes, imaged in terms borrowed from Jacobean and Restoration drama as lechery, extravagance, hell-raising, gambling and revengefulness, aristocratic, gentle and royal vice reaches out to draw provincial virtue into its web of corruption. The weakness in the major characters – Amy, Nigel – shows us a provincial society sapped by its own vanity and unable to resist the viciousness of the centre, not even recognising it as such. Embedded in this group – which will have to be represented in my study by the previous analysis of *Peveril* – is one novel that attempts to shore up imaginatively the vertiginous social collapse of the other three with the creation of a community so strong in its own culture and so remote geographically – yet still subsuming familiar Scotch positives – that it can not only resist the corruption of the centre but reform it. This is *The Pirate*, a novel that seems to make the best sense if it is seen as a rewriting, with far greater emphasis but much less surety, of the themes of group ii, with a hero drawn from group iii.

'The Pirate': Scott's 'Tempest'

The arrival of the stranger in an enclosed community is a frequent starting-point in Scott's novels. If the stranger brings the influence of modern civilisation with him, does his advent initiate the long process of social disruption that leads to a more efficient but less lovely and humane society? Scott's diary of the lighthouse-yacht would allow us to propose such a scheme with a good show of reason. He frequently records the backwardness of agriculture, land tenure, housing and finance. In the contemporary Zetland, strangers, like Scottish plough-men[12] are brought in to great effect, and Scott fully approved. Nevertheless, this is the opposite of the novel. The economic facts of life are made little of, and attempts to reform the Zetlanders fail deservedly. The Zetland of the novel is not really related to the Zetland Scott saw in 1814 but to the emotions of 1821. The most important key to the novel is the realisation that Scott was here reworking *The Tempest*, with his own materials and in his own way.

The very large number of references to the play bear witness to this. There is Mertoun's 'dark hour' (chapter 2); the epi-graph to chapter 6 – 'If by your art you have Put the wild waters in this roar, allay them'; the 'song of the Tempest' (chapter 5); Triptolemus (= Trinculo?) getting a wetting in the stream (chapter 11); the mermaid's song with its echoes of 'Full fathom five' – 'Fathom deep beneath the wave/String-ing beads of glorious pearl'; an echo of Prospero when Brenda refers to Norna's story as 'baseless visions' (chapter 23); a reference to the loss of Trinculo's bottle (chapter 24); Claud Halcro's reference to another Ariel song when he says: 'I bid you welcome to these yellow sands' (chapter 30); Triptolemus' complaint that 'He asks for drink and they bring him sour whey . . . you ask for meat and they bring you sour sillocks', a reference to Prospero's 'banquet'; an epigraph from another 'old play', which mentions Miranda and Prospero; Norna's Prosperian rhetoric – 'My throne is a cloud, my sceptre a meteor, my realm is only peopled with fantasies' (chapter 33); and, above all, the epigraph to the whole novel

> Nothing about him –
> But doth suffer a sea change.

'He' is Cleveland. The sea change is the change that over-takes Cleveland somewhere in the novel, which puzzled early critics, who remarked that he was one man at the beginning and another at the end. Cleveland himself remarks on the change:

I came hither rude and wild, scarce knowing that my trade, my desperate trade, was more criminal in the sight of man or of Heaven than that of those privateers whom your law acknowledges. I was bred in it, and, but for the wishes you [Minna] have encouraged me to form, I should have perhaps died in it, desperate and impenitent (chapter 40).

'Desperate' is mentioned twice. If that were not enough, a sentence from *Tales of a Grandfather* makes it clear why Scott chose to write about a pirate: 'pirates [are] men who might be termed enemies to the human race and [have] done deeds which [seem] to exclude them from intercourse with mankind'.[13] It is not the romance, the derring-do, even the criminality of the Pirate (Scott is at pains to make him a very gentlemanly pirate) but his apartness; not his guilt but his being beyond the pale – he is not so far from the Covenanters, Effie, Elshie, Edgar and Rob.

The Tempest moves through the common last-plays pattern of sin–suffering–repentance–redemption. *The Pirate*, allowing for the fact that Scott's is a secular imagination, which cannot relish images of supernatural power or the notion of grace, exhibits a similar pattern. The most important difference is that there is no single agent of grace in Scott's tale: the redemptive power is found within the human community. Cleveland, rude and wild, is civilised by the seemingly simple and artless society of Zetland. The community of Zetland in the novel is an imaginary one: it does not represent 'really' either the Zetland Scott had seen or even one from the previous century; it is an imaginary construct based on the best features of Scottish society of past and present, with the darker sides that Scott knew of, and drew frequently, omitted; an utopian and not a realistic account.

A good way of entering the novel is to take Cleveland's temptation scheme (chapter 31). The pirate ascends a hill with Jack Bunce and they gaze at the world below them. Bunce offers him a world of riches and power:

Yonder she lies . . . I wish to God she was in the bay of Honduras –
you, captain, on the quarter deck, I your lieutenant, Fletcher your
quartermaster and fifty stout fellows under us . . .

   . . . Your Don, rolling as deep in the water as a grampus, loaden
with rum, sugar, and bales of tobacco, and all the rest ingots,
moidores and gold dust.

Cleveland at the same time is looking at

trumpery small craft, which is only loaded with stock-fish, and
ling, and smoked geese, and tubs of butter that is worse than tallow.

The obvious moral choice put before Cleveland is enhanced by
the scriptural memories (the devil's temptation of Christ).
Cleveland makes his choice correctly:

These poor men make the sea a means of honest livelihood and
friendly communication between shore and shore, for the mutual
benefit of the inhabitants; but we have made it a road to the ruin
of others, and to our own destruction here and in eternity. I am
determined to turn honest man, and use this life no longer.

Bunce has attempted to place the pirate's life in as attractive
a light as possible – power, adventure, wealth. But his dis-
paraging references to the loads of the 'trumpery small craft'
bring to mind all the modest but undoubted human values
that have been associated with the island life: all the 'manners'
that rise from its simple hunting and pastoral economy. Scott
had worked hard to create a romantic social paradise in the
first half of the book so that the pirate Cleveland could be
sustained by its image in the hour of his temptation. The
action that involves Cleveland hardly ever interpenetrates
with the passages that extol the social values of the island.
He does not have to face the difference between his own code
and that of his host community in any particular moment of
recognition. But the change is effected, although we do not
see the interior stages of its process. It is rather as if the reader is
assumed to have undergone Cleveland's experience for him.

   The assertion that Zetland is an ideal society needs explanation. It is not ideal in the way that a utopian writer would
recognise. Scott can imagine an ideal only within a context of
experienced possibility, which for him must include frailty,

venality, self-deception and egotism. The ideal community will have to reckon with all of these, and hold them in check, order them in such a way that the balance of positives outweighs the negatives. There is a whole habit of mind here shown, for instance, in the 'portrait' of Magnus Troil with its balancing of opposites: 'He was an honest, plain Zetland gentleman, some-what passionate, the necessary result of being surrounded by dependants; and somewhat over-convivial in his habits, the consequence, perhaps, of having too much time at his disposal; but frank-tempered and generous to his people, and kind and hospitable to strangers' (chapter 1). Good and bad are related to the same causes, and balance each other – passion and frank-ness, conviviality and hospitality. In this way any scepticism that might have been generated by the character is anticipated and rebuffed. It is the same with the references in the early chapters to the petty deceptions that the Zetlanders practise on Mertoun; the slightest hint of the economic and physical hardships that form a constant backdrop to the delineation of the local manners. There is just enough to convince us that the picture is truthful, but not enough to change the direction of the novel fundamentally.

The atmospheric descriptions of the sea coast lead naturally into the romantic evocation of the Norse legends and sagas, and the descriptions of the hardships of life outdoors to that of the fun and folk games that occupy the Zetlanders during the winter.

The two most important ways by which the theme of com-munity is approached might be summed up as 'hospitality' and 'property'. The earliest chapters simply propose hospitality as an established fact. Mertoun received that 'warm and cordial hospitality for which the islands are distinguished'. At the same time, he is cheated by the villagers of Yarlshof. We feel that the two facts are somehow related, that boundless hospi-tality and dishonesty in economic relations are not mutually contradictory. The principal scenes in which hospitality is seen are the two house scenes at Burgh Westra for St John's Eve, and at Stourburgh.

In the scene in which the various travellers come to shelter from the storm at Stourburgh, the factor's house, Scott so manages point of view as to give a complex and convincing demonstration of the difference between this community and others (chapters 4–6). First we follow Mordaunt's experience: the warm hospitality of Burgh Westra, which he leaves, the 'hospitable household', 'the warm kindness', followed by the highly worked description of his journey on foot across the island in vile weather. Scott makes us entirely sympathise with Mordaunt when he sees the house and desires its shelter. The hospitality of the islands is made to seem not only a fine thing, but one that is, in these latitudes, as much an economic and social necessity as it is in other unfavoured regions. The hospitality that is asked as a right is not sentimentally conceived.

Then Scott shifts the point of view so that we can sense the outraged feelings of the unwilling hosts, and feel that their attitude is much closer to our 'normal' way of looking at things. We can feel Yellowley's fears for his property, and know why he presents his gun at Mordaunt. At the same time, Baby's language, with its repeated cries of 'caterans', 'thiggers' and 'sorners' reminds us of the changing manners of Scott's own society – these were the words by which the old beggars were officially reprobated. The Yellowleys are something more than simple misers, and Scott's original readers must have been to a certain extent sympathetic to them too. This episode with its humour and its constantly changing point of view, convinces us of the realness of the Zetland hospitality, and its uniqueness.

The open-heartedness with which all are invited, and the material profusion, might arouse our scepticism about the feast at Burgh Westra. But Scott again anticipates disbelief. Mrs Baby's cry that 'The very hill-side smells of their wastefulness, and a hungry heart wad scarce seek better kitchen to a barley scone, than just to waft it in the reek that's rising out of yon lums' (chapter 11), prepares us to accept as normal and natural, by opposition to this unnatural thrift, the profusion that follows. The description of the mansion itself, more ship than house, with all its rich associations of trade, smuggling and wrecking, shows us how it is that these obviously poor people can afford so much luxury. It is in the two fishing-scenes, however, that the feasting is shown most obviously to be paid for.

During the feast, the boats set off for the haaf-fishing. The scene in which this occurs is moving in the restraint with which the anxiety of the fishermen's wives is drawn as they watch their men put out to sea. The effect of the contrast and juxta-position is to make us believe in the truthfulness of the feasting – that not only does it not ignore the 'real' hard life of the Zetlanders, but it is in some way accounted for by it. The scene of the whale hunt is in many respects the central action of the novel (chapter 17) for many of the thematic threads are drawn together in it. And within the scene the point to start from should be the moment when the violence of the whale-fishers' reaches its peak:

the unfortunate native of the deep was overwhelmed by all kinds of missiles – harpoons and spears flew against him on all sides – guns were fired, and each various means of annoyance plied which could excite him to exhaust his strength in useless rage. When the animal found that he was locked in by shallows on all sides and became sensible, at the same time, of the strain of the cable on his body, the convulsive efforts which he made to escape, accompanied by sounds resembling deep and loud groans, would have moved the compassion of all but a practised whale-fisher. The repeated showers which he spouted into the air began now to be mingled with blood, and the waves which surrounded him assumed the same crimson appearance. Meanwhile the efforts of the assailants were redoubled.

The violence of the scene, which follows so close upon the feasting, convinces us that we are learning something of impor-tance about the given community: violence in acquisition balances the furious profusion of the feast. In chapter 21 we learn that Troil's share from the professional whale-fishing is three whales. The cross-referencing reminds us of the two fishing scenes and tells us how the wealth we have seen ex-pended is got. Another thread brought into the hunt is the 'communal' theme: all lend a hand to hunt the whale, and all who share in the labour and danger share the spoil. If we know Adam Smith, we refer this primitive socialism to the 'hunting' stage of society, and will know that it must be overthrown by agriculture or will thwart the establishment of that next phase. It also reminds us of the strict equality with which Cleveland's possessions were divided at Yarlshof, and cross-references with the important theme of property. It also repeats the frequently mentioned theme of hostility to strangers. The whale is an analogue of Cleveland himself, washed up by the sea. Basil Mertoun makes the connection in so many words: 'you may cheat a stranger as you would flinch a whale' (chapter 2). Ultimately the scene is linked to Scott's comparisons between English and Scottish society. The closer-knit any community is, the more xenophobic it is likely to be and the less time it will have for 'general philanthropy'. The English were charitable, coldly and from principle, to strangers; while the Scots tended to limit their charity to the circle of their own home, family, parish. The difference was mirrored in the different poor-law administrations.[14]

The hospitality theme opens out into the property theme. To Triptolemus, with his advanced ideas of the meaning of *meum* and *tuum*, they are obviously related. The *normal* rights of a householder do not apply here: Mordaunt asks him: 'what right have you to will anything about it?' He must not ask, but receive the strangers in his house. To Baby's complaint, as he feeds the fire a log, Mordaunt remarks

You should not grudge the fire what the sea gives you for nothing.

Triptolemus cannot understand the system of land tenure:

I till a piece of best ground; down comes a sturdy beggar that wants a kailyard, or a plant-a-cruive, as you call it, and he claps down an enclosure in the middle of my bit shot of corn, as lightly as if he was baith laird and tenant; and gainsay him wha likes, there he dibbles in his kail-plants (chapter 30).

There is the same confusion over the border between private and communal property with the Shetland ponies:

There is, indeed, a right of individual property in all these animals, which are branded or tatooed by each owner with his own peculiar mark; but when any passenger has occasional use for a pony, he never scruples to lay hold of the first which he can catch, puts on a halter, and having rode him as far as he finds convenient, turns the animal loose to find his way back again . . . this general exercise of property was one of the enormities which in due time the factor intended to abolish (chapter 11).

This commonalty is one of the most attractive and utopian features of the island community. When the misers attempt to hoard the fairy gold and save it for their own personal use instead of applying it to the general good, Minna comments: 'the youngest child in Orkney could have told you that fairy treasures, if they are not wisely employed for the good of others . . . do not dwell long with their possessors' (chapter 30).[15] The utopian elements of island life are guaranteed not only by the internal management of paradox, but also by reference to an external philosophy of society, however implicitly. Economically, Zetland society is primitive; before division of labour or of land into private holdings, still at the hunting and fishing stage, before allodial tenures are converted into feudal, before the division of ranks, for no great variety of fortunes exists. The Scottish Enlightenment taught us that such societies are indeed more simply virtuous, socialist and egalitarian and so we are inclined to believe the picture. Yet this is the first time Scott has ever presented such a society. Previously he has been inclined to stress the other side of the coin – the necessarily accompanying material poverty as in the scenes at Glennaquoich. However, Scott is able in *The Pirate* to combine 'primitive' social arrangements with tolerable material comfort by a cunning extension of the whale-hunting theme: the Zetlanders live by scavenging, wrecking, carefully disguised piracy, and are enabled to enjoy the benefits of 'civilisation' while not partaking in its norms. We have seen previously how Scott has affirmed the necessity of society's moving from simple and natural states to complicated and artificial ones. *The Pirate* turns this on its head with Scott's most extreme opposition of the values of the old community to those of the new.

In the novel, artificial values are represented by strangers – Yellowley and the two pirates. On the whole they also represent perversions of civilised life. The elder pirate, in a speech heavy with memories of *Timon of Athens*, discloses a view of commercial relations that argues a far from harmoniously regulated society:

Everything in the universe is bought and sold, and why not wind if the merchant can find purchasers? The earth is rented, from its surface down to its most central mines – the fire, and the means of feeding it are currently bought and sold – the wretches that sweep the boisterous ocean with their nets pay ransom for the privilege of being drowned in it (chapter 7).

Arguments over property give rise to most of the dissension on the island: Cleveland's chest, the 'gold chaplet' and 'silver box', his clothes in the yagger's possession, by their traditional balladic typology, imply the various forms of urban wealth.

The love story in the novel repeats the property theme. At the beginning of the novel Zetland is a paradise of sexual as well as economic innocence. Mordaunt is on innocent fraternal terms with the two sisters and makes no distinction between them. But with the coming of Cleveland, whom Norna calls 'reptile', 'adder', dissension arises, causing, with the introduction of sexual passion, differences between Mordaunt and the girls, and between the sisters themselves. Mordaunt is compelled to choose between them as he has not done before. As this theme develops, the tale of Ulla Troil–Vaughan is introduced. The parallels between this tale and the story of Minna suggest repetition, inevitability, something as in *Lammermoor*. Innocence cannot endure is the suggestion. Yet here, in this novel, the community is strong, it will remain itself, assimilate and transform the alien.

Cleveland's change of heart is mirrored in the journey that we make with him from Zetland to the pirate ship. The comparison is made principally in terms of social organisation. While Zetland is imaged as both patriarchal and egalitarian, the

pirate ship has all the features that Scott associated with
popular democracy: disorder, anarchy, strong drink, the illusion
of popular rule and the reality of despotical oligarchy. It is
on this – just as much as on the dangers and immoralities of
the piratical life – that Cleveland wishes to turn his back.

The somewhat mysterious and sudden change in Cleveland –
almost as magical as parts of *The Tempest* – is one way in which
Scott underlines his feeling for the importance of the bond
between community and character – how much character
(morality and personality) depend on circumstances. The
changes that Zetland brings about in Cleveland are credible
because of the insistence that it was external circumstances
that made him what he was. There is a moralising passage in
which Scott makes this clear: 'Cleveland . . . belonged . . . to
the . . . class . . . who are involved in evil rather by the con-
currence of external circumstances than by natural inclination
. . . one also who often considered his guilty situation with
horror, and had made repeated, though ineffectual efforts, to
escape from it' (chapter 39).

Cleveland's rescue by this community is Scott's most romantic
creation. There are many parts of the novel that recall Wordsworth: Minna, who 'learned from the book of Nature' and had
'high feelings for the solitary and melancholy grandeur' of her
island home, reminds us of Wordsworth's pedlar. But there is a
more fundamental resemblance; the island community, with
its legends, traditions and bleak, stark landscape, possesses
the same power to nourish and revivify as Wordsworth's
mountains and mountain communities. The novel will not
perhaps sustain critical comparison with *The Prelude* or *Lyrical
Ballads II*, either formally or philosophically. Yet they are
at one in ascribing spiritual values to communities that oppose
to the prevailing, or advancing, norms of an arrogant (and
southern), urban plutocracy, which seems about to dissolve
into its opposite, their own blend of local and traditional
pieties, as eternal as the landscape in which they are rooted.

Development

Two like 'Redgauntlet'

Of all the novels, *Redgauntlet* is the most elusive. I believe that the meaning of the novel is to be found in answers to a number of questions that Scott developed from the novels discussed so far. He accepted the fact that the cultural and political centres were weak, that forces of avarice, violence and anarchy seemed to be in the ascendant. On the whole, the solution of *The Pirate*, the purification of corruption through an appeal to 'basic' local culture, cannot be sustained. Nevertheless, although in some novels the defeat of the entire society is entertained, life does continue, individually and communally. What then of the lives of the individuals, of those who are excluded and of those who manage to survive? What are the resources and weaknesses of the individual? What friends does he have? And, above all else, there is a deepening of the question raised in the article from *Blackwood's* – where are the gains and losses in the transition from a 'status' to a 'contract' society?

Scott's novelistic answer is pessimistic; he envisages a good deal of pain and only a limited deal of freedom and satisfaction. The tendency of these novels is towards the delineation of small areas of compromised autonomy, which are surrounded and limited by social and political forces largely hostile, or at best indifferent, to the sort of solutions hoped for in group II novels: a vision not unlike that of Dickens in *Little Dorrit* and *Great Expectations*.

But can *Redgauntlet* really be read like this? Why is the simpler description of the novel as a contrastive cultural analysis still rejected? Some support for the arguments being advanced here can be gained from an analysis of two novels that are approximately contemporary with *Redgauntlet – Anne of Geierstein* and *The Fair Maid of Perth*. Common themes and character types are brought into sharp focus by repetition and we are bound to ask why Scott used similar people and situations in novels set in widely varying temporal and geographical co-ordinates. His primary interest cannot, logically, have been

193

in rendering the objective reality of the particular age. Indeed, if *Anne*, the more confused and less attractive of the two, were the sort of historical novel Lukacs would have us believe, which historical epoch is it about? Not about the fall of Burgundy, for Burgundy plays too little part in the novel; nor about Switzerland, nor the Wars of the Roses, nor the Kingdom of Provence, nor the Germany of the Empire or the Vehmique Tribunal. None of these are irrelevant, but neither can they act as a focus for the novel's interests. If it were really about the Swiss Republic, why would it leave the Swiss halfway through and return only perfunctorily in the closing pages?

Scott's writing habits are responsible for making *Anne* look more like a novel really concerned with the politics of the past than it is. As in *Woodstock* and *Peveril*, he is unable to keep out certain preoccupations that are at best secondary. For example, one conviction that Scott had inherited from the historians was the idea that a republic could exist only in certainly narrowly defined conditions. The land area had to be small and the citizens virtuous – unselfish, patriotic, agrarian, uncontaminated by commerce and large fortunes. There are frequent reminiscences of Smith and Ferguson as Scott describes the manners of the Swiss:

the spoils of victory had invested the Swiss with some wealth, and had taught many of them new wants (chapter 1).

'[Drunkeness] is a vice,' said the Englishman, 'which I have observed gains ground in your country, where within a century I have heard it was totally unknown.'
'It was so,' said the Swiss, 'for wine was seldom made at home, and never imported from abroad; for indeed none possessed the means of purchasing that, or aught else, which our valleys produce not' (chapter 3).

Such were then the sober manners of the Swiss, afterwards much corrupted by their intercourse with more luxurious regions (chapter 5).

Behind this, a lesson in political economy is being pointed: yet it is all by the way, for the political morality has little connection with the novel's main action and metaphors, which do not impinge upon the Swiss.

One indication of the novel's intention is the highly wrought opening scene with its Romance symbolism. A frequent image in the Waverley novels is 'stopping someone falling over a cliff'. We have seen Lilias using it to Darsie; Edward Glendinning uses is to Roland in *Abbot*: 'I have arrived in time to arrest thee on the verge of the precipice thou wert approaching' (chapter 28). In *Anne*, the image, which is generally used to represent friendship, the human solidarity that protects individuals from the consequences of their own ignorance or folly, is blown up into a full-scale episode.

The story opens with travellers, toiling through Swiss mountains in the company of an uncertain guide, a lad who knows something of the mountains but not much. After a short time, the weather deteriorates and the mountains are covered with a thick mist. The road is so winding and contorted that the travellers lose their way: 'they lost any vague idea which they had previously entertained concerning the direction in which the road led them'. The elder Philipson implicitly introduces the expected 'pilot' image when he wishes for 'that mystical needle . . . that points ever to the north'. So far, we have been given a typical yet individualised maze image. The condition of the protagonists is established as one of disorientation, although we have no way of knowing what it means. As the travellers go on, the image is intensified: a landslide completely destroys any semblance of orderliness:

The bank of earth, now a confused mass of ruins inverted in its fall, showed some trees growing in a horizontal position, and others, which, having pitched on their heads in their descent, were at once inverted and shattered to pieces, and lay a sport to the streams of the river which they had heretofore covered with a gloomy shadow (chapter 1).

We note here the suppressed political metaphor. Arthur resolves to climb along 'a narrow ledge, the very brink of the precipice'. The precipice is to be for Arthur what the Solway is for Darsie. Instead of the terror of the tide, there is Arthur's disabling vertigo. Before he has gone far, the cliff falls away under his feet, and he is left clinging to a tree, unable to move, paralysed with fear. It is from this position that the girl rescues him. The writing is so very figurative and elaborate in these opening chapters that it seems to ask us to find a purpose in it. A good clue to the purpose is contained in the following paragraph:

Meanwhile, the young man's spirits were strongly braced for the performance of his perilous task. He laid a powerful restraint on his imagination, which in general was sufficiently active, and refused to listen, even for an instant, to any of the horrible insinuations by which fancy augments actual danger. He endeavoured manfully to reduce all around him to the scale of right reason, as the best support of true courage. 'This ledge of rock,' he urged to himself, 'is but narrow, yet it has breadth enough to support me, these cliffs and crevices in the surface are small and distant, but the one affords as secure a resting place to my feet, the other as available a grasp to my hands, as if I stood on a platform of a cubit broad, and rested my arm on a balustrade of marble. My safety therefore depends on myself. If I move with decision, step firmly, and hold fast, what signifies it how near I am to the mouth of an abyss?'

Such confidence has only been invoked to be shattered, of course. A short while later, the young man is totally unable to command his feelings in this way. Arthur has that confident belief in the power of the individual to control his own behaviour in spite of any external circumstances that was Darsie's at the opening of *Redgauntlet*. His attainment of safety is accompanied by awkwardness and embarrassment (looking a fool in front of a girl) similar to Darsie's when he was disguised as a woman. In *Anne*, however, experiences that were matter for a chapter or two in *Redgauntlet* are developed at leisure throughout the whole of the novel. Experiences like this are repeated: Arthur's failure at the boyish sports of the Swiss, his terror at crossing the bridge into the castle of Geierstein, his bewilderment on being confronted with the wandering figure of Anne during the night in Graffslust, his feeling of vertigo when he looks into the dungeon of Brisach. Scott is so determined to have his hero look an idiot that the intention sometimes over-rides the actual creation, as in the Graffslust episode, where the emotions Arthur experiences – enough to deprive him of speech – are ill-proportioned to the event that gives rise to them.

Maze images abound, and dream images. The reader is partially involved, because he does not know the (Radcliffean) meaning of the mysteries but his experience is alienated from that of the protagonist by certain rhetorical devices. For example, as Arthur approaches the castle of Arnheim, he notices the following rustic scene: 'a lad in rustic dress was employed in the task of netting a brood of partridges, with the assistance of a trained spaniel [whose duty it was] to drive the partridges under the net'. Watching the sport is Annette, Anne's maid; it is her job to watch out for Arthur and guide him to the castle. As she does so, it naturally occurs to the reader that Arthur is a partridge, and so on. We cannot suspect Anne of any sinister intention, but the distance between reader and protagonist is increased.

Nevertheless, just as Alan and Darsie suffer together, Arthur is joined in his experiences by his father. The elder Philipson undergoes his own disorienting experience in John Meng's Golden Fleece Inn. His bed is let down through a trap, and he himself is bound and taken 'passive and unresisting' to answer the charges of the Vehmique Tribunal. While in Italy he had spoken ill of the Vehm, and had offended the Germans by his contempt for their eating habits. The scene is reminiscent partly of Alan's experience in the cellars of Tom Trumbull's, partly of Darsie's *faux pas* at the Brokenburnfoot dance. Later, as she helps Arthur secretly in Brisach, Anne re-enacts the part of Lilias; later still, she repeats Lilias' words: 'I was then acting under the agency of others, not my own' (chapter 22). All three principal characters take part in experiences that are disturbing, which do not leave them free to act as they will and seem to invade the roots of their capacity to be individuals. All of them are foreigners – Anne doubly so. The ambiguity surrounding her, culminating in the suggestion that she has a *doppelgänger*, mirrors uncertainty about her true role.

Arthur's maladroitness in the Swiss mountains and in everything connected with them is a reworking of Alan Fairford's bewilderment when outside the familiar law world of Edinburgh. Like Alan, he has moments of success that show us that he is no mere weakling: he can bend the bow of Buttisholz because his education qualifies him to do so. He is constantly overshadowed by Rudolph, yet when they meet on horseback, not clambering among the rocks with two-handed swords, it is Arthur who – at home on the plains – kills his man.

Another theme repeated from *Redgauntlet* is restraint, and the claims of parental authority. This is developed through the opposed figures of Donnerhugel and Philipson. Arthur plays the part of Alan, as Donnerhugel observes: 'Good King Arthur . . . thou art a dutiful observer of the fifth commandment, and thy days shall be long in the land' (chapter 10). Donnerhugel is principally characterised by his opposition to parental authority. It is Donnerhugel who encourages the youth of the Swiss party to prepare for and precipitate war with Burgundy. One of the most suggestive moments is when Rudolph asks Philipson what he thinks of the Swiss youth. To Philipson's guarded reply, he returns:

I judge thou wouldst not buy a steed which thou hadst only seen covered with trappings, or encumbered with saddle and bridle, but wouldst desire to look at him when stripped and in his natural state of freedom . . .

. . . thou hast seen our Swiss youth but half, since thou hast observed them as yet only in their submissive attendance upon the elders of their cantons (chapter 10).

Horse and bridle are very usual images in Scott for will and authority. Donnerhugel posits a Rousseauist attitude, that the real man is natural and free, not subject to restraint. Switzerland, with its emphasis on freedom, equality, frankness, encourages this idea. Switzerland is hardly a historical depiction at all but a symbol of a state that is on the one hand primitive and natural but on the other unreal and illusory. The mists,

mountains, legends and illusions deprive the background of its
solidity, at least for Arthur who, with Anne, is a firm supporter
of parental authority. Biedermann makes the symbolism of
the mountains explicit as he bids farewell: 'Thou hast learned
among us to keep thy foot firm on the edge of a Helvetian
crag, but none can teach thee so well as thy father to keep
an upright path among the morasses and precipices of human
life' (chapter 12). On the other hand, as an explicit dialogue
between Anne and her maid informs us, 'the distinction of rank
binds men to certain duties'; Anne and Arthur, like Lilias
and Alan, are unable to act spontaneously. Their embarrass-
ments, hesitations and awkwardnesses are a result of a lack of
congruity between their inherited roles and their present
situations. When they meet as lovers, they are extremely
formal, which shocks Annette 'whose ideas of love partook
of the freedom of a more Arcadian country and its customs'
(chapter 21). 'Real', 'historical' Switzerland slides off constantly into this imaginary world of freedom and spontaneity.
Respect for the actual Switzerland stops Scott from making it
complete. Instead he makes a more complete Arcadia in the
Kingdom of Provence, in which the King plays lover and
shepherds and shepherdesses sing of love to each other.
This is highly free and natural, and artificial and unreal.
It is an extension of Mt Sharon in *Redgauntlet*. ' "Peace," said
Arthur, as he looked around him, "is an inestimable jewel;
but it will soon be snatched from those who are not prepared with heart and hand to defend it" ' (chapter 29). This
is the Quaker businessman's problem too: if he wishes to carry
on his business in a violent society, he must be prepared
to invoke the ultimate sanctions of the law. Does this have
further, more personal implications for Scott, the recluse–
novelist of Abbotsford, the Edinburgh man of law, the Radical-
beating shirra? Such speculations are on the verge of critical
permissibility, yet the persistence with which quietism is
considered and rejected in these later novels does lead to their
formulation.

These are the sorts of interest that *Anne of Geierstein* offers;

yet I have deliberately refrained from advancing a coherent scheme of meanings for the novel, since there is little close connection between the scenery, the plotting and the symbols. The scenes briefly discussed here have an interest, but one related mainly to other novels rather than to their own internal structure. With F. R. Hart, I would tend to see the novel as something of an after-echo of *The Fair Maid of Perth*.[16]

This novel too is set in a region of (temporally not spatially defined) lawlessness. However, authorial intention is more insistent and obvious, and is expressed in an almost over-deliberate play with doubling and imagery. The sense of control and distance that this gives is reinforced by the current of ironic authorly comment throughout the work. Scott tells us to have no romantic expectations about this society. Although the conditions of life cannot have been very different from those described in *Waverley*, Scott's mood is less tolerant, more dismissive and suggestive of disillusionment with all social arrangements:

Hamlets were seen . . . which, like many earthly things, made a fair show at a distance, but, when more closely approached, were disgustful and repulsive, from their squalid want of the conveniences which attend even Indian wigwams. They were inhabited by a race who neither cultivated the earth nor cared for the enjoyments which industry procures (chapter 27).

Even more distancing reflections are permitted as the battle approaches. Reflections are made on man's hypocrisy:

those who had so lately borne palms in honour of the great event which brought peace on earth and goodwill to the children of men, were now streaming to the place of combat; some to take the lives of their fellow-creatures, or to lose their own; others to view the deadly strife, with the savage delight which the heathens took in the contests of their gladiators (chapter 34).

Rationalism undercuts romanticism in one of its securest areas – the clans' hospitality:

the Clan Quhele conducted themselves with that species of courteous reserve and attention to the wants of others, which is often found in primitive nations, especially such as are always found in arms; because a general observance of the rules of courtesy is necessary to prevent quarrels, bloodshed and death (chapter 28).

Another and similar irony in the novel underlines what the author considers the 'real' or 'egotistical' basis of actions. Dorothy is one of those members of the lower classes who love to relate 'sinister intelligence' because they 'love the attention which a tragic tale ensures to the bearer, and enjoy, perhaps, the temporary equality to which misfortune reduces those who are ordinarily accounted their superiors' (chapter 19). Dwining saves a child's life out of 'vanity and the love of his art' (chapter 22); Glover has a greater respect than other burghers for the Highlanders, but this is because he knows that nowhere are there men 'by whom a man may more easily make an honest penny'; the triumph of Torquil of the Oak's sons in Hector's chieftainship is based on their own 'having been raised to an eminent rank in the clan by his succession'. Such ironies provide a rhetorical framework that gives shape to the fable.

F. R. Hart has drawn attention to the 'linking images' of the novel, particularly those of 'head' and 'hand', action and thought, the ruling and acting classes in society. Other images not only assist in this process but indicate some of its meaning, and direct attention outwards to other novels, to *Redgauntlet* for example. Some of the images or concerns that link the two novels are: horses, dreams, labyrinths, manhood and names. Characters too have their analogues: Glover and old Fairford, Henry Smith and Alan, Conachar and Darsie, Joshua Geddes and Catherine/Father Clement.

Part of the purpose is made very obvious in the first few chapters, almost too obvious, for the language is slack and abstract, though not devoid of significance. These chapters are about power, authority, social status, and their opposites – lawlessness and anarchy. Everyone's status is the thing first defined, particularly through dress. Later in the novel this preoccupation becomes more integrated with the action; men are defined by their crafts – Smith's talk is full of references to steel, fire and blows as Glover's is to hands, gloves and skins. A major structural device makes the same sort of point. The

action is confined to three days of the year: St Valentine's
Day, Shrove Tuesday and Palm Sunday. These holy days are
used with effect for a number of purposes. Large numbers of men
are brought together for normal and traditional purposes.
Then Scott is able to point to the collapse of the traditional
way of life into disorder and anarchy. St Valentine's day, with
its nice blending of religious, social and cultural elements,
turns into a brutal attempted rape. Names too are indicative
of status: men are called after their place, their station, their
craft or their master. A man's social position is bound up with
his name: they can be lost together. At the end of the novel,
Smith refuses to change his name and enter the Douglas'
service, while Conachar/Eachin/Hector says to Catherine:
'I was called Conachar when I was happy, and Eachin when I
was powerful. But now I have no name, and there is no such
clan as that thou speak'st of; and thou art a foolish maid to
speak of that which is not, to one who has no existence' (chapter
36). While Smith's many names ('like a heathen deity') show
his success in stamping many areas of life with his personality,
Conachar's show his failure to find himself in any role. His
failure is like Darsie's, the ambiguity over names being crucial
with both of them. Both are heirs to ancient families brought up
in burgher obscurity, both are connected with a fatal legend,
both are called upon to act in alien quarrels. In Darsie's case
the picture is softened, the determinism seems less rigorous.
He is not made into a coward, yet is insulted by the plot.
Conachar is bound by the legend to be a coward, but Scott
refers it to having been brought up in 'Glover' surroundings –
just as Darsie is called by Herries 'a forest plant . . . brought up
in a green house'. Conachar can settle neither in Perth nor as a
Highland chief; and it is the *ability to take a role that defines
manhood*. Lack of ability to take a role is expressed as, among
other things, cowardice.

The King is an analogue of Conachar. We are told directly
that 'his merits were not of a kind suited to the part he was
called upon to perform in life' (chapter 9). Various images are
used to describe his character: a vessel adrift, a chameleon,

a mirror and 'a timid horseman, borne away by an impetuous steed, whose course he can neither arrest nor direct'. All these images are very conventional, and Scott has used them many times before. But they are made more cogent by physical embodiments of them in the novel. Smith and Douglas, like Herries, both control strong and powerful horses. Oliver Proudfute cannot control his horse Jezabel. Shortly after she had thrown him on the moor, the image of the King as incompetent rider is introduced. Proudfute's deficiency in 'animal courage' is a comic version of Conachar's; his disabling excess of imagination about warfare is similar to the young chief's (chapters 8 and 29). Both of them are linked to the Prince, who in Ramorny's image: '[indulges] a powerful imagination as an unskilful horseman permits a fiery steed to rear until he falls back on his master and crushes him' (chapter 30). Scott was perhaps incapable of producing a single complex character, a Lord Jim; the synthesis of the various attitudes we are invited to adopt to these four linked characters is the nearest Scott can approach to a unified analysis of a coward.

Imagination, cowardice, uncertainty of self and role are all inter-related. When Conachar claims he has 'no existence' his words are not mere melodramatic hyperbole. They represent a clear statement of the novel's main theme: that a man must find his identity within that station of life which nature, birth, education and convention have called him to, or not at all. Rothsay's death is a confirmation of his failure to find his identity. Scott has little interest in the origins of Rothsay's character deficiencies: his activities would be hardly intelligible to someone who had not read *Henry IV*. Scott is interested in his end, and wants to know what the significance of his legendary death is when compared with other legends – that of the cowardly Highlander and the brave burgher. The Prince is presented as a man who, as he does not live his allotted role (his disguisings and masquerades symbolise this) cannot feel himself. This is why he relies upon Sir John Ramorny for 'guidance and direction'. Some of the elements of his flight repeat those of Darsie's and Alan's adventures: he flies from a

place of restraint; there is a journey undertaken on the spur of
the moment, a flight across water, a horse ride at night, a
lonely habitation, fever and illness, dressing up as a woman.
Whatever significance these events have is illuminated by a
number of grim jokes. Rothsay will not be killed, he will 'cease
to exist'. His fever will make it seem 'the effect of nature'.
Rothsay's death is heavily moralised: his life has been excess,
his death privation; his life license, his death imprisonment.
But it is a moralisation of the theme of the relation between
'manhood' and the social order.

The novel persistently asks the question: what does it mean
to be a man, and alive at a time like this? Questions are important – the first part of the book is alive with questions and
choices. Henry Smith constantly has to decide whether to fight
or not, and for whom. Sometimes he fights 'for manhood's
sake', sometimes not to be disgraced. With Louise the glee
maiden, the moral problem is so overpowering that he approaches
a moment of impotence, he 'remained stupefied at what had
passed'. Ramorny, Conachar and Rothsay experience similar
moments of dream-like impotence; Ramorny when he has
lost his hand, and hand is everywhere in the novel the symbol
of power to act. Smith's legendary saying, 'I fought for my
own hand', is behind this imagery. His hand both makes his
position and keeps it. On his belt he had 'a dirk . . . as if to
defend the purse which (burgher fashion) was attached to the
same cincture'. The same point is taken up in Charteris' bear-
ings: 'a hand holding a dagger or short sword with the proud
motto: This is my charter.' Yet Smith always behaves according to a code of behaviour, he acts only as traditional and
communal pressures have him. Scott creates an anti-Smith,
Bonthron, who is only brute strength, and has Smith defeat
him. Both men are short and brawny (chapters 2 and 15). While
the Smith's victory is pre-determined, it is clearly a magical
sort of victory: he wins because he is convinced of the justice
of his cause; tradition and belief buoy him up, while Bonthron
is isolated, guilty and depressed (chapter 23).

Once again we are in regions where myth and magic are of

much more interest than traditions of historiography. Scott would not have been able to write exactly the novels he did if he had not had at his disposal his rich historical knowledge. Without it, they would have lacked their substantiality. Yet his distinction as an artist is as creator of myths, romances and symbols. If this is true, then Scott's art 'about society' must be interpreted within the myths, and not within the information and philosophy that subserve them. In this novel, our interpretation of the myths is facilitated by the presence of questions about moral choices: these are the central threads that link the seemingly inchoate experiences into a whole.

Catherine Glover is another character who needs to make moral choices. As Henry's choices are to do with 'manhood', Catherine's centre on the notion of 'womanhood'. As heroine, she will, it is expected, make a happy marriage. In the novel, she is expected to marry Smith. She should behave according to her sexual role. When she kisses her Valentine, we guess that her own 'real' wishes blend with the demands of custom and authority. An irony at the expense of women warns us not to take Catherine too seriously. Her womanliness is associated with feminine vanity. When she asks leave to dress herself, Glover jokes that those were 'the only words like a woman that thou hast uttered for these ten days' (chapter 5). When she hears of Smith's death, she runs half-dressed through the town 'surprised at last into owning [herself] a woman' (chapter 19). Her role is to marry Smith: fictional convention, plotting and authorial asides make this clear at every point. However, our expectations are kept tense, for there are two possibilities of her rejecting this role. There is the threat to her father and Smith if she does; and she would be happy to renounce a world that does not live up to her ideals. Her admonitions to Henry not to fight are presented unsympathetically. Glover accuses her of lack of realism: 'she believes that the whole world is one great minster church'. Scott also hints that her behaviour is self-deceiving. She uses her beauty to make Conachar do her bidding although she will not offer him her love. She uses the power that society gives her over her Valentine, even though she would like to deny the other consequences. Her beauty is power: 'At such a period in society the power of beauty was almost unlimited' (chapter 2). She cannot retreat from society any more than can Joshua Geddes, with whom she is linked through pacificism. The key moment for her is when she has to recognise the human fallibility in her mentor, the Lollard Father Clement who would have her become Rothsay's mistress so that she can effect his plan of Church reform. This experience makes her submission to her role as Smith's wife convincing: she recognises that men 'rarely advance in civilisation and refinement beyond the ideas of their own age'. All those who fail in the novel are those who step outside their roles – those who fall below their positions, and those who attempt to be wiser than their age, Dwining and Father Clement. For a character who experiences real fulfilment in the performance of his role we should turn to Smith. Here there is no reflection and depth; Scott has little skill in the elucidation of motives and the fine delineation of states of mind. His art is of surface and action; the elements of the novel's surface, powerfully rendered individually, are joined and juxtaposed in such a way that they take on an additional, symbolic meaning. Chapters 33–4, Henry's involvement in the Palm Sunday battle, demonstrate this principle at work.

Henry is like Alan Fairford. For most of *Redgauntlet*, Alan is out of place and ill-at-ease. He is most completely sure of himself when he can operate in his own theatre, in his terms, using his own language. This is Smith's Palm Sunday battle: he fought for his own hand. Previously he has fought because his culture and community have demanded it. But in this fight, personal motives are present – and the plot skilfully makes the contest between Henry and Conachar unavoidable. Much more is intended by the fight than a demonstration of the hero's military prowess. Much play is made with Henry's being both armourer and warrior. Although it is partly realistic, at another level, with the insistence on pattern, coincidence and repetition, there seems to be something magical about the arming of the heroes. The magic enacts psycho-sociological truths. Henry's capacity and excellence as Smith are presented through the semi-magical trial of strength with the Highland smith. They play with each other's names; worsted, the Highlander confesses 'she has lost her name of the Hammerer'. Henry refuses to sell the armour for gold, but will give it to anyone who 'will face [him] for the best of three blows'. In the battle Norman offers Smith a blow with a dagger of his own making, calling at the same time: 'You taught me the blow.' But Henry 'wore his own good hauberk' and the blow is deflected. Torquil of the Oak suspects witchcraft when he finds his foster-son in armour of the enemy's making.

The technique and language is of ballad and folk tale; yet the total effect of the last two chapters is more sophisticated. The framework of the whole fight is of disillusioned ironic commentary on the savagery of the times – so a serious invocation of magic cannot be countenanced. Torquil nullifies any suggestion of the supernatural even as he makes it. Henry's magical power can only be interpreted in a way that seems to fit the tone and imagery of the whole novel. I would suggest that Henry's fighting for his own hand is equivalent to Steenie's asking for his ain; his magical power is nothing more than his limited integrity, his honesty, self-respect and complete assumption of his given role.

Yet we are in no doubt at the end that Catherine's election of Smith, and the novel's endorsement of his type of success, represent a willed limitation of feeling, sympathy, imagination and idealism. Smith is not-Bonthron, but only just; he is still brutal and unimaginative. The society of each of these novels imposes limits upon individuals' growth and freedom. Community is maintained with difficulty, and at great cost to those who cannot adapt readily to expected patterns.

Art and nature: 'St Ronan's Well' and 'Count Robert of Paris'

The final novels have a deserved reputation for unreadability; yet the decline was not a simple downward curve, for the last novel, *Count Robert*, most repays attention. There is a certain inconsequentiality about it, baffling to the reader who cannot decide why narrative threads are dropped and taken up. But Scott's novels are frequently imperfect structurally; their strength resides in their ability to derive significance from local passages of great power and vividness. This strength the other two late novels lack: there, a determination to summarise the necessary events as soon as possible is combined with a desperate, irrelevant padding. But in *Count Robert*, in spite of its remoteness, there are scenes in which some of Scott's former power is displayed – a power related to Scott's discovery in the story of a theme that held a significance for him.

The story of *Count Robert* appears to have three distinct phases. In the first, a simple Anglo-Saxon mercenary exile, Hereward the Varangian, is insinuated into the confidence of the Byzantine Emperor Alexius Commenus, his sturdy independence being contrasted with Grecian despotism and subtlety. In the second phase the interest is centred on the influx of the Crusaders, the attempts of the Greeks to stem the tide from the west, the contrast between the court and the Western chivalry and a plot worked up against the Emperor. In the final phase the interest shifts once again to Alexius and his former rival Ursel, found to be alive and well and produced to stifle the palace plot. Count Robert and Hereward do not disappear from the plot, but they cease to be at its centre. A perfunctory detailing of national animosities and duelling preserves a formal continuity, but a forced and unsatisfactory one.

There is however an obvious and pervading unity of intellectual commentary. Constantinople was for Scott a city of art, yet an art in which something has gone wrong. Chapter 2 alone has the following comments:

the inflated language of the Greeks

A triumphal arch decorated with the architecture of a better though already degenerate age

the artist determined to be wealthy if he could not be tasteful

figures carved in a distant and happier period of the art glanced from the walls, without assorting happily with the taste in which these were built

These comments, by no means inevitable to the plot, probably indicate the presence in the author's mind of some pressing intellectual considerations, presumably related to art, artifice and taste. The novel as a whole bears out this early impression: constantly, in his critical and commenting moods, Scott refers us to examples of super-artificiality, tastelessness and vulgarity. But this is no sign of intellectual superiority or of the novel's success or seriousness of purpose as a novel. Do such comments unite with the fable, with metaphors, characters, as they must if the work is to validate any claims to serious attention? There are in fact two or three scenes in the novel where, the reader's attention being aroused by the uncommonness of the writing, significance and fable are united in a very definable way, quite unusually in this late period.

Chapter 7 introduces the birds of hammered gold – a device, in Scott's interpretation, to impress the barbarians rather than to keep the Emperor awake. Part of the Palace of the Blaquernal contains a room guarded by

six deformed Nubian slaves, whose writhen and withered countenances formed a hideous contrast with their snow-white dresses and splendid equipment. They were mutes, a species of wretches borrowed from the despotism of the East, that they might be unable to proclaim the deeds of tyranny of which they were the unscrupulous agents. They were generally held in a kind of horror rather than compassion, for men considered that slaves of this sort had a malignant pleasure in avenging upon others the irreparable wrongs *which had severed themselves from humanity* (my italics).

The passage is of some importance, for it helps to shape our attitude not only to the later Ursel passages, but also to the throne room that they guard. The marvellous imitation of nature that the gold bird represents is paralleled by the crime against nature that the slaves imply. It is true that Scott describes them as mutes, but the melodramatic evasiveness of the passage suggests that it is castration that he has in mind. These creatures have been rendered unnatural artificially, as steel, gold and precious metals have been made into the likeness of birds, trees and lions. That man and machines share an area of common ground suggests where the impetus of the novel comes from.

The machinery comes to stand for much of the mingled ingenuity, sophistication and illiberality that characterises the Grecian Empire. In chapter 14, it is amusingly demolished by Count Robert in a scene that anticipates his being decoyed into the dungeons by the Greeks and his slaughter of the tiger set to guard him.

Alexius made the signal that the ceremonial of the grand reception should immediately commence. Instantly the lions of Solomon, which had been newly furbished, raised their heads, erected their manes, brandished their tails, until they excited the imagination of Count Robert, who, being already on fire at the circumstances of his reception, conceived the bellowing of these automata to be the actual annunciation of immediate assault. Whether the lions, whose forms he beheld, were actually lords of the forest, – whether they were mortals who had suffered transformation, – [a note in keeping with the fairy story told by Agelastes and with the more horrible transformation undergone by the mutes] – whether they were the productions of the skill of an artful juggler, or profound naturalist, the Count neither knew nor cared . . . He strode to the nearest lion, which seemed in the act of springing up, and said, in a tone loud and formidable as its own, 'How now, dog!' At the same time he struck the figure with his clenched fist and steel gauntlet with so much force, that its head burst, and the steps and carpet of the throne were covered with wheels, springs, and other machinery, which had been the means of producing its mimic terrors.

A second passage, which is in some ways a repetition of this scene, comes in chapter 25. Agelastes, the philosopher and one of the most 'active artificers' in the plot that has deceived the Countess of Paris, is attempting to convince Brenhilda that all religious conceptions are meaningless. As he does so, a face remarkably similar to that of the devil whose existence he has just disproved appears in the mirror he is looking into. 'Mirror' suggests that it is his own reflection, and at the same time raises doubts about the substantiality of the vision. In fact, it is later explained as the reflection of an Orang Outang that has escaped from the dungeons. When Agelastes attempts to exert his 'philosophic control' over the creature (it is worth remembering that Agelastes' slave has previously described him as 'a man who commands his own passions') and touches him on a sore spot, it loses its fear of man and strangles the philosopher to death. The passage is whimsically macabre, but it also possesses an unequivocal, unsubtle, symbolism.

Agelastes is a principal plotter against Robert and against Alexius; he also deceives Hereward. He plays the part of a stoic, disguising his luxurious, sensual nature. His character is defined by his demesne. Brenhilda has been abducted to the 'Philosopher's Gardens', and it is there that the Varangian guides Count Robert. The gate is opened by a dwarfish negress whose countenance might argue 'malice and a delight in human misery'. Brenhilda tells her attendant that although she was deceived by Agelastes' assumption of learning and rectitude, the 'gloss' has now rubbed off and the 'ugly picture remains in its native loathsomeness'. Here are reminders of the scene with the mirror, of his death, of the throne room theme of appearance and reality. Hereward leads Count Robert through the garden:

The path winded beautifully through the shades of an Eastern garden, where clumps of flowers and labyrinths of flowering shrubs, and the tall boughs of the forest trees, rendered even the breath of noon cool and acceptable.
. . . He crept . . . through the same labyrinth of foliage . . . (chapter 18).

The beauty of the garden, with its subtle transformations of nature, recalls Alexius' mechanical toys, and, as labyrinth, the under-world of the Blaquernal. Agelastes is a type of this civilisation. Sylvan, or Man of the Woods, is a representative of nature, indeed, in one specific passage, the spirit of Nature: 'It was probably this creature, seldom seen, but when once seen never forgotten, which occasioned the ancient belief in the god Pan' (chapter 16). Scott was, it seems, uncertain about the precise place of Sylvan in the creation, for he refers to it as 'a specimen of that gigantic species of ape – if it is not some animal indeed more nearly allied to ourselves – to which, I believe, naturalists have given the name orang outang'. Throughout the novel, the animal is invested with emotions more human than (I believe) it actually possesses. In fact, the animal occupied an interesting place in eighteenth-century lore, particularly in the works of Monboddo. His *Of the Origin and Progress of Language* can nearly be read as an anticipation of Darwinism: yet Monboddo was no evolutionist, rather a believer in the Great Chain of Being. Primitive tribes and apes were figures used by Monboddo to make comments about civilised psychology, which were truer, he felt, than the superficial optimism of the Enlightenment. The Orang Outang was – in his account – no precursor, but man himself in his most primitive aspect, denied only the gift of speech. Scott was not trying to fictionalise Monboddo's widely satirised ideas; rather, their very unclarity and controversiality enabled him to make use of the background of half-knowledge as he felt inclined.

In these two episodes, art and nature, civilisation and nature, clash violently; the offended powers of nature take their revenge upon the policy that sought to overawe them. There is not only a connection of meaning, as will be shown in detail below, but one of technique: both episodes are somewhat fantastic, abrupt and violent. Both have symbolic meanings, which are so overt that the episodes become little more than parables in which the characters, or actors, are only puppets.

In the third episode to be examined here, this technique is reversed, as is the meaning. This is the awakening and restoration of Ursel, in chapters 26–7. Ursel was a rival to Alexius, who caused him to suffer 'a painful operation' on the eyes and to be plunged into a lightless dungeon of the Blaquernal. Over a number of years, Ursel has come to believe that he is blind. Although this is explained at the level of plotting, it does seem to have a deeper significance, pointed to by the remarkable unexpectedness of the scene, the 'philosophical' language with which Scott surrounds it, the repetition of the art/nature and reality/illusion themes, and the powerful Shakespearean echoes (particularly of *King Lear*).

It is true that Scott was too willing to fall back on rhetoric; nevertheless, he was attempting to register a psychological state of some subtlety, something of an anticipation of those Dickensian prisoners who find the return to freedom too painful to bear. First, Ursel is shown a lamp, but he is unable to make sense of the sign: 'Of something like light I am sensible; but whether it is reality or illusion I cannot determine.' Medicine is called in, to bring the bewildered prisoner to his senses; twice this is called 'restoring nature':

Douban . . . remained by the bed of the patient until the dawn of morning, ready to support nature as far as the skill of leechcraft admitted.

The balmy restorer of nature came thus invoked.

Nevertheless, the illusion has taken so firm a hold of Ursel's mind that the prison alone remains a reality, the restored world an illusion:

'Traitor,' said Ursel, 'and deceiver of old, bring no one hither! and strive not, by shadowy and ideal forms of beauty, to increase the delusion that gilds my prison house for a moment, in order, doubtless, to destroy the spark of reason . . .'
    'Thou thinkest then,' [said the doctor] 'that the seeming release of last night, with its baths, and refreshments, was only a delusive dream, without any reality?'
    'Ay – what else?' answered Ursel.
    . . . the prisoner . . . remained with his eyes obstinately shut, regarding the imperfect recollection he had of sights which had been before his eyes the foregoing evening, as the mere suggestion of a deluded imagination.

When the conviction of restored sight and liberty is finally borne upon him, Ursel ascends the roof of the Blaquernal to

verify the truth of his restored eyesight by looking out once more upon the majestic face of nature.
    On the one hand the scene which he beheld was a masterpiece of human art . . . affected him at first with great pain. His eyeballs had long been strangers to that daily exercise which teaches us the habit of correcting the scenes as they appear to our sight by the knowledge which we derive from the use of our other senses. His idea of distance was so confused, that it seemed as if all the spires, turrets and minarets which he beheld, were crowding forward upon his eyeballs, and almost touching them.

I find these passages something more than hack-work, and they are certainly part of a coherent larger scheme. There is a grand division in the book between the two antagonistic opposites of art (the city, civilisation, politics) and nature (simplicity and integrity). Art is the city itself, and the palace, with its rituals and its mazy underground world of Eastern despotism. Alexius is the most accomplished of all the plotters and is a symbol of anti-nature forces of the city. Alexius is the man who orders lime added to the Crusaders' flour. The eunuchs and the dungeons are agents of his will. Ursel is his victim: he is the man so blinded by 'artificial society' (Scott draws on *The Republic* and the fable of the cave to deepen his allegory) that when nature is shown to him he cannot believe his own senses. Restored to life, he is capable of no greater fulfilment than can be found in the cloister.

Opposed to this world are the three layers of naturalness represented by Sylvan, Hereward and Robert. The primate is completely solitary, wordless and primitive. The uncertainty of his zoological status is very useful, for it allows him to merge into the character of Hereward. Hereward has an 'instinctive sympathy' with the animal; Anglo-Saxon is the language used for communication with the brute; he is sometimes referred to as 'Man of the Woods', and Hereward is a 'Free Forester' and also a man of the woods in his native country; thanks to Norman oppression, the society of the Anglo-Saxons had reverted to a more primitive model: 'they made a step backwards in civilisation, and became more like to their remote ancestors of German descent' (chapter 20). The simplicity and integrity of Hereward and Bertha, his betrothed, are represented by their steadfast refusal to accept alien names. At times, Scott overdid the 'blunt' Englishman in Hereward, a creation that partly anticipates the sickening jingoism of Kingsley. Count Robert is further up the scale of social progress. He is rough when compared to the Greeks, but is compared to Hereward as a cut to an uncut diamond: 'In the one case, the value was more artificial, in the other, it was the more natural of the two.' This trio is made capable of destroying, snubbing, avenging itself upon, and proving morally superior to, the effete civilisation of the Greeks. Hereward and Count Robert are seen through the glass of history; they partly represent the virtues of Western civilisation, that pattern of society that grew out of the manners of those marvellous old Franks. They are also societal and not *natural* man in a Rousseauist sense. But the undeniable schematism of the story, the shading of Robert into Hereward into Sylvan, represent for Scott a remarkable excursion into sentimental primitivism, for surely we are being confronted with a version of the noble savage who is to be found in so many of the plays and novels of the later eighteenth century.

It has been argued that Scott's novels are best understood, in the majority of cases, as symbolic and poetic romances, and not as realistic novels of manners. It is fairly clear that a work like *Count Robert* is not realistic; but *St Ronan's Well* is so temptingly similar to realistic social satire that it has usually been classed as such, and as an egregious failure.

An early criticism was that *Well* characters were drawn with too heavy a sarcasm.[17] A more contemporary turn of critical phrase is this: 'That the characters associated with the social satire of the novel do not appear in a summary of the narrative structure is indicative of Scott's lack of success in weaving together a novel of manners and a tragedy'.[18] Actually, this author's account of the 'narrative structure' is the merest summary of the novel's pre-history – the seduction–love–madness plot. Almost everything of interest in the book is left out, so to call this the 'structure' of the novel is mere question-begging.

There is a strong and obvious Gothic element in the novel – the marriage, the suborned witness and so on. There is an air of incredibility about the episode, which Scott does not trouble to erase. Indeed, he seems to play up to it: Bulmer, recounting the history of the marriage, relates how Tyrrel had assured him that the union could never be accounted binding because of the deception, and continues:

I wonder this had not occurred to me; but my ideas of marriage were much founded on plays and novels; where such devices as I had practised are often resorted to for winding up the plot, without any hint of their illegality (chapter 26).

Hannah Irwin, recalling her life with Clara before the catastrophe, says:

I was elder than Clara – I should have directed her reading, and confined her understanding; but my own bent led me to peruse only works which, though they burlesque nature, are seductive to the imagination. We read these follies together, until we had fashioned out for ourselves a little world of romance, and prepared ourselves for a maze of adventures (chapter 32).

The unreal 'romances' of Clara and Bulmer/Tyrrel's marriage, its playbook origins and its disguises, are related to a wider theme in the novel: the separation of art and nature.

Cusac writes that Clara dies to expiate her looseness; being upper-class she has to pay a heavier price than Effie Deans.[19] Yet in neither version of the novel does the seduction receive any great weight of emphasis. Clara's death is in fact the outcome of her maker's expressed prior determination 'to be cruel', to make a tragedy.[20] And the tragedy is the expression of Scott's feelings about society, or 'a society' or 'some trends in society'.

The book is introduced on an elegiac note reminiscent of *Michael*. The old village of St Ronan's is described in such a way as to present us from the outset with the opposition of art and nature. Later on, though earlier in time, we shall find nature perverted and thwarted, but here her ultimate strength and 'reassuming' power is stressed:

a stranger had a complete and commanding view of the decayed village, the houses of which, to a fanciful imagination, might seem as if they had been suddenly arrested in hurrying down a precipitous hill, and fixed as if by magic in the whimsical arrangement which they now presented. It was like a sudden pause in one of Amphion's country dances, when the huts which were to form the future Thebes were jigging it to his lute. [It is worth observing here how 'art', an appropriately artificial prose style, and the idea of the city merge.] But, with such an observer, the melancholy excited by the desolate appearance of the village soon overcame all the lighter frolics of the imagination . . . On some huts, the rafters, varnished with soot, were still standing, in whole or in part, like skeletons, and a few, wholly or partially covered with thatch, seemed still inhabited, though scarce habitable . . . Nature, in the meanwhile, always changing but renewing as she changes, was supplying, by the power of vegetation, the fallen and decaying marks of human labour. Small pollards, which had been formerly planted around the little gardens, had now waxed into huge and high forest trees; the fruit trees had extended their branches over the verges of the little yards, and the hedges had shot up into huge and irregular bushes; while quantities of dock, and nettles, and hemlock, hiding the ruined walls, were busily converting the whole scene of desolation into a picturesque forest bank (chapter 1).

At the end of *St Ronan's* the watering-place is razed to the ground and the village 'returns to its primitive obscurity' (chapter 39). The very deliberateness of the introduction prepares us to be aware of the important contrasts that will be offered in the story.

Against this sombre background, the guests at the well are introduced to us as virtuosos and dilettantes, offering amateur sketching, geologising, needlework and versifying. Less trivial examples of artifice are introduced. There is Mr Winterblossom, whose name is indicative of artificiality:

he was possessed of some taste in the fine arts, at least in painting and music, although it was rather of the technical kind than that which warms the heart and elevates the feelings. There was, indeed, about Winterblossom nothing that was either warm or elevated. He was shrewd, selfish and sensual: the last two of which qualities he screened from observation under a specious varnish of exterior complaisance (chapter 3).

Art and artificiality join insensitivity and lack of feeling. In its essential conception, the character of Winterblossom is similar to that of Agelastes. A different sort of art, but one equally inimical to health, is that of Dr Quackleben, where the relation to the main theme is unmistakable:

A skilful physician, Mrs Blower, knows how to bring down that robust health, which is a very alarming state of the frame when it is considered *secundum artem*. Most sudden deaths happen when people are in a robust state of health. Ah! that state of perfect health is what the doctor dreads most on behalf of his patient (chapter 7).

The idea that Winterblossom's social role does not reflect his true self is an extension of the art theme, for the universal art of St Ronan's is play-acting. Clara Mowbray expresses this theme overtly when she says: 'I do carry on the farce of life wonderfully well. We are but actors, you know, and the world but a stage' (chapter 9). This is meant to sound second-hand, shallow and delusive. However, in the world of the novel it is appropriate that one in Clara's position should have such an opinion. When Lady Binks expresses her poor opinion of Clara's behaviour, Lady Penelope retorts 'My Lady Binks, I am very sure, is too generous and candid to "Hate for arts which caused herself to rise".' Arts, that is, of play-acting: 'Few knew that this wild, hoydenish, half-mad humour was only super-induced over her real character, for the purpose of – getting well married' (chapter 6). The chapter of theatricals at Shaws (chapter 20) is to indicate, against a background that is partly formal garden and partly wild nature, the baselessness of their lives:

This plan of exhibition, where fine clothes and affected attitudes supplied all draughts upon fancy or talent, was highly agreeable to most of the ladies present.

Honest Mrs Blower's comment is allowed to remain un-challenged:

in my mind . . . it's a mere blasphemy for folk to gar themselves look otherwise than their Maker made them; and then the changing the name which was given them at baptism is, I think, an awful falling away from our vows; and though Thisby, which I take to be Greek for Tibbie, may be a very good name, yet Margaret was I christened and Margaret will I die.

The last part is very similar to a disgruntled authorial aside:

their own little Jackies and Marias – for *Mary*, though the prettiest and most classical of Scottish names, is now unknown in the land

suggesting that the intention is to satirise a variety of affect-ation. It is related to the vanity of the elder Scroggie's urge to relinquish his name in favour of that of Mowbray, and the younger Scroggie's bulldoggish desire to retain it – another link with *Count Robert*. The obvious and declared intention of making the masque symbolic of social dis-ease is shown in Clara's comment: 'Supported as well . . . as such folk support the disguise of gentlemen and ladies during life; and that is, with a great deal of bustle and very little propriety' (chapter 23).

The opposition of art and nature had been in the eighteenth century very much connected with a fading of enthusiasm for the idea of progress. There is one moment in *St Ronan's* that must have been very familiar to the experienced reader of late eighteenth-century literature:

I tell you, sir, that besides its being forbidden, both by law and gospel, it's an idiotical and totally absurd practice, that of duelling. An honest savage has more sense than to practise it . . . It is unknown in Africa among the negroes, in America . . . the heathen natives, who, heathen as they are, live in the light of their own moral reason, and among whom ye shall therefore see better examples of practical morality than among such as yourselves (chapter 34).

The implications of this primitivism should not be pressed too far because Scott's standpoint was still 'social' and not 'natural' in the Rousseauist sense. Touchwood, the praiser of the noble savage, has purely social criteria and wishes to enforce norms of social decency. This is not a reactionary stance, for he is a reformer and attempts to change the habits of those who (like Jaup with his midden) 'held out for the practices of their forefathers' (chapter 28).

Nature stands as a background to *St Ronan's*. It expresses the mood of the action – autumnal, cold. Its permanence causes reflection on the transitory vanities of the world, but it is not man's home. Man's home is society, the natural life is an illusion. Before her fall, Clara was a child of nature: 'scarce sixteen years old, and as wild and beautiful a woodland nymph as the imagination can fancy – simple as a child' (chapter 25). Her ignorance and innocence betrayed her, for she was unsupported by a social role: 'Her motions were under no restraint, save that of her own inclination; . . . and her only companion . . . served for company indeed in her strolls through the wild country on foot and on horseback, but never thought of interfering with her will or pleasure.' Her freedom and trust in simplicity led her to 'disguise herself' as a 'country wench' and her attack by 'a country fellow' looks forward to Etherington's attack on her virtue, also in disguise. Her later behaviour during the action of the novel proper is in no sense a criticism of society but a reaction to the absence of it: Mowbray's primitivist joke 'you turn every day more shy of human communication – we shall have you take to the woods one day, and become as savage as the Princess Caraboo' (chapter 11) anticipates the tragic ending where Clara does take to the woods and dies.

Scott's handling of the story makes it clear that it is lack of society, or inadequate society, that makes Clara unable to support her identity as Miss Mowbray of St Ronan's. Meg Dodds says 'the puir thing is hurried here and there, and down to the Waal, and up again, and nae society or quiet at hame' (chapter 15) and the author makes this long aside: 'she had never been under the restraint of society which was really good, and entertained an undue contempt for that which she some-times mingled with; having unhappily none to teach her the important truth that some forms and restraints are to be ob-served, less in respect to others than to ourselves' (chapter 7). Clara has been betrayed by society because, apart from being 'unnatural', in a particular way, it is also 'unsocial'. There is a strain in the novel that refers to the human characters as animals: bulls, bucks, mastiffs, cats, monkeys, lions and wolves. Society is in the course of degenerating into a primitive state of nature.

Scott doubtless wished to criticise the particular phenomenon of the watering-place. More importantly, it served him as an image for a type of society that he had been circling round ever since *The Antiquary*. Its springs were vanity and avarice, its characteristics anonymity, affectation (implying the rejection of a true social role) and impermanence. Order, tradition and hierarchy were all missing.

Scott was faced with a vision of a society that was growing

progressively more uncomfortable for him. And yet for its discontents he had no remedy of which he was thoroughly confident. Rather as the Jacobean dramatists retreated to medieval concepts and language when confronted with the economic restructuring of their society, Scott resorted to concepts that had already become outmoded. The late eighteenth century, in one of its phases, had reacted against urban civilisation, and had sought fresh sources of inspiration in the uncorrupted goodness of the heart of primitive peoples. We can see Scott playing with the edges of this concept, using its language to express his own dissatisfactions. But he did not really believe that primitive peoples lived in a state of nature: they lived in society. The French Revolution had been an adequate reminder of what would happen were social controls to be removed and the heart trusted to.

Hereward is partly a noble savage: yet he cannot be totally accepted as this. Agelastes informs him, flatteringly, that he wants to see something 'fresh from the hand of nature'. Hereward replies: 'You see not that in me . . . the rigour of military discipline, the camp – the centurion – the armour – frame a man's sentiments and limbs to them, as the sea crab is framed to his shell' (chapter 7). It is in key with the account of the rigid discipline to which the outlawed Anglo-Saxon tribes subjected themselves.

Primitivism of a sort there is: but the primitivism of one social organisation as against another, not of unsocial, as against social, beings. Here again we may notice the influence of the Scottish school. Smith's distinctions were not between the state of nature and the state of society but between primitive and civilised societies, those of hunters, farmers, manufacturers and traders. One society was more advanced than another, but it was not more social.

The way in which civilisation was progressing was of course disturbing Scott. His borrowing of themes that had long ago lost their currency allowed him to structure his forebodings. Despairing asides are common in his later years, like this one from the *Journal*:

The state of society now leads so much to great accumulations of humanity that we cannot wonder if it ferment and reek like a dung-hill. Nature intended that population should be diffused over the soil in proportion to its extent. We have accumulated in huge cities and smothering manufactories the numbers which should be spread over the face of a country – and what wonder they should be corrupted. We have turned healthful and pleasant brooks into morasses and pestiferous lakes [the imagery reminding us of the transformation of the well of St Ronan's] – what wonder that the soil should be unhealthy?[21]

Or this – completely incidental – comment from *Castle Dangerous*: 'he who has been for many years the slave of agriculture, or (still worse) of manufactures, – engaged in raising a single peck of corn from year to year . . . the monotonous toil of modern avocations' (chapter 7). There is also Scott's fear of political alterations. The allusions to slow growth/sudden change, art/nature in this passage from *Count Robert* possess a covert reference to contemporary politics:

But nature has her laws, which seem to apply to the social as well as the vegetable system. It appears to be a general rule, that what is to last long should be slowly matured and gradually improved, while every sudden effort, however gigantic, to bring about the speedy execution of a plan calculated to endure for ages, is doomed to exhibit symptoms of premature decay from its very commencement (chapter 1).

Another strand in the novels is the neo-stoical contempt for acquisition and luxury that had always been latent in Scott, as in Smith and Ferguson. The commercial society of Constantinople is made repulsive, and the Greeks are cowards. In his chapter 'Of the influence of Commerce on Manners'[22] Adam Smith had written that the inhabitants of rich commercial societies 'By having their minds constantly employed on the arts of luxury . . . grow effeminate and dastardly'.

Both novels have themes of some importance, and their construction is not haphazard. Images of life and vitality in the social order confront those of debility and decay. Yet we can complain that so much symbolism and distancing was inappropriate. Only at one point – Lady Penelope's vicious attitude to poor-relief (chapter 32) – is the symbolic world of 'artifice' made to interpenetrate with the 'real' world of social conflict and injustice.

It is a minor criticism, though, that Scott provided too few bridges between the two worlds, the world of the novel and the world of post-Waterloo Britain. Other novels, including some of Scott's most distinguished, offer only the obscurest of clues to their deeper meanings. It is perhaps particularly difficult to make an image of the contemporary world that symbolises rather than copies the real world, when it is representation that readers instinctively expect. With *St Ronan's* the real failure is 'that there is too strong a pull towards representation, too little metaphor and too heavy a dependence on a borrowed theme.

Scott's metaphors about society are of two types; the most successful of his novels combine the two. One type is 'man in a landscape' – a character in relation to mountains, rivers, cliffs, sea shores; plains, parks and gardens; walls, streets, houses, palaces and cellars. The other is 'man in his family': parents and children. Together, they allow for a layering of images that define man's place in the world of phenomena, and his activity in a world of events. They tend to coalesce, as the spatial world becomes, in the later novels, a place of cliffs, bogs, mists, quicksands and winter, while family relations decline; mothers and fathers threaten and betray their sons and daughters.

I have suggested throughout this work that the metaphorical and mythical were the only ways in which Scott could begin to approach the tragedy of conflict and loss, displacement and alienation that has been a major part of man's experience of the modern world. Does this mean that a connection is implied between – say – Conachar, annihilated in a foaming river, and the real-life personal tragedies of countless numbers of men and women in the nineteenth-century economic and demographic revolutions? Yes; although Scott's very lack of specificity as to class makes his symbols wider of application than merely to the displaced poor. His gentry may be materially more comfortable, but their sense of the strangeness of the world may be just as complete.

There is a corollary to the notion that it is only through symbol that Scott could do justice to his ever-deepening sense of wrong and loss: he was not fully aware, though he was partially, of what he was doing. One fulfilment of this theoretical expectation can be found in the very large number of myths and symbols that have a sexual origin. If Scott had realised their full significance, he would surely have been moved to cancel them. For confirmation I would like to consider one more scene from *Redgauntlet*. Darsie we know is a wanderer, rootless. It is not until Lilias' explanation (chapter 18) that we know the plot-origin of his condition. When they were two and three years old, the children were playing in a walled garden. Herries scaled the wall and stole Lilias, while their mother defended Darsie; Herries was unwilling to offer Lady Redgauntlet 'any violence'. Instead, he gave her one of his dark looks (the same looks that Darsie has inherited). Darsie and his mother had to leave the garden; a few years later, she died and Darsie was smuggled to Edinburgh to live in the grey stone walls of the Fairfords. Overt sexuality is absent here, but we cannot miss the hint given by the 'walled garden'.

The figures in the primary myth are split up among the characters. Herries is (Claudius, Murdstone) the successful supplanter of Darsie in his mother's affection; although Lilias' absence substitutes for her mother's. The actual father is already dead, and Darsie's guilt is increased by his remaining in the garden while his sister is forced to leave. The situation is full of fear and guilt. The garden also represents mother love, the womb, the background of loving security from which Darsie is torn. In future, Darsie will no longer be able to draw on love and affection as of right; he has to pay for it with his pocket book. Scott coalesces the image of the birth trauma with the oedipal situation to intensify the emotional charge of the

224

wider, or more public, area of concern, something like the trans-
fer of people from 'community' to 'anomie', from status to
contract. The story of the kidnapping is bracketed by two
items concerning Lilias, which draw our attention to the sexual
angle. There is the evasive incest motif, in which Darsie is at
first frightened by what he considers Lilias' excessive sexuality
('He took her for the most frank-hearted and ultra-liberal lass
that had ever lived since Mother Eve eat the pippin without
paring') and later embarrassed by his near escape from a forbidden situation. Afterwards there is the odd incident in which
Lilias is supposed to have challenged George III at his coron-
ation. In both cases, female sexuality is aggressive, and rendered
more so by Darsie's female disguise. The story is brought up to
date by Cristal Nixon's desire for Lilias. This is officially explained as an avaricious desire for the property of an heiress,
yet Darsie's reaction and the manner of Nixon's death (cut
through the skull) convince us that there is more to it. Disgust
and an outraged sense of propriety are added to the fear and
guilt already present. The situation is taken up and repeated
in the other side of the novel, with 'Father Buonaventura'. The
plotters object to the presence of Charles' mistress because she
is a spy. Such a thing is of course mentionable, but the real
objections go deeper, and are contained in the double meaning
of 'Father'. By now, sexual misconduct has become Scott's
automatic symbol for 'Charles Stuart's' betrayal of his subjects.
And in his objections to the liaison, Dr Grumball uses a Latin
tag that Scott had employed a year or two earlier to describe
George IV's court:

no man of experience will ever expect the breath of a court to be
favourable to morals – sed si non caste caute tamen. One half of
the mischief is done by the publicity of the evil which corrupts
those who are near its influence and fills with *disgust and apprehension* [NB, my italics] those to whom it does not directly extend.[23]

The Jacobites in the novel are no rebellious force, not even a
pathetic, irrelevant rebellious force; they are a socio-political
version of the child expelled from the garden of mother love
by the demon father. Their irresolution is a perfect match for

Darsie's, and in the plot he and they fittingly agree to reject Herries and Charles Stuart.

Redgauntlet has here escaped from the classification earlier imposed upon it. Not only is it a novel like *The Fair Maid*, recording the insistent demands of conformity, but also one of those fables that, like *Peveril*, worry about class hostility. Looking at an episode that has been totally neglected in my account – Peter Peebles' persecution of his elderly tenant and debtor, which is finally revealed as the ultimate cause of his own downfall – we see that there is also an imaginative connection with group II and III novels.

The novels can and do stand by themselves. Nevertheless, critical interpretation does need the clues supplied by each novel's position in the series, in its group and in relation to the author's changing experience. This is appropriate, because Scott allowed his people, fables and symbols to accrete meaning and emotional charge, to be transmitted as ready-made units from one work to another. 'Charles Stuart', as we have seen, is one example: the Pretender of *Redgauntlet* is the successor only slightly of the same historical person shown in *Waverley*, much more of his ancestor and namesake, Charles II, of *Peveril* and *Woodstock*. 'Charles Stuart' had come to mean to Scott a king/father whose weaknesses induce disastrous failures of trust in his subjects/children. There are numbers of orienting images that Scott can use more or less as counters because he has used them at length previously: maze, dream, pilot, horseman, river, precipice. Sometimes Scott senses that his performance fails the potential of an image, and it will be repeated – the 'wedding' image of *The Black Dwarf*. Sometimes a setting, landscape or historical background is done quite perfunctorily, strength being drawn from previous works. The 'Covenanting' and 'persecution' backgrounds of *Lammermoor* are very sketchy because *Old Mortality* and the *Heart of Midlothian* are assumed to be in the background; nevertheless, actions and events of that period are vital to establishing the guilt of the Ravenswoods: without them, the novel is totally different.

Scott's principal emotion about 'society' was a well-grounded and progressively strengthening anxiety. To contain, fix or exorcise this anxiety his mind went over and over a comparatively small number of character types, symbols and actions. As comparative optimism, urgency or desperation dictated, now one and now another element not only came into the foreground but was invested with such a large proportion of the available emotional energy that the story bulged around it and contracted at other places. How unlike each other *Antiquary* and *Lammermoor* are, and yet how easily the one can be transformed into the other with a little re-emphasis. The enormous tonal differences in the two works indicate how rapidly the author's mood had changed. At first reasonably confident of, and then only longing for, a society that was not only stable but also just, tolerant and comfortable, he was more and more forced to see one in which age-old human vices worked loose what he referred to as 'the bonds of society', initiating a world that, hostile to community, forced individuals into reliance on increasingly slender personal resources.

APPENDIX

TO THE EDITOR OF

THE EDINBURGH WEEKLY JOURNAL

Sir, – I have been so little edified by your late reflections on the disturbance at Manchester, expressed in a style unusually different from the quiet and sensible tone of your ordinary politics, that I was about to discontinue my subscription to your Journal. At length it occured to me, that the passages of which I complain must have been thrown out by way of challenge, in order to bring forward some investigation of that affair a little more radical and serious than your own time has permitted you to offer. As the trumpet has been sounded therefore, and no more able champion appears in the lists, I take the freedom to send you this brief vindication of the Magistrates of Manchester, to whose firmness and spirit we are, I think, likely to be indebted for benefits which will not soon be forgotten.

To proceed with some regularity, I beg to consider the conduct of the Magistrates of Manchester under the double point of view of Law and Expediency. In other words, I hope first to shew that they had a full right to dissolve this meeting of radical reformers; and secondly, that it was highly essential to the peace of the country, and a peremptory part of their sacred duty, to do so in the time, place and manner which they actually did.

The first of these propositions is essential to the second; for I, no more than you, Mr Editor, approve of vigour beyond the law. While we are permitted to retain our laws, they must be our guides as well as our guardians, and nothing can be farther from my thought or wish than to recommend that they should be infringed under pretext of defending them. But the truth is, our ancestors were not unwise enough to make laws which did not afford the means of protecting and enforcing themselves, and that they afford the right of defence as well against the brute (I should have said *physical*) force of a mob, as against the armed hand of a despot.

But to the point. I fancy it will be hardly denied that magistrates have some more serious occupation than to weigh light bread, or hear causes betwixt oyster-women and coster-mongers. They are the GUARDIANS OF THE PUBLIC PEACE, declared so by a hundred statutes, and recognised as such by all law-books. In this capacity, they are not only entitled, but bound, to put down and disperse all assemblies which may tend to a breach of the peace; by the civil power, if it is found efficient, and if not by the assistance either of the regular soldiery or armed citizens. Without such a power, their office and ensigns of magistracy would become a mere laughing stock to every dozen of sturdy fellows who might be disposed to oppose physical force to empty proclamations. I should be ashamed to labour the point further, yet it seems to me, Sir, that you have totally laid it out of view.

Assuming therefore, the power of the Magistrates to disperse any riotous assembly, let us enquire into the nature of this which was convoked by Mr Hunt and his friends. I apprehend you will find it had every character which could stamp upon it danger and illegality. The very numbers assembled, and the great distance from which most of them assembled, was a circumstance calculated (and designed) to strike terror into every thinking person. From fifty to one hundred thousand men, more or less, were convoked from every quarter of that populous district – men and women diverted from their daily labour for many miles around – a peaceful town traversed by thousands and thousands of strangers, whose banners and watchwords expressed the most desperate resolution to carry their purposes by force – the hand of industry arrested, and at least prepared for violence – shops shut and commerce suspended – while the whole town and the immense property which it contains was placed at the mercy of this immense multitude or, I may say, of any mischievous individual among them who should first set the example of riot, plunder or murder. Upon my word, Sir, I should have thought the Magistrates extremely remiss if they had not bestirred themselves to disperse such an assembly, and to send, or, if you please, to drive home, to their own dwellings the thousands of strangers who, having no business whatever at Manchester, unless to make part of so formidable an assembly, were liable to be dismissed by the local authorities so soon as their presence should appear dangerous to the city. The risk arising from the numbers alone assembled, without any just or reasonable cause, entitled, at common law, the Magistrates to disperse them, even if they had not had deeper and more serious grounds of apprehension. You may have seen, Sir, in your walks through our own city, that the scolding of two barrow-women, the overthrow of a cart, or any other trifling incident a little out of the common run, has attracted a crowd of spectators; and you may also have observed that so soon as this increases to a degree which interrupts the passage in the public street, a constable appears with his batton, and requires the people composing the crowd to pass each on his own way. I don't suppose this ever struck you as being very tyrannical, or that you were tempted, in the zeal of your new principles, to elbow the officers, and assert the right of encumbering the street as long as you thought convenient. But if the civil power can lawfully disperse these little groups, which idle curiosity and mere chance so frequently assemble in the streets of a populous city, is it possible to conceive that mobs of many thousands can be assembled from distant quarters without the magistracy possessing the same right to assert the good order and quiet of their town?

Hitherto I have said nothing of these men's purposes or the circumstances of the country but both were such as to call on the Magistracy to exert their discretional powers with which the law has vested them, for the express purpose of suppressing riotous or seditious meetings. The avowed object of the meeting was the overthrow of the British constitution – not the repeal of this, that, or the other grievances, real or supposed – this terrific convocation had not for its object the preventing of the enclosure of a common, or the raising the price of labour, or the lowering the price of bread, or the destruction of machinery, or the wreaking vengeance on some obnoxious character – those usual and petty objects of riotous assembly were as much beneath the purpose of Mr Hunt's meeting as their numbers were superior to those of ordinary mobs. Their avowed intention was to agitate, and, if possible, inforce the total alteration of the British constitution, by introducing *Universal Suffrage and Annual Parliaments*. I will not stop to enquire whether this object be attainable, or desirable when attained. It is sufficient for my present purpose, that it is totally inconsistent with the existence of the present constitution of these Kingdoms, and is, as matters now stand, an object so highly illegal, as to approach to treason. Nevertheless, to attain this most unlawful purpose was the object of an assembly of from fifty to an hundred thousand men, assembled in regular bands, and moving under banners, some of which expressed their determination to carry their purpose at the risk of life itself. Nor must we omit the strong circumstances, that many displayed the peculiar badges and insignia which the atrocities of the French Revolution rendered dear to atheistical banditti, and the terror of every peaceable man. Cockades and banners are not trifles, Sir, when they become the badge of peculiar opinions. A white ribband made treason in the year forty-five, to display a red cap announces a republican ever since 1792. Surely the Magistrates were at least entitled in law, to request persons assembled in such force, with such insignia, and for a purpose so illegal, to disperse and go about their business, without waiting for the extremities to which their flags announced their willingness to proceed.

Let me bring this matter to your bosom, Sir. You are, I believe, a considerable printer. Suppose a friend to the liberty of the press was to convoke, by open proclamation, in your own Pandaemonium, every journeyman and printer's devil about

Edinburgh, for the purpose of getting rid of you and the other master printers; and carrying on the business in future on their own account. I apprehend, Sir, that such a convention would strike you with some awkward feelings – that you would think your pica and Ruthven-presses were in some danger – and that you would see no illegality in dispersing by fair means or foul, those who had chosen your own premises for the scene of devising your ruin. But this, Sir, is just the case of Manchester, where the territory under the protection of the Magistrates was filled with strangers, assembled for the avowed purpose of destroying the constitution under which the authority subsisted.

But the Magistrates had yet stronger reasons for considering the meeting as leading to a most dangerous issue. It is a fact, which Hunt himself has ackowledged, that large bands of those very men whom he assembled in a mass, were in the habit of assembling by night, for the purpose of 'playing at soldiers', that is, of being regularly drilled; and it is equally certain that in a late instance, these nocturnal recruits nearly murdered two men whom they suspected as spies. Of the very same description were the violent proceedings which followed the Spafields meeting, as well as the desperate and bloody expedition of Brandreth, the chosen captain of the same species of insurgents, whose execution of the wilful and unprovoked murder of an unoffending lad, was the subject of deep regret and loud lament, and whose memory is cherished as the proto-martyr of the cause of radical reform. If further a proof were wanting of their sentiments and purposes, I refer you to the assassination of Birch, perpetrated on acccount of that active officer having arrested one of their demagogues at a general meeting, convened by the same leaders who were to preside at Manchester. In one and all of these cases, the radical reformers gave distinct testimony to the spirit which possesses them; so that I may venture to say to you, in language to which you are no stranger, 'this fairy which you say is a harmless fairy, has done little better than play the Jack with us'.

These previous events, indicative of the temper and purpose both of the multitude and their leaders, could not be left out of view by the Magistrates, when estimating the character of the present meeting, and most unquestionably led them to the fair conclusion, that it was convened for an illegal purpose, and in an illegal manner, as well as connected in spirit and character with previous meetings, which had terminated in violence and bloodshed, and deliberate assassination.

It seems to be your opinion, Sir, that the Magistrates were not entitled to take into consideration the conduct of the Radicals upon former occasions, or the violence which they then displayed, but that, limiting themselves to the case before them, they ought to have waited the issue of this special Manchester meeting before attempting to suppress it. This maxim is no doubt true in a Court of Justice, where the Judge ought to confine his attention to the case before him, without suffering his mind to be influenced by the character of the parties. Thus I once heard an eminent Counsel, when pleading the cause of a person so notorious that he was generally called scoundrel G——, rebuke indirectly the Judge, who applied repeatedly to the other party, by way of distinction, the term of 'honest man'. 'My client is an honest man too, my Lord,' said the Counsel with his usual energy, to the great amusement of all who stood bye. And unquestionably, were a man to be tried for being at the Manchester meeting, he would be answerable for no other proceedings than what then took place. But it is a widely different question whether the Magistrates, in deliberating concerning the line of conduct which they were to adopt, had the right to consider the probabilities arising out of the crimes and violences which had elsewhere arisen out of similar convocations. Without doing so they could not exercise any power of preventive police, and if compelled to wait until the assembly proceeded to actual violence, they might indeed punish the rioters, but they could not prevent the riot.

Thus impressed, the Magistrates took every precaution in their power to prevent the meeting taking place. They published a steady and sensible proclamation, announcing their opinion of the illegality of the meeting, commanding and conjuring all good subjects to abstain from it, and putting as far as they

could every human on his guard that in doing so it would be
at his own peril. I own it does not occur to me that they could
have done more for the safety of that very numerous and
unthinking class whom sheer curiosity leads to such places of
rendezvous, and whose presence adds so much to the courage of
the mob. This wise and temperate proclamation was answered
by Hunt in what he called his counter proclamation, in which
he bade the Magistrates defiance, treated them with the utmost
scorn and insolence, and summoned all men to keep the appoint-
ment which this precious King of Clubs had assigned them.
Thus circumstanced, I say, it became a question to be tried
betwixt the Magistrates of Manchester and this turbulent individual, whether they should enforce the reverence due to the
law and the office of preserving the public peace, or submit to
be the insignificant and degraded scarecrows to which it was
his object to reduce them.

Yet on the very day of the meeting, when the vast concourse
of people had more than realised the fears entertained by all
good subjects, when repeated informations had been lodged with
the Magistrates on oath, stating the well grounded apprehensions of the informers, they seem to me to have proceeded
with a steadiness and moderation highly deserving the applause
which they have received from the Secretary of State. The
proclamation of the Magistrates had made all Manchester and
its neighbourhood acquainted with their opinion of the illegality
of the meeting, and they were both steps which would have
rendered it illegal by special statute had it been otherwise harmless. They read the Riot Act, charging the persons to disperse
on peril of what might follow – they waited till an hour elapsed,
which by special statute renders them guilty of felony who
remain assembled – they caused the Riot Act to be a second
time read – and finally, they ordered their civil officers, supported by as numerous a band of special constables as ever were
assembled, to advance for the purpose of putting into execution
their warrants against the ringleaders of this unlawful assembly.

The orator was at this very moment engaged in ridiculing the
Magistrates and the measures they had taken, in exhorting his

numerous assemblage to be firm – and they were firm, in so much that no force which could be exerted by the officers and constables could make way through the crowd, who linked their arms fast together and held all attempts to break through them in derision. You, Sir, or any honest gentleman seated in his elbow-chair, may think it an easy thing for peace-officers to make their warrants effectual in such cases, but fifty thousand men and more, to five hundred make a fearful odds where arms are equal. It was then in support of warrants legally granted, and in order to disperse an assembly most illegally convened, that the cavalry were finally ordered to advance. Not the regular soldiers, however, but a body of armed citizens, who, from a hundred reasons, might be supposed to act with as much moderation as the circumstances admitted.

Here I might rest the defence of the Magistrates on the point of law; because if they legally called in the assistance of the military their case is made out, and excesses, had any been committed in the execution of their orders, must be answered for by the perpetrators. But the truth is, that the Yeomen seem to have acted with very great forbearance, as well as courage, considering the circumstances of unprecedented danger and difficulty in which they were placed. The mob had bid them formal defiance; for, in such cases, we all can guess the meaning of the three cheers with which Mr Hunt, himself setting the example, and at the same time bidding his adherents not fear such soldiers, directed his rabble to receive the Yeomanry. Yet, notwithstanding this provocation, it is certain that the Yeomanry only made way through that vast mass by the weight and pressure of their horses and without using their weapons. I say this is certain; because as they advanced in line and in a compact body until they reached the scaffold, it is absolutely impossible that they could have used their swords. When the arrest was made, they were received by a violent shower of brick-bats and stones; and, from the necessity of the case, as well as the natural feelings of self-defence and retaliation of injuries, probably some sabre blows were given. But the stabbing, and cutting, and hewing, which has given you so much tribulation, could not, Sir, have, in the nature of things, taken place. It is not difficult for any one to guess the degree of execution which the cavalry might have made among these infatuated people, had they been in the bloody temper so gratuitously assigned to them. The hospitals must have been filled with the wounded – the church yards with the dead. But, instead of such a horrible carnage, it appears that among the numerous cases in the hospital there were only two – mark this, Sir – only TWO cases of sword-wounds, which, with two or three others so slightly hurt as only to require a single dressing, summed up the cutting and hewing and slashing of this fearful day, which has extracted so many syllables of dolour. The other injuries received were by the precipitate retreat of the mob themselves, or by their opposing their persons to the pressure of the Yeomanry when in execution of their duty – circumstances inseparable from the dispersion of a mob by cavalry, wherever that shall take place.

With respect to the blows actually given, we have Mr Hunt's own evidence that they were of the most gentle nature. In his modest epistle to Lord Sidmouth, he avers that he received several blows with a sabre on his own most politic pate. Now, as not a drop of Mr Hunt's blood was spilt, nor a scratch to be seen on his person, it follows either that the worthy patriot's person is as impenetrable as his understanding, or that the vindictive swords of these savage Yeomen must have fallen as lightly as the bags of cotton which Sancho Panza chose for his weapons of combat when challenged by the Squire of the Mirrors. And better evidence than Hunt's establishes positively that the Yeomen in general used only the flat of the sword, and were studious to intimidate rather than to hurt their antagonists. And thus the commands of the Magistrates – legal in themselves – were most temperately and humanely executed.

I promised to shew, Sir, that the Magistrates had reason as well as law upon their side, but the arguments which I have used to prove the latter point go far to decide the former also. If this immense convocation was assembled upon principles hostile to the constitution under which we live – if such assemblies professing the same objects had already recourse to open force, – if their numbers were immense, and their spirit, as expressed by their mottoes, bent to do or die, – if they met in opposition to the entreaties and commands of the Magistracy, and remained assembled in defiance of the civil authority after the riot act had been read, – it surely remains no matter of question whether they should or should not be dispersed before worse came of it. – But Mr Hunt, you will say, had recommended peaceable measures to his followers; and indeed I will hold that gentleman acquitted of everything that might involve personal danger. But who is Mr Hunt, that expects his word to be taken as a guarantee for the conduct of sixty, seventy or eighty thousand men, whose object and language were alike desperate? Be he knave or fool, or a mixture of both, be he as cowardly as he is absurd, I would no more take his word for the good conduct of his followers, than that his horses should not run away with his curricle. Who was to ensure the Magistrates, that when this pacific orator laid the reins out of his hand, his place of driver would not be occupied by a second young Watson, by the emulator of the fame of Brandreth or the assassin of Birch. If he could answer for the hours of daylight, could he or an hundred such demogogues insure against the riots which were almost certain to take place at night, – the friend of riots, of plunder and of murder? And was all this risk to be incurred in compassion to fools and madmen, who, a thousand times forewarned, would have no compassion on themselves?

In truth, Sir, the meeting was looked upon on both sides as an experiment – a touch-stone of the spirit of the Magistrates, and of the courage of the mob. It was to ascertain how far the latter might go, and what respect was to be in future paid to the former. The radical reformers do not disguise their resolution to have recourse to *physical force* – they only aver that they do not as yet consider it the suitable time to do so. When their deluded followers have been permitted to meet in huge bodies, useless for all purposes of deliberation, but intended to strike terror into others, and inspire courage into themselves, – when they have been accustomed to the sight of a degraded magistracy and an inactive soldiery – it is then they would probably think matters ripe for a *Jacquerie*, a servile war, or a second edition of Jack Straw's rebellion of the commons. Will men of sense and property, will the Magistrates and Government act legally, wisely, or humanely, in suffering matters to be brought to this pass? and is it not better to smother in its first sparkles a fire which may rise to a height so frightful?

I know, Sir, it is the custom with good-humoured and candid men like yourself, to consider those meetings as contemptible and unworthy of serious notice, because their avowed object is equally absurd and unattainable. A herd of the lowest and most ignorant manufacturers, you will say, demanding privileges which could not exist along with any regular government are acting under motives too absurd and visionary to be considered as objects of serious correction. The noble fabric of our constitution, you will say, can never be endangered by the machinations of such madmen. Therefore, let them play at soldiers, and let them assemble some forty, fifty, or an hundred thousand together, they are too ridiculous to be terrible, and when they have fretted their hour they will go home again. Now, Sir, this is the argument of the silly nurse, who gave the child the knife because it cried for it, in hopes it would go to sleep instead of putting its new acquisition to exercise. As surely as one wave of an advancing tide sweeps farther up shore than its predecessor, so sure does a multitude once accustomed to assemble, and to place confidence in its numerical strength, proceed from one aggression to another, until at length it is necessarily repressed by the arm of violence.

Concerning the supposed insignificance of these men, if such a phrase can be applied to such an immense assembly, whose numerical force alone must always make it formidable, give me leave to tell you a story. – A worthy laird of my acquaintance having got a little jolly one night with some old acquaintances, went to bed without the ceremony of putting out the candle. Next morning his landlord made a formal remonstrance to him concerning the danger to which he had exposed his tenement. 'Dear me, Johnie Graeme' answered the worthy guest, 'wouldest thou persuade me, man, that a bit farthing candle would set a low to a mickle three story sclated house like this of thine?' Apply your story yourself, Sir, and admit the Magistrates of Manchester did well to extinguish, I will not say this small spark, but this fire of loose straw, before it caught more solid nutriment.

One word more and I have done. I am old enough to remember Lord George Gordon, a sort of Hunt in his way, having the same enlightened zeal for the protestant faith which our modern reformer displays for the cause of freedom, and seeking to secure it from supposed danger by a similar convocation of the lieges. This noble and sapient person assembled twenty or thirty thousand people in St George's fields for the purpose of petitioning Parliament not to repeal the penal acts against popery. If the Lord Mayor or the Magistrates of the Borough had, like the Magistrates of Manchester, considered that the assembly of such a mob was in itself dangerous, and if they had forcibly dispersed them, it is possible a man or two would have been trampled to death, or some other casualties might have taken place. And it is certain that the well intentioned Magistrates must have seen their characters run the gauntlet through every newspaper, *candid* and *uncandid*, and have heard their conduct bewailed in the one with treacherous moderation, and execrated in the other with open malignity. – But mark the reverse. – A million of property would NOT have been destroyed – a thousand lives would NOT have been lost – and the city of London would not have been on fire in thirty six places at one and the same fearful moment.

Magistrates, Sir, acting to the best of their judgement, and in the exercise of an office rendered dangerous as well as unpopular by their opposition to popular clamour, are particularly entitled to the fair construction of the periodical press, and I am very sorry you have, in the present instance, pronounced your judgement upon the conduct of those of Manchester without at least waiting for a clear statement of the case. Nothing encourages the mischievous portion of the mob so much as the presence of idle by-standers – nothing tends so much to harden and confirm the seditious as the seeming compassion of those, who, though they will not venture to approve their doctrines, are sure to censure every step taken to suppress them.

Such doctrines are sometimes promulgated by those editors who wish to gain a little popularity and a few subscribers at the expense of 'clawing the humour' of the public. I will acquit you, as a man of sense and integrity, from such a charge. Yet let me add, the policy is as doubtful as it is mean. More violent doctrines catch the crowd, who are not to be soothed with such luke-warm and indirect encouragement. And the unlucky Editor, in endeavouring to trim between two opinions, becomes despised and disregarded by the partizans of both.

> I remain, Sir,
> Your Friend and Reader,
> L.T.

September 8, 1819.

On 24 August, the *EWJ* had contained Ballantyne's opinion that 'the proceedings of the Magistrates [were] ill-arranged, and the conduct of the Yemonary . . . rash and precipitate.' The following week, he had written: 'We see nothing like a reason for altering our opinion that the Magistracy and the Yeomanry were deeply to blame.'

Later, writing of Scottish newspapers, Scott commented about the *EWJ*: 'went wrong in the first blast of the Manchester business but I whipd it in' (*Letters*, vol. VI, p. 106). We could be fairly convinced that this letter must have been written by Scott because Ballantyne would have been unlikely to allow any one else so much space to air opinions that he himself considered wrong. There was no L.T. in the Edinburgh Post Office directory for this year; but L.T. fits the pseudonym under which *Ivanhoe* was written – Lawrence Templeton.

There are, however, more undeniable indications of Scott's authorship. In a private letter to James, Scott used the same phrase as on p. 231, line 1 above: 'they are in the case in hand avowedly assembled for the overthrow of the constitution' (*Letters*, vol. V, p. 484). A slightly earlier letter (*ibid.* vol. V, p. 483) makes the point about Hunt's lack of wounds; while the phrase 'fire of loose straw' had been used still earlier (*ibid.* vol. V, p. 467). L.T.'s threat to discontinue his subscription is an echo of Scott's threat to dissolve the partnership: 'I cannot continue a partner where such mistaken views are inculcated at a crisis of peculiar danger.' The image Scott uses on p. 228, line 9 – 'trumpet [sounds] . . . able champion appears in the lists' is perhaps a secret reference to *Ivanhoe,* and another reminder to James of which side his bread was buttered on.

The comparison of Radical reformers with the Gordon mobs is an interesting anticipation of the theme of *Pevreil of the Peak.*

NOTES

1. 'WAVERLEY' AND 'REDGAUNTLET': DEFINITION OF A CRITICAL PROBLEM

1 S. S. Gordon, 'Waverley and the Unified Design', in Walter Scott: Modern Judgements, ed. D. Devlin (London, 1968).
2 The Letters of Sir Walter Scott (Letters), ed. H. J. C. Grierson (12 vols., London, 1932–7), vol. I, p. 335.
3 Ibid.
4 J. Russell, Reminiscences of Yarrow (Selkirk, 1894). The original of Davie is found on p. 115.
5 J. G. Lockhart, Memoirs of the Life of Sir Walter Scott, Bart (Edinburgh, 1837), vol. III, p. 206.
6 D. D. Devlin, The Author of Waverley (London, 1971), pp. 114–15.
7 R. K. Gordon, Under Which King? (Edinburgh, 1969), p. 151.
8 A. O. J. Cockshutt, The Achievement of Sir Walter Scott (London, 1969), p. 206.
9 D. Daiches, 'Scott's Redgauntlet', in Devlin, Walter Scott.
10 Report . . . Select Committee . . . Salmon Fishing in the United Kingdom. (1824) (VIII), pp. 120–2, 113–14.
11 H. Cockburn, Letters addressed to several persons, chiefly on the Affairs of Scotland (London, 1874), p. 183.

2. SCOTT AND THE ENLIGHTENMENT

1 See for example D. Forbes, 'The rationalism of Sir Walter Scott', The Cambridge Journal (April 1954).
2 Nothing like a complete survey of this school can be attempted here. For the reader who would like to know more the following works can be recommended: G. Bryson, Man and Society: The Scottish Enquiry of the Eighteenth Century (Princeton U.P., 1945); W. C. Lehman, Adam Ferguson and the beginnings of Sociology (New York, 1930); W. C. Lehman, John Millar of Glasgow (Cambridge, 1960).
3 Lockhart, Life, vol. I, p. 43.
4 Ibid. vol. I, pp. 58–9.
5 David Hume, Essays, ed. L. A. Selby-Bigge (Oxford, 1963), p. 561.
6 Adam Smith, The Theory of Moral Sentiments (London, 1853), p. 225.
7 W. Bagehot, 'The Waverley Novels', in Literary Studies (London, 1895), vol. II, p. 104.

8 W. Scott, *Life of Dryden* in *Miscellaneous Prose Works* (*MPW*) (28 vols., Edinburgh, 1836; 2 vols., 1871), vol. III, p. 428.

9 Edited by G. Campbell Paton for the Stair Society. These are the lectures for 1823, which Hume did not personally deliver.

10 Lehman, *John Millar*, p. 35.

11 W. Scott, *Minstrelsy of the Scottish Border* (Edinburgh, 1812), p. lxxv.

12 John Bruce, *Elements of the Science of Ethics on the Principles of Natural Philosophy* (Edinburgh, 1787), p. 1.

13 D. D. Devlin, *The Author of Waverley* (London, 1971), pp. 40–1.

14 William Robertson, *Works* (Edinburgh, 1822), vol. IV, p. 234; vol. VII, p. 300; see also vol. VIII, p. 90.

15 W. Scott, 'Review of Southey's *Kehama*', *MPW*, vol. XVII, p. 306.

16 W. Scott, 'Essay on Romance', *MPW*, vol. VI, p. 174.

17 *Ibid.* p. 165.

18 See C. B. Tinker, *Nature's Simple Plan* (London, 1922); Lois Whitney, *Primitivism and Progress in the Eighteenth Century* (Baltimore, 1934).

19 Robertson, *Works*, vol. VIII, p. 102; cf vol. VII, pp. 318–22.

20 Scott, *MPW*, vol. XVIII, p. 356.

21 *Waverley*, chapters 11–12, 16.

22 *Tales of a Grandfather*, Second Series, *MPW*, vol. XXIII, pp. 232–4; p. 219.

23 Ferguson, *An Essay on the History of Civil Society* (Basil [*sic*], 1789), p. 2.

24 For Scott, see the whole of chapter 1 of *Tales of a Grandfather*, Second Series; cf. J. Millar, *The Origin of the Distinction of Ranks* (London, 1799), pp. 137–70; Robertson, *Works*, vol. VII, p. 358.

25 Lord Kames, *Sketches of the History of Man* (London, 1787), vol. I, p. 93.

26 J. Millar, *An Historical View of the English Government* (London, 1812), vol. I, p. 127.

27 *Tales of a Grandfather*, Second Series, p. 229.

28 In the *Edinburgh Annual Register* (not reprinted).

29 *Westminster Review* (April 1829), Article I, p. 257.

30 D. Stewart, 'Introduction', in Robertson, *Works*, vol. I, p. 61.

31 Millar, *Historical View*, vol. I, pp. 86–7.

32 Scott, *Life of Napoleon*, vol. I (*MPW*, vol. VIII), p. 58.

33 J. E. Duncan, 'The Anti-Romantic in *Ivanhoe*', *NCF*, 9 (1955), 293–300.

34 Dugald Stewart, *Political Economy* in *Collected Works* (Edinburgh, 1854–8), vol. II, p. 42.

35 Millar, *Historical View*, vol. II, p. 162.

36 Gilbert Stuart, *View of Society in Europe in its progress from rudeness to refinement* (Edinburgh, 1793), p. 27.

37 Millar, *Historical View*, vol. I, pp. 86–7.

38 *Tales of a Grandfather*, vol. VI (*MPW*, vol. XXVII), p. 37.

39 *Pitcairn's Criminal Trials*, *MPW*, vol. XXI, p. 233.

40 Stuart, *A View of Society*, p. 33.

41 Christopher Hill, *Puritanism & Revolution* (London, 1958).

42 Lockhart, *Life*, vol. I, p. 173.

43 James Tod, *Annals and Antiquities of Rajasthan*, ed. W. Crooke (Oxford, 1920), vol. I, pp. 153–4.

44 *Ibid.* p. 154.
45 Scott, *Culloden Papers*, *MPW*, vol. xx, p. 10; Robertson, *Works*, vol. ix, p. 18.
46 *Tales of a Grandfather*, VOL. vi, p. 95.
47 Millar, *Historical View*, vol. ii, pp. 304–5.
48 *Tales of a Grandfather*, vol. v (*MPW*, vol. xxvi), p. 35.
49 'Provincial Antiquities', *MPW*, vol. vii, p. 228.
50 Adam Smith, *The Wealth of Nations*, ed. E. Cannan (London, 1950), vol. i, pp. 434–7.
51 *Tales of a Grandfather*, vol. v, p. 44.
52 *Life of Napoleon*, vol. i, pp. 57–8.
53 *Ibid.* pp. 23–4, 59.
54 *Ibid.* pp. 38–9.
55 Bagehot, 'The Waverley Novels', p. 98.
56 Millar, *Ranks*, p. 5.
57 *Ibid.* p. 9.
58 *Westminster Review* (April 1828), 252.
59 *Life of Napoleon*, vol. v (*MPW*, vol. xii), p. 330.
60 Millar, *Ranks*, pp. 295–6; Robertson, *Works*, vol. vii, p. 322.
61 *Life of Napoleon*, vol. i, pp. 197–9.
62 Ferguson, *Civil Society*, p. 284; similar comments can be found in Beattie, Monboddo, Dugald Stewart, Kames *et al.*
63 See Lawrence L. Bongie, *Hume – Prophet of the Counter Revolution* (Oxford, 1965).
64 James Mackintosh, *Vindiciae Gallicae* (London, 1791), p. 116.
65 James Mackintosh, *A Discourse on the Law of Nature and Nations* (London, 1838), p. 18.
66 *The Wealth of Nations*, chapter 11.
67 *Moral Sentiments*, p. 264.

3. SOME POLITICAL TOPICS

1 *Letters*, vol. vi, p. 25.
2 NLS MS 1583.
3 *Edinburgh Annual Register 1814*, p. 49.
4 *Ibid.* p. 57.
5 *Edinburgh Annual Register 1815*, pp. 57–71.
6 *EAR 1814*, p. 57.
7 *Ibid.* p. 360.
8 Cf. 'Provincial Antiquities', *MPW*, vol. vii, p. 251.
9 *EAR 1814*, p. 74.
10 Cf. Whig comments reported in *EAR 1815*, p. 56.
11 For Malthus' influence on other writers, see D. G. Barnes, *History of the English Corn Laws* (London, 1930), chapter 6. The two works of Malthus in question are *Enquiry into the Nature and Progress of Rent* (London, 1815), and *Grounds of an Opinion on the Policy of Restricting the Importation of Foreign Corn* (London, 1815).
12 *EAR 1815*, p. 68.

13 Malthus, *Rent*, p. 47.

14 *EAR 1815*, p. 59.

15 *Letters*, vol. VII, p. 275.

16 'A View of the Changes . . .', *Edinburgh Annual Register for 1808* (pub. 1810), p. 372.

17 *Journal*, ed. J. G. Tait (Edinburgh, 1950), p. 73.

18 *EAR 1815*, p. 31.

19 'A View of the Changes', pp. 350–2.

20 Russel Kirk, *The Conservative Mind* (London, 1954), p. 111; see also Crane Brinton, *Political Ideas of the English Romanticists* (Oxford, 1926), pp. 116–17.

21 Francis Jeffrey, 'Proposed Reform of the Court of Session', *Edinburgh Review* (1807), 462.

22 Brinton, *loc. cit.*

23 Scott, 'A View of the Changes', p. 365; Jeffrey, 'Proposed Reform', p. 487.

24 J. Bentham, 'On the Proposed Reform in the Administration of Justice in Scotland', *Works*, ed. J. Bowring (Edinburgh, 1843), vol. V, p. 14.

25 Kirk, *The Conservative Mind*, pp. 112–13.

26 Scott, 'A View of the Changes', pp. 342–3, 371; Bentham, 'On the Proposed Reform', pp. 5–6, 19.

27 *Life*, chapter 22.

28 *Journal*, p. 282.

29 *Letters*, vol. VI, p. 190.

30 *The Croker Papers*, ed. L. J. Jennings (London, 1885), vol. I, p. 316.

31 *Malachi Malagrowther, MPW*, vol. XXI, p. 2.

32 'Report of the Select Committee of the House of Commons on Scottish Banking' (May 1826), p. 66.

33 'Report', p. 140.

34 An unpublished fragment, NLS MS 1583 (n.d.; from internal evidence sometime before April 1820).

35 *Letters*, vol. VII, p. 110.

36 *Life*, chapter 47.

37 Edgar Johnson, *The Great Unknown* (London, 1970), vol. I, p. 688.

38 R. J. White, *Waterloo to Peterloo* (London, 1957).

39 NLS MS 876 (n.d.); NLS MS 1000 (n.d.); NLS 'Fragment on Excise' MS 876 fo 19. MS 1000 is a proof corrected by Scott; 876 fo 19 is clearly a continuation of 876, the sheets of which are numbered 1–11.

40 *Life*, vol. VII, p. 247.

41 *Life of Napoleon*, vol. VIII (*MPW*, vol. XV), p. 304; see also vol. I, pp. 57, 75, 77, 89.

42 *Letters*, vol. VI, p. 36.

43 *EAR 1814*, pp. 64–5.

44 *Letters*, vol. IV, p. 414.

45 *Ibid.* p. 456.

46 *Ibid.*

47 *Letters*, vol. IV, p. 494.

48 T. R. Malthus, *The Principles of Political Economy* (London, 1820), p. 505.

49 E.g. *Letters*, vol. IV, pp. 393, 446–7.

50 *Ibid.* pp. 495–6.

51 E.g. T. C. Curwen, 'Speech on the Movement of the Poor Law Committee' (1817), pp. 52, 57–61.

52 *Letters*, vol. IV, p. 413.

53 'Report . . . Select Committee of the House of Commons' (1817), chapter 6, pp. 21–3.

54 S. Dowell, *A History of Taxation* (London, 1884), vol. II, p. 254.

55 *Life*, vol. VII, p. 248.

56 *The Annual Register* (1830), p. 51.

57 Sir Henry Parnell, *On Financial Reform* (London, 1830), p. 51.

58 'Sir H. P. on Financial Reform', *Westminster Review* (April 1830).

59 *Letters*, vol. IV, pp. 183, 231, 227, 235; vol. VI, p. 279; vol. VII, p. 275; vol. XI, p. 166.

4. SCOTTISH SOCIETY 1770–1832

1 G. Donaldson, 'Scottish History and the Scottish Nation', *Edinburgh University Journal*, 21, 4, p. 319.

2 D. Craig, *Scottish Literature and the Scottish People 1680-1830* (London, 1971), p. 152.

3 *Tales of a Grandfather*, vol. V, p. 349.

4 NLS MS 3653 fo 8.

5 *The Autobiography of Thomas Guthrie* (London, 1877), p. 9.

6 J. Robertson, *General View of the Agriculture of Inverness* (London, 1808), p. 74.

7 Sir John Sinclair *et al.*, *The Statistical Account of Scotland* (Edinburgh, 1791–7), referred to as *Old Statistical Account* or *OSA*, vol. V, p. 19.

8 *OSA*, vol. VI, p. 259.

9 T. Douglas, Earl of Selkirk, *Observations on the Present State of the Highlands* (Edinburgh, 1805), p. 25.

10 *Ibid.* p. 26.

11 Robertson, *Inverness*, p. 73.

12 *OSA*, vol. III, p. 182.

13 *Ibid.* vol. V, p. 250.

14 Lockhart, *Life*, chapter 62.

15 T. Craig-Brown, *The History of Selkirkshire* (Edinburgh, 1886), vol. I, pp. 242–3.

16 *The New Statistical Account of Scotland (NSA)*, ed. J. Gordon (Edinburgh, 1845), vol. III, p. 65.

17 NLS MS 3653 fos 188–98.

18 G. Robertson, *Rural Recollections* (Edinburgh, 1829), p. 494.

19 J. Anderson, *Observations on the Means of Exciting a Spirit of National Industry in Scotland* (Edinburgh, 1777), p. 50.

20 M. Gray, *The Highland Economy* (Edinburgh, 1957), pp. 99–100.

21 R. Southey, *Journal of a Tour in Scotland in 1819* (London, 1829), pp. 40–1.

22 D. Stewart of Garth, *Sketches of the Character, Manners and Present State of the Highlanders of Scotland* (Edinburgh, 1825), vol. I, p. 122.

23 Robertson, *Inverness*, p. 86.

24 *Report on Agriculture*, Parliamentary Papers (1821), vol. V, pp. 125, 323.

25 W. Cobbett, *Cobbett's Tour in Scotland* (London, 1833), pp. 84–7.

26 Robertson, *Rural Recollections*, pp. 70–5.

27 *NSA*, vol. III, p. 179.

28 *OSA*, vol. VI, pp. 332–3.

29 *Ibid.* vol. XI, p. 238.

30 *Blackwood's Magazine*, 3 (April 1818), 83. For attribution, A. L. Strout, 'The Authorship of Articles in B.M. Nos XVI–XXIV', *The Library*, n.s. 11: 'The pieces by William Laidlaw may have been by . . . Scott.'

31 'Effects of Farm Overseers', p. 87; for piecework, see *Letters*, vol. IV, pp. 447–8.

32 J. Anderson, W. S., *Prize Essay on the Present State of the Highlands of Scotland*, Transactions of the Highland Society (Edinburgh, 1827), vol. VIII, pp. 16–17.

33 Robertson, *Inverness*, p. ix.

34 Stewart of Garth, *Sketches*, vol. I, p. 139.

35 Scott, *Culloden Papers*, *MPW*, vol. XX, p. 93.

36 H. Cockburn, *Memorials of his Time* (Edinburgh, 1856), p. 172.

37 *OSA*, vol. III, p. 376.

38 NLS MS 3109 fo 93.

39 *OSA*, vol. III, p. 74, for A. Grant's leases at Monymusk.

40 J. Chisholm, *Sir Walter Scott as a Judge* (Edinburgh, 1918), p. 54.

41 Stewart of Garth, *Sketches*, vol. I, p. 120.

42 Robertson, *Inverness*, p. 95.

43 Lockhart, *Life*, vol. III, p. 153.

44 *Ibid.* p. 206.

45 E. R. Creegan, *Argyll Estate Instructions 1771–1805* (Edinburgh, 1964), p. 23.

46 *Ibid.* p. 74.

47 J. Macdonald, *General View of the Agriculture of the Hebrides* (Edinburgh, 1811), p. 102.

48 *NSA*, vol. XIV, pp. 235–6.

49 *Letters*, vol. II, p. 361.

50 *MPW*, vol. XIX, p. 170.

51 *Letters*, vol. IX, p. 378.

52 *OSA*, vol. V, p. 178.

53 *Ibid.* vol. VI, pp. 139–41.

54 J. Smith, *General View of the Agriculture of the County of Argyll* (Edinburgh, 1805), p. 14.

55 The holder of an entailed estate could not grant leases, or borrow money on the estate to improve it.

56 A. Allison, *The Principles of Population and their connection with human happiness* (Edinburgh, 1840), p. 55.

57 *Edinburgh Review* (February 1826), 422.

58 See for example Silver of Netherley, reported in Robertson's *Rural*

Recollections, pp. 485–7. Other remarks here are based on an examination of the lives of seventeen nabobs defined as such in *The Political State of Scotland in 1788* (anon.), ed. Sir C. Adam (Edinburgh, 1888).

59 H. Levin, *The Contexts of Criticism* (Harvard, 1958), p. 181.

60 R. C. Gordon, *Under Which King?* (Edinburgh, 1969), pp. 98–109.

61 L. J. Saunders, *Scottish Democracy 1815-1840* (Edinburgh, 1950), p. 112.

62 *Extracts from the Records of the Burgh of Glasgow* (Glasgow, 1914), vol. IX, pp. xv-xvi.

63 J. Hogg, *Statistics of Selkirkshire*, Transactions of the Highland Society, vol. IX, p. 300.

64 J. Russell, *Reminiscences of Yarrow* (Selkirk, 1894), p. 45.

65 Craig-Brown, *Selkirkshire*, vol. I, pp. 242–3.

66 *OSA*, vol. XI, pp. 524–8.

67 Parliamentary Reports on Factory Children: (1816), vol. III, pp. 13–19, 167–73; (1831–2), vol. XV, reports on Arbroath, Dundee and Aberdeen.

68 A. Aspinall (ed.), *The Correspondence of George IV* (Cambridge, 1938), pp. 539–44; also *Letters*, vol. VI, pp. 101, 190.

69 *OSA*, vol. XII, p. 357.

70 T. Somerville, *My own Life and Times 1741-1814* (Edinburgh, 1861), p. 368.

71 Robertson, *Rural Recollections*, p. 105.

72 *OSA*, vol. III, pp. 156–7.

73 Parliamentary Report, Agriculture (1833), vol. V, p. 128.

74 Parliamentary Report, Poor Relief (1818), vol. V, p. 65.

75 NLS MS 3112 fo 111A.

76 T. Chalmers, *The Christian and Civic Economy of Large Towns* (Glasgow, 1821), vol. I, p. 25.

77 W. P. Allison, *Observations on the Management of the Poor in Scotland and its effects on the Health of Great Towns* (Edinburgh, 1840).

78 *Letters*, vol. XI, pp. 127–8.

79 Allison, *Observations*, p. 183.

80 *Letters*, vol. IV, p. 449; Allison, *Observations*, pp. 188–9.

5. QUEEN CAROLINE AND KING CHARLES

1 *Life of Napoleon*, vol. I, p. 215.

2 *Ibid.* p. 24.

3 *Letters*, vol. VII, p. 271n.

4 *The Letters of Charles Dickens*, ed. M. House and G. Storey (Oxford, 1965), vol. I, p. 576.

5 *Letters*, vol. VI, p. 310.

6 *Ibid.* vol. VI, p. 335.

7 *Ibid.* vol. VI, p. 378.

8 *Ibid.* vol. VII, p. 82.

9 *Ibid.* vol. VII, p. 34.

10 *Ibid.* vol. V, p. 225.

11 *Ibid.* vol. VI, pp. 217–18.

12 *Edinburgh Weekly Journal* (24 January 1821). Scott's MS is to be found as NLS MS 3775.

13 *Letters*, vol. VII, p. 198.

14 *Ibid.* vol. VI, p. 309.

15 *Ibid.* vol. VI, p. 76.

16 *Ibid.* vol. VI, p. 307.

17 In the National Library of Scotland, docketed 'from the collection of Davidson Cook'.

18 *Letters*, vol. VIII, pp. 321–2.

19 *Malachi Malagrowther, MPW*, vol. XXI, p. 372.

20 *Letters*, vol. VI, p. 177.

21 *Ibid.* vol. VIII, p. 376.

22 Johnson, *The Great Unknown*, p. 832.

23 Cockshutt, *The Achievement of Sir Walter Scott*, p. 77.

24 F. R. Hart, *Scott's Novels* (Charlottesville, 1966), p. 105.

25 *Letters*, vol. VI, p. 307.

26 *Ibid.* vol. VI, p. 325.

27 *Ibid.* vol. VI, p. 329.

28 I am indebted to David Lodge's discussion in his *The Modes of Modern Writing* (London, 1977).

6. DEVELOPMENT

1 Cf. *A Legend of Montrose*, ch. 17: 'The power of man at no time appears more contemptible than when it is placed in contrast with scenes of natural terror and dignity.'

2 *NSA*, vol. III, Roxburghshire, pp. 166–76.

3 *Blackwood's Magazine* (January 1818), 414.

4 Ian Grimble, *The Trial of Patrick Sellar* (London, 1962), p. 5.

5 *Ibid.* p. 9.

6 Stewart of Garth, *Sketches*, pp. 156–7n. Sutherland was meant.

7 *Letters*, vol. I, p. 336.

8 *Ibid.* vol. IV, p. 269.

9 D. Davie, *The Heyday of Sir Walter Scott* (London, 1961), p. 120.

10 R. C. Gordon, '*The Bride of Lammermoor:* a novel of Tory pessimism', in Devlin (ed.), *Walter Scott*.

11 *Tales of a Grandfather*, vol. III (*MPW*, vol. XXIV), p. 212.

12 Lockhart, *Life*, vol. III, pp. 152–3.

13 *Tales of a Grandfather*, vol. IV (*MPW*, vol. XXV), p. 41.

14 E.g. *Letters*, vol. IV, p. 456.

15 This scene can be compared to the clothes-line scene in *The Tempest*. Tronda 'yelloched and skirled, that you would have thought her a whole generation of hounds'.

16 Hart, *Scott's Novels*, p. 224.

17 Lockhart's note to the 1832 Introduction.

18 M. H. Cusac, *Narrative Structure in the Novels of Sir Walter Scott* (The Hague, 1969), p. 46.

19 *Ibid.* p. 47.
20 *Letters*, vol. VIII, p. 29.
21 *Journal*, pp. 488–9.
22 A. Smith, *Lectures on Justice, Police, Revenue & Arms*, ed. E. Cannan (Oxford, 1896), Book V, chapter 1.
23 *Letters*, vol. V, p. 225.

INDEX

Index

Index

253